Excelsior

Douglas

TRIUMPH

VINCENT

Velocette

ROYAL ENFIELD

ARIEL

A·J·S

SUNBEAM

BSA

Greeves

Norton

Excelsior

TRADE MARK

BIRMINGHAM
FOUNDED IN COVENTRY
1874
MADE IN ENGLAND

Douglas

TRIUMPH

VINCENT

Velocette

ROYAL ENFIELD

ARIEL

A·J·S

BSA

SUNBEAM

Greeves

Norton

Great British
Motor Cycles
of the Fifties

Great British
Motor Cycles
of the Fifties

Bob Currie

CHANCELLOR
PRESS

First published in 1980 by The Hamlyn Publishing Group
This edition published in 2000 by
Chancellor Press, an imprint of Bounty Books,
a division of Octopus Publishing Group Ltd,
2-4 Heron Quays, London E14 4JP
An Hachette UK Company
Reprinted 2005, 2007, 2008, 2009

ISBN 9 780753 703786

Produced by Toppan (HK) Ltd
Printed in China

Most of the illustrations in this book are from the archives of Motor Cycle Weekly.
For additional material the publishers are grateful to Jasper Spencer-Smith, Cyril Ayton
and A.J. Wood and other owners who made their machines available for photography.

CONTENTS

INTRODUCTION

'Bikes of today are all very well,' complain the traditionalists, 'but they have no character – Yamahas and Suzukis, and shaft drive, and self-starters, and winkers; they cannot be called *real* motor cycles. Now, take an old B31 Beesa . . .'

Each enthusiast has his own reasons for looking back to the 1950s with a particular kind of affection. Japanese competition was then no more than a speck on the horizon, Germany and Italy were turning out some attractive machines, but above all it was the traditional British single and vertical twin which dominated the motor cycle scene, both at home and abroad.

However, during the early 1950s, buying a new machine was not so simple as all that. The demand was certainly there and, on the face of it, Britain's manufacturers should have been raking in fat profits. But those who are forever carping that British industry should have been investing more heavily in new equipment during this period, would be advised to take a closer look at the country's economic situation.

The struggles of the Second World War had left the nation in a sorry state, and the immediate need was to build up reserves of foreign currency. For that reason, factories both big and small were constantly being urged to export more and more of their production. Metals were in short supply, and stocks were only obtainable by flourishing a government permit – and, usually, such permits were granted only if the firm concerned could produce an order from an overseas customer.

Nor were export markets easy to find, because often other countries would either refuse entry to British products or (as in the case of the USA) place a heavy import duty on them. There were quotas and trade agreements to be negotiated and honoured, and it was not really surprising that our factories should find their major overseas markets in the countries of the Commonwealth. Indeed, in 1950, the first year of this decade, Britain's biggest customer for motor cycles was Australia.

However, the American market was just beginning to move, thanks in some measure to the efforts of Edward Turner and the Triumph company. Over a very long period, American riders had grown accustomed to the oversize, overweight vee-twins of their own industry, but wartime experience had shown them that bigness is not necessarily a virtue, and that there was a deal of enjoyment to be had from a relatively light, and vastly more manoeuvrable British machine.

Nevertheless, the vast distances of the United States permitted bikes to run at higher sustained speeds than was possible in Britain's crowded land, and it was this factor which led British factories to introduce such models as the 650 cc Triumph Thunderbird, and the BSA Golden Flash of the same capacity.

It might appear that every factory worthy of the name felt honour-bound to follow Triumph's lead and include a vertical twin in its post-war range, but that is not strictly true because there were some firms striking out along individual lines – Douglas, for instance, with a 350 cc transverse flat twin and torsion-bar springing, Sunbeam with an in-line, overhead-camshaft twin and shaft final drive, and Velocette, casting aside its pre-war traditions and staking everything on a little water-cooled, side-valve twin in a pressed-steel frame.

In the industry as a whole, there was a tendency towards grouping. Ariel and Triumph had long been linked under Jack Sangster's banner, and now the giant BSA firm joined in, taking Sunbeam with it. The London-based AMC group, already makers of AJS and Matchless, added Francis-Barnett, then James.

What with material shortages, international tariff problems, labour difficulties, and the continual demand for more bikes than they were able to produce, the factories just had not the resources available to cope. That is why, with the inevitable disruption a London Show would have caused, there was no major Earls Court Show in 1950.

A year later, the position had eased just slightly and, with a flourish of trumpets, Earls Court was again the major attraction of the 1951 autumn. It was not quite such a glittering affair as it had been in earlier times, though, because the year had brought a world shortage of nickel and, by government edict, austerity finishes were the order of the day.

Some trends were becoming evident, as the visitor wandered from one stand to another. More and more firms were adopting rear springing, albeit plunger type instead of the full pivoted rear fork (although Triumph managed to get extra mileage out of their old rigid frames, by adding a rear wheel which encompassed rudimentary springing within the hub). The traditional hearth-brazed lug frame was being ousted by the all-welded frame, due to advancements in steel-tube technology through wartime experience.

In trials and scrambles, the big four-stroke single was pre-eminent, but whereas in earlier days competing machines were mainly roadsters stripped of lighting and equipped with suitably knobbly tyres, purpose-built competition bikes were now emerging, exemplified by the 500T Norton, BSA Gold Star, or G80C Matchless.

The time-honoured Magdyno, a combined magneto and dynamo that had originated in the early 1920s, was on its way out and, instead, the alternator (the rotor of which could be mounted directly on the engine shaft, so avoiding the necessity of providing a separate drive) was making headway.

It was not all big stuff, of course. There had long existed a demand for a simple, ride-to-work lightweight, and in the course of any trip by (steam) train, nearly every signalbox along the way would be seen to have a small two-stroke, usually an Excelsior or a James, propped up against the outside stairway. Mostly these were much of a muchness, powered by reliable if none too exciting Villiers two-stroke units, but in 1948 the BSA Bantam had come upon the scene, initially for export only but later for general sale; the Bantam was a frank copy of the pre-war German DKW (as was the 125 cc Royal Enfield 'Flying Flea', used initially by the Airborne Forces but continued into civilian production as the Model RE), but was none the worse for that.

Enthusiasts had for so long regarded Triumph as wedded to

Heavy by present-day standards, but quite a lightweight in its own period, the Royal Enfield 346 cc Bullet is seen here in 1951 Trials guise (road-going, and scrambles versions were listed at the same price). The Bullet was the machine which overcame the trials rider's mistrust of rear springing

the vertical twin idea, that the introduction in 1952 of the 150 cc ohv Terrier single came as a distinct shock. But the wily Edward Turner, who was not only Triumph's chief designer but also the factory's overall boss, knew what he was about, because in the

An unusual shot of a Royal Enfield Bullet at speed in a Vintage MCC road race meeting. The rider is Steve Linsdell, of Bedfordshire, whose standard-looking but exquisitely tuned 1952 Bullet won most 350-cc class races in which it was entered from the 1977 season onwards

years to come the same basic layout was applied first to the 199 cc Triumph Tiger Cub, then to the 250 cc BSA C15 and eventually, by way of the 343 cc BSA B40, to the ultimate 498 cc Victor. It was scaled downward, too, to produce the 75 cc BSA Beagle and, smaller still, the 50 cc Ariel Pixie (these only prove that even as eminent a designer as Edward Turner can put a pencil wrong, just once in a while!)

At the start of 1950, the British motor cyclist was still bedevilled by fuel rationing, but in June of that year came the welcome news that restrictions on private motoring were being lifted at last. True, branded fuel had yet to return, and all that the pumps contained was the dreaded 75-octane 'Pool', but at least coupons were to be torn up and the enthusiast could make the most of the summer – always bearing in mind that at 3s (15p)

a gallon, it paid to check the carburettor for economy!

The familiar names did return, of course, and once more a rider could fill up with Shell, BP, or whatever his favourite brand might be; but then came the Suez Crisis in 1956, fuel was again in short supply and back came all the fuss and bother of ration books and coupons. Cost of administering the scheme, according to a parliamentary reply, was around £20,000 a week. Not until late May of 1957 did fuel rationing end, and by that time successive price increases had raised the price of 100-octane fuel to just over 5s (25p) a gallon.

By the mid-1950s pivoted-fork rear springing had become universal, mainly because proprietary rear-spring units by Girling or Woodhead-Monroe, were readily available to manufacturers. Villiers, who had hitherto built engine units of up-to-197 cc only, expanded their range to include a new 224 cc single of a more modern, rounded appearance than before. Then came a 250 cc single and, more interesting still, a 250 cc two-stroke vertical twin. At last, the small factories – Cotton, DMW, Panther, and that new firm with such unorthodox ideas as a cast-light-alloy frame beam, Greeves – could offer a wider range of models to the public.

The lowest powered transport in the first part of the 1950s had been provided by a wide selection of clip-on engines, designed to turn an existing pedal cycle into a moped of sorts. Of these, the BSA Winged Wheel, and the Cyclemaster, were complete powered rear wheels. Others (they even included the Firefly, a totally unexpected product of the illustrious Vincent company) were clamped above the front or rear wheel, or under the bottom bracket, there to drive direct on to the tyre by a friction roller.

The wartime 98 cc autocycle had all but disappeared, with the New Hudson as the last survivor, and in its place had come a lighter type of autocycle known as the moped. This, in turn, was to eclipse the clip-on, and it has to be admitted that British industry was late in foreseeing the trend. Oh, we tried, with Phillips and Norman both producing attractive-looking mopeds, but the Villiers 50 cc 3K engine was no match for the imported power units.

By the mid-1950s, a move towards enclosure and a general tidying-up was well in evidence with Vincent, of all people, leading the field. Their Black Prince and Black Knight models featured elaborate enclosure formed in a new wonder material, glass fibre (and the appearance of the machines was considered so futuristic that a squad of Vincents served to mount the Thought Police, in a film based on George Orwell's novel *1984*).

Soon, Triumph joined in, draping the rear of the new 350 cc 3TA Twenty-One twin in a pressed-steel cover, and announcing the bike as 'The Motor Cycle with a Wheel in Tomorrow'. However, it was left to Ariel to produce the biggest surprise of all. Designed by veteran Val Page, who had been responsible for

An exhibit from the 1952 Earls Court Show – a Vincent Black Shadow in touring trim, attached to a Garrard S90 single-seat sidecar. By rotating the front-fork auxiliary-damper upper mounting, the fork trail could be adjusted for solo or sidecar work

Cotswold farmer Ron Langston was a real all-rounder, equally at home as a road racer, scrambler, or solo or sidecar trials ace. High above the town of Kinlochrannoch, he balances his Ariel through the Scottish Six Days Trial of 1958

revitalising the Ariel programme as far back as 1926, the newcomer was the Leader, a two-stroke twin from a factory that had built its reputation upon four-strokes.

Unfortunately, the riding public tended to admire the Leader from a distance – and leave it at that. To help recover at least some of the tooling-up cost, the Ariel firm produced, for 1959, another version known as the Arrow. In essence, this was the Leader, but with simplified upper works, and shorn of the side enclosure and built-in legshields that, it had been hoped, would have endeared the original design to the city-gentleman type of customer.

Certainly the city-gent rider, the chap who commuted to work over shortish distances and did not want the bother of dressing-up in bulky motor cycle clothing, did exist. It was just that the Ariel Leader (and for that matter, the LE Velocette) was not quite what he wanted.

The Italians knew what he wanted, and were able to provide it with such untraditional confections as the Vespa and Lambretta. Ironically, Britain had foreseen the post-war scooter boom, and even in the mid-1940s BSA had been toying with a little side-valve model with semi-automatic transmission; that model, the BSA Dinghy, never did reach the production stage and neither did a later design, the very stylish 200 cc Beeza exhibited at Earls Court in 1955.

One scooter which did sell in small quantities was the Swallow Gadabout, a Villiers-engined two-stroke built by a famous sidecar company. But the Swallow was a shade too early, and it had gone by the time scooter mania got a hold on the country.

At long last, in 1958, the BSA group did indeed produce a pair of scooters, powered respectively by a verson of the 175 cc Bantam engine, and by a fan-cooled 250 cc overhead-valve vertical twin. Available to choice under a BSA-Sunbeam or Triumph Tigress name, the scooters were not at all bad, but they could have been better (the side panels, for example, should have been made quickly-detachable, as on the Lambretta, but instead were held in place by a dozen or so fiddly little screws).

They should have been introduced sooner, too, and once again Britain seemed to have climbed onto the bandwagon after the music had stopped.

Still, with the trading restrictions of the past largely overcome, British industry was in top gear and on full throttle as the 1950s drew to a close. Home registrations for January, 1959, were 90 per cent up on the same month of 1958, and 41 per cent higher than the average of the previous five years. And June's figures, aided by a glorious summer, were a fantastic 150 per cent better than those of the previous year.

As 1960 dawned, so the number of machines on British roads constituted an all-time record. A news item from Hong Kong mentioned that a new Japanese motor cycle had been seen in that city. Known as the Honda Dream, it was a 300 cc overhead-camshaft twin, with such exotic features as a pressed-steel, spine frame, electric starter motor, and built-in direction indicators. It would never catch on, of course . . .

However, about this book. The road tests are word-for-word reprints from contemporary issues of *Motor Cycle*, supplemented by potted histories of the model or type under test. To give as fair a picture as possible of the 1950s scene as a whole, I have not concentrated on the bigger-capacity models to the

exclusion of the lightweights – and if it might seem that there are a couple of surprising omissions; well, there are reasons.

To take the case of AJS and Matchless, Donald Heather, who ran the London part of the AMC group, refused for many years to provide road-test machines to the press. It was a policy which could not have done his firm much good, and yet it was not relaxed until the closing years of the 1950s. Then there was the BSA Gold Star. Again, this company never did supply an example for road-testing, and their reasoning was that the Goldie was not a true quantity-production model but, instead, was a rather specialised version of the standard 350 or 500 cc singles, built specifically for trials, scrambles, or clubman racing.

Those apart, however, I believe the models selected really were, in their special day and age, among the Best of British.

Bob Currie

BLACK SHADOW

The Series A 998 cc (84 × 90 mm) Vincent-HRD Rapide vee-twin which made headline news on its introduction in 1936 was, in essence, a double-up of the same factory's 500 cc high-camshaft single. The Rapide was designed jointly by Phil Vincent and Phil Irving and was – or so the legend goes – the outcome of a happy accident in which two tracings of a Comet engine had been placed on top of each other in narrow vee formation.

With much external oil piping, the Series A became known as the 'plumber's nightmare', but when the first post-war Vincent-HRDs were launched early in 1946, it was seen that the company had lived up to the promise it had made in its wartime advertising. It was far more than just a general tidying-up of the earlier design, for the two Phils had evolved something new in motor cycles. Advertised as 'The little big twin', the new Series B Rapide was indeed a lightweight thousand.

Motor Cycle tried out the prototype in May, 1946, and commented: 'It has the wheelbase of a five-hundred, and the weight of a five-hundred, and it handles like a TT five-hundred.' The short wheelbase was the whole key to the model's behaviour, and it was mainly achieved by discarding the conventional tubular frame of pre-war years and, instead, suspending the engine from a fabricated beam which served, also, as the oil tank.

Highlight of the Vincent stand at the 1952 Earls Court Show was this 998 cc Series C Black Shadow with various parts sectioned to show the internal workings and construction. The Series C had only another 18 months of life, before being superseded by the Series D range

Of course, the engine had to be redesigned to accept the stresses of acting as part of the frame, and to suit the new layout the cylinder angle was widened from 47 to 50 degrees. As before, the rear sub-frame pivoted under the control of springs beneath the saddle, but now the wheelbase had been reduced from 58.5 in of the Series A, to 56 in.

Two brake drums were used on each wheel, the rear wheel could be reversed in the fork ends to give a choice of final-drive sprockets, and a completely new servo clutch was intended to eliminate the pre-war problems of the standard Burman component.

Now, it so happened that one of the employees of Vincent-HRD's factory at Stevenage (which, incidentally, had been a horse-drawn carriage works in Georgian days) had been a certain George Brown, who was a road-racing man of considerable ability. George approached Phil Irving with a plot, whereby a Series B Rapide would be given extra-special tuning, to permit it to compete with honour in sprints and such-like where a 1,000 cc class was operative. Phil agreed, and a bike was duly equipped with oversize carburettors, high-lift cams and other goodies, and polished internally to reduce oil drag.

This, then, was the machine which in due course came to be revered on tracks all over Britain as Gunga Din, first of a line of George Brown specials that was to continue with Nero and, eventually, Super Nero.

But Gunga Din was more than just a formidable sprinter. It was a mobile test bed, and from it Vincent-HRD evolved a road-going super-sportster aimed at retaining the low-speed sweetness of the Rapide, but adding somewhere around 15 mph to the Rapide's speed of 110 mph. Cylinders, cylinder heads and crankcases of the newcomer (announced in February, 1948) were given a special baked-on black finish, and the model was given the appropriate name of Black Shadow.

The incredible mixture of high speed and docility was obtained by a specification which included a compression ratio of only 6·45 to 1, and a 3·5 to 1 top gear ratio which meant that, at the bike's designed top speed of 125 mph, the engine shaft was turning over at a lazy 5,800 rpm. As on the Rapide, the clutch was a servo type, brought into action by a conventional single-plate clutch, but to cope with the additional power output there were six springs, as compared with the three employed in the Rapide.

Next move of the Stevenage team was to produce an out-and-out speed version of the Black Shadow twin. This was the Black Lightning, at first reserved for export only, and claimed to produce a maximum speed of 140 to 150 mph. Certainly the Black Lightning was given a great send-off, with one of the first to reach the USA being used by Rollie Free to gain the American national maximum speed record at 150·313 mph. In Belgium, the same week, Rene Milhoux broke the Belgian flying kilometer record at 143·2 mph, and the world sidecar standing mile at 94·0 mph.

The Series B Black Shadow, meanwhile, was soon succeeded by the Series C, introduced for 1949, the main feature of which was the patented Girdraulic front fork, a parallel-ruler design with additional hydraulic damper units; the upper mountings of the damper units could be rotated, to afford solo or sidecar trail, as required.

Another Series C refinement was the fitting of a small and fat hydraulic damper unit between the two springs controlling the cantilever rear suspension. This, then, was the Black Shadow as tested by *Motor Cycle* in their 11 August, 1949, issue. In effect it was the 1950 version, except in one very important respect.

For some time, Vincent-HRD dealers in the USA had been bombarding Phil Vincent with requests for him to drop the 'HRD' part of the machine's name. This he was very reluctant to do because, after all, he had entered the motor cycle manufacturing world, back in 1928, by purchasing the redundant 'HRD' trade-mark originally made famous by Howard R. Davies. But, argued the Yanks, folks that side of the Atlantic had the weird idea that 'HRD' meant that, somehow, the company was related to Harley-Davidson.

There being no room (or at any rate, very little room) in business for sentiment, Phil at last gave way, and from 1950 onwards the machines were known as plain Vincent. That meant not only a new tank transfer but, also, new timing chest and rocker-cap castings bearing the Vincent name. The opportunity was taken to switch from sand-cast to die-cast covers, giving an improved finish and, also, a slight saving in weight.

The next year's Shadow adopted a forged steel instead of bronze idler pinion in the timing train, in an effort to quieten the mechanical noise. There was, too, a metering device in the oil feed to the rocker gear, but the characteristic 'tap-tap-tap' was shushed but slightly.

It must be said that the Vincent was an acquired taste, a hand-built machine that was the post-war equivalent of the Brough Superior, and a glance at the 1951 Buyer's Guide shows why the Black Shadow was by no means a big-volume seller. The cost, all in, was a daunting £402 10s, which may not sound very much in these inflationary times, but must be compared with the contemporary 1,000 cc Ariel Square Four at £281, or the sporty 499 cc BSA Gold Star Clubman at £253.

By the mid-1950s, the number of potential customers with that kind of money to spare had fallen considerably, and the Vincent firm tried to keep going by producing a number of less-costly items, such as (of all things) a 50 cc bicycle auxiliary known as the Firefly, a water-scooter with a disastrously-designed glass-fibre hull, and a range of lightweights which were mainly of NSU origin.

There was to be one startling last fling in the big-machine field, with the announcement late in 1954 of the Series D range, almost wholly shrouded in futuristic glass-fibrework, including inbuilt legshields, handlebar windscreen, and facia panel. There was a whole family of new names, too – Black Prince (instead of Black Shadow), Black Knight (instead of Rapide), and Victor (instead of the single-cylinder Comet). It was a bold move, but it met with little success, and in September, 1955, came the announcement that the factory was closing down. 'The product', said Philip Vincent, in explanation 'will not stand a higher retail price. Continuing escalating production costs have brought the company to the position where there is no financial return from the manufacture and sale of motor cycles.' It was understandable, but a pity, for all that.

Above: *in 1950, Manchester dealer Reg Dearden constructed a Shorrock-supercharged 998 cc Black Lightning. The intention was that road-racer Les Graham would make an attempt on the world motor cycle land speed record with it but, tragically, Graham was killed in the 1953 Senior TT, and the record-breaking project was abandoned*

Below: *most potent of the production Vincent models, the 998 cc Black Lightning was sold in racing trim only. This is the 1953 version*

998 c.c. Vincent-H.R.D

An Ultra-high Performance Mount for holding and a Cruisi

MERE mention of the name "Black Shadow" is enough to speed the pulse. Since the machine's introduction last year as a super-sports brother to the already famous Rapide, the sombrely finished "Shadow" has achieved wide distinction. It is a connoisseur's machine: one with speed and acceleration far greater than those of any other standard motor cycle; and it is a motor cycle with unique and ingenious features which make it one of the outstanding designs of all time.

So far as the standards of engine performance, handling and braking are concerned—the chief features which can make or mar an otherwise perfect mount—the mighty Black Shadow must

Every line of the 998 c.c. vee-twin Black Shadow is suggestive of powerful urge. Cruising speed is anything up to 100 m.p.h. !

be awarded 99 out of 100 marks; 99 because nothing, it is said, is perfect

The machine has all the performance at the top end of the scale of a Senior T.T. mount. At the opposite end of the range, notwithstanding the combination of a 3.5 to 1 gear ratio, 7.3 to 1 compression ratio and pool quality fuel, it will "chuff" happily in top at 29-30 m.p.h. Indeed, in top gear without fuss, and with the throttle turned the merest fraction off its closed stop, it will surmount average gradients at 30 m.p.h.

In Britain the machine's cruising speed is not only limited by road conditions, it is severely restricted. It is difficult for the average rider in this country to visualize a route on which the

Black Shadow could be driven for any length of time at its limit or near limit. During the test runs speeds of 85-90 m.p.h. were commonplace; 100 m.p.h. was held on brief stretches and, occasionally, the needle of the special 150 m.p.h. Smith's speedometer would indicate 110. No airfield or stretch of road could be found which would allow absolute maximum speed to be obtained in two directions, against the watch. Flash readings in two directions of 118 and 114 were obtained, and in neither case had the machine attained its maximum. Acceleration from 100 m.p.h., though not vivid, was markedly good.

The compression ratio of the test model, as has been remarked, was 7.3 to 1. This is the standard ratio but models for the home market and low-octane fuel are generally fitted with compression plates which reduce the ratio to 6.5 to 1. The greater part of the test was carried out on "pool," though petrol-benzole was used when the attempts were made to obtain the maximum speed figures.

Steering and road-holding were fully in keeping with the exceptionally high engine performance. A soft yet positive movement is provided by the massively proportioned Girdraulic fork. There is a "tautness" and solid feeling about the steering which engenders confidence no matter what the speed and almost irrespective of the condition of the road surface. Corners and bends can be taken stylishly and safely at ultra-high speeds. There was no chopping, no "sawing"; not one of the faults which are sometimes apparent on high-speed machines. Bottoming and consequent clashing of the front fork were, however, experienced once or twice. Low-speed steering was rather heavy.

Any grumble the critics may have had with regard to the Vincent rear suspension has been met by the fitting of the hydraulic damper between the spring plunger units. So efficient is the rear springing now, that never once was the rider bumped off the Dualseat or forced to poise on the rests. Even at speeds around the 100 m.p.h. mark, only the absence of road shocks gave indication that there was any form of rear-springing, such was the smoothness and lateral rigidity.

Straight-ahead steering was in a class by itself. The model could be steered hands off at 15 m.p.h. with engine barely pulling or just as easily at 95 to 100 m.p.h. The steering damper was required only at speeds over 115 m.p.h.

Used in unison, the four brakes (two per wheel) provided immense stopping power. Light pressure of two fingers on the front-brake lever was sufficient to provide all the braking the front wheel would permit. One of the front brakes, incidentally, squealed when in use. The leverage provided at the rear brake is small, and the brake operation was heavy.

The compact engine-gear unit remained exceptionally clean throughout the 700-mile test. Only a faint smear of oil and slight discoloration of the front exhaust pipe close to the port indicated that the model had been ridden at all

Black Shadow

Engine starting from cold was found difficult at first. Cold starting was certain, however, provided that only the front carburettor was flooded and the throttle control was closed. When the engine was hot, there was no difficulty.

After a cold or warm start the engine would immediately settle down to a true chuff-chuff tickover. Throughout the course of the test the tickover remained slow, certain and one-hundred per cent reliable. No matter how hard the previous miles had been, the twistgrip could always be rolled back against its closed stop with a positive assurance that a consistent tickover would result.

The engine was only tolerably quiet mechanically. At idling speeds, there was a fair amount of clatter, particularly from the valve gear. But so far as the rider was concerned all mechanical noise disappeared at anything over 40 m.p.h. All that remained audible was the pleasant low-toned burble of the exhaust and the sound of the wind in the rider's ears.

Bottom gear on the Black Shadow is 7.25 to 1. Starting away from rest can seem at first to require a certain amount of skill in handling the throttle and clutch. The servo-assisted clutch had a tendency to bite quickly as it began to engage.

The Riding Position

The riding position for the 5ft 7in rider who carried out the greater part of the test proved to be first-class. The saddle height is 31in which is comfortable for the majority of riders. The footrests are sufficiently high to allow the rider complete peace of mind when the machine is heeled over to the limit, and were sufficiently low to provide a comfortable position for the 5ft 7in rider's legs.

Now famous, the 25½in from tip to tip, almost straight, Vincent-H.R.D. handlebar provides a most comfortable wrist angle and a straight-arm posture. All controls are widely adjustable—the gear pedal and brake pedal for both height and length. Both these controls, incidentally, move with the footrests when the latter are adjusted.

The gear change was instantaneous but slightly heavy in operation. Snap gear changes could be made as rapidly as the controls could be operated. The clutch freed perfectly throughout the test and bottom gear could be noiselessly

Extreme lateral rigidity is a feature of the massively - proportioned Girdraulic fork. The trail can be altered for sidecar work in a few minutes

selected when the machine was at standstill with the engine idling. However, because of the pressure required to raise the pedal it was sometimes necessary to select neutral by means of the hand lever on the side of the gear box, and also to engage bottom gear by hand.

In the 700 miles of the road test the tools were never required. In spite of the high speeds there was no apparent sign of stress. Primary and rear chains remained properly adjusted. There was very slight discolouring of the front exhaust pipe close to the port and a smear of oil from the base of one of the push rod tubes on the rear cylinder. The ammeter showed a charge at 30 m.p.h. in top gear when all the lights were switched on and the road illumination was better than average. An excellent tool-kit is provided and carried in a special tray under the Feridax Dualseat.

There are many ingenious features of the Vincent-H.R.D. which brand it as a luxury mount built by highly skilled engineers who at the same time are knowledgeable motor cycle enthusiasts. The Black Shadow finish is distinctive, obviously durable and very smart; and only a minor reason why the "Shadow" attracts a crowd of interested passers-by wherever it is seen!

Information Panel

SPECIFICATION

ENGINE : 998 c.c. (84 x 90 mm) vee-twin high camshaft o.h.v. with gear box in unit. Fully enclosed valve gear. Dry-sump lubrication : tank capacity, 6 pints. Four main bearings. Roller-bearing big-ends. Specialloid pistons. Cast-iron liners shrunk into aluminium-alloy cylinder barrels. Aluminium-alloy cylinder heads.

CARBURETTORS : Amal : twistgrip throttle control and twin-handlebar-mounted air levers.

TRANSMISSION : Vincent-H.R.D. 4-speed gear box with positive-stop foot control. Gear ratios ; Top, 3.5 to 1. Third, 4.2 to 1. Second, 5.5 to 1. Bottom, 7.25 to 1. Servo-assisted clutch. Primary chain, ⅜in pitch triplex, enclosed in aluminium-alloy case. Secondary chain, ⅝ x ⅜in with guard over top run. R.p.m. at 30 m.p.h. in top gear ; 1,392 approx.

IGNITION AND LIGHTING : Lucas magneto with auto-advance. Miller dynamo : 7in head lamp : stoplight. Dynamo output, 50 watts.

FUEL CAPACITY : 3¼ gallons.

TYRES : Front, 3.00 x 20in. Avon ribbed : rear, 3.50 x 19 Avon studded.

BRAKES : Twin on each wheel : drums 7in diameter x ⅞in wide.

SUSPENSION : Girdraulic front fork with twin helical compression springs and hydraulic damping ; link action ; pivot-action rear springing hydraulically damped.

WHEELBASE : 56in. Ground-clearance, 5in unladen.

SADDLE : Feridax Dualseat. Unladen height, 31in.

WEIGHT : 476 lb fully equipped and with approximately ¾ gallon of fuel.

PRICE : £315 plus purchase tax (in Britain only) £85 1s. Price includes Smith's speedometer.

ROAD TAX : £3 15s a year (£1 0s 8d a quarter). Half rate if used only on standard ration.

DESCRIPTION : *The Motor Cycle* dated February 19th, 1948.

PERFORMANCE DATA

MEAN MAXIMUM SPEED : Bottom : 68 m.p.h.
Second : 87 m.p.h.
Third : 110 m.p.h.
Top : Not obtained.

ACCELERATION :					10-30 m.p.h.	20-40 m.p.h.	30-50 m.p.h.
Bottom	...	...	...	...	2.4 secs	2.8 secs	3 secs
Second	...	...	...	...	3.6 secs	4.2 secs	3.4 secs
Third	...	...	...	...	—	5.8 secs	4.8 secs
Top	...	...	...	...	—	—	7.6 secs

Speed at end of quarter-mile from rest : 96 m.p.h.
Time to cover standing quarter-mile : 14.2 secs.

PETROL CONSUMPTION : At 30 m.p.h., 96 m.p.g. At 40 m.p.h., 91.2 m.p.g. At 50 m.p.h., 86.4 m.p.g. At 60 m.p.h., 70 m.p.g.

BRAKING : From 30 m.p.h. to rest, 26ft 6in (surface, coarse, dry chipping).

TURNING CIRCLE : 14 ft.

MINIMUM NON-SNATCH SPEED : 21 m.p.h. in top gear.

WEIGHT PER C.C. : 0.48 lb.

SUNBEAM

S8

Despite the black-out restrictions, the ever-present shortages, and the inevitable queueing for the necessities of life, there was a definite lightening of the skies over Britain in November, 1944, a general feeling that the Second World War could not last much longer. And if anything could lift the spirits of motor cyclists, it was the advertisement which appeared in the November 2 issue of *Motor Cycle*.

'The Sunbeam post-war programme is settled!' it declared, 'Everything is ready! Planned. Agreed. Finalised. And now the Masterpiece is under lock and key. Behind closed doors. Replete with a crop of big surprises. Waiting for the "Cease fire" to sound and production to begin!'

The first of the promised surprises, though, came with the name at the foot of the advertisement, for it was issued by Sunbeam Cycles Ltd, Birmingham 11 – an indication that the Sunbeam name, acquired by AMC in the late 1930s, had changed hands yet again and was now in the BSA fold.

Erling Poppe, who was at one time in partnership with Gilmour Packman as co-manufacturer of P & P motor cycles, had long left the motor cycle field to become a designer of diesel vehicles. But during the war period he had been recruited on to the BSA design team.

One Erling Poppe project, which reached prototype stage but was never produced, was an ingenious scooter known as the BSA Dinghy. For the second project, the new Sunbeam, he was given the freedom to design whatever he liked – always provided that it was clean to ride, comfortable, smooth, and reliable.

BSA had already been experimenting with an in-line vertical twin, and the prototype engine, installed in Erling Poppe's office, was undoubtedly the inspiration for what followed. Nevertheless, Poppe brought a totally new approach to the scheme, and the Sunbeam as announced in March, 1946, was very definitely from the drawing board of an automobile engineer, rather than a motor cycle engineer.

No fewer than 30 patents had either been granted, or were pending. Shaft final drive, overhead camshaft engine, rear springing – all the 'dream' features mentioned in the correspondence columns of the wartime motor cycling press had been incorporated, and in theory it should have had the customers queueing up to offer their hard-earned cash. And yet . . .

Echoing car practice, the cylinder barrels of the Sunbeam were cast integrally with the crankcase. Drive to the overhead camshaft was by chain at the rear of the block. A pancake-type direct current generator (dynamo) was located at the front end of the assembly

Yes; and yet . . . Right through the ages, there have been plenty of examples of a maker striving to provide everything for which the public had been clamouring; except that, when it came to the crunch, the same public was apt to hang back and see what the other man thought of it, before going off to buy something humdrum but familiar.

The 487 cc (70 × 63·5 mm) Sunbeam engine followed car practice in combining the cylinder and crankcase in one light-alloy casting (cylinder liners were of austenitic iron, pressed into the block). A ribbed sump plate was bolted to the underside of the crankcase, and the high-tensile cast-iron crankshaft was inserted from the rear. Transmission was by way of a car-type single-plate clutch to an integral four-speed gearbox, and then by shaft to an underslung-worm rear wheel drive. On the first prototype, a rigid frame was employed, but before production began this was replaced by a frame with plunger rear springing.

The front fork was a telescopic type, with hydraulic damping of each leg, but it departed from normal practice by enclosing the springs in a separate, central housing. Rider comfort was aided by a cantilever-sprung saddle, the spring of which was concealed in the frame top tube. Still more comfort was promised by the use of 4·75 × 16 in tyres (massive, in the eyes of the 1946 public, who refused to be convinced that a bike with boots that big could handle properly).

The overhead camshaft was driven from the rear of the unit and operated the valves (which were set at an angle of 22·5 degrees, and worked in wedge-shape combustion chambers) through the medium of rocker arms. Power output was a very modest 24 bhp at 6,000 rpm and, on road test, the first S7 clocked a none too inspiring 72 mph.

Well, fair enough. The S7 was intended to be a luxury tourer, and for those who wanted a brisker performance a sports engine with 90-degree valves was under development. Indeed, a prototype sportster was built and, with larger carburettor than the S7, a lighter flywheel, and an 8 to 1 compression ratio, it returned an impressive 94 mph.

That was much more like it! Or it would have been, but the

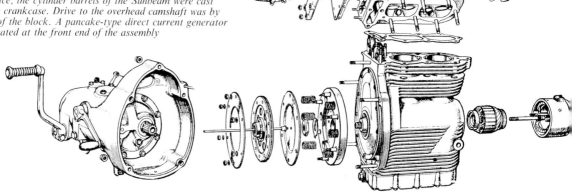

Sunbeam had an inbuilt disaster area. That underslung-worm drive to the rear wheel was incapable of transmitting very much power. Even in day-to-day use it became uncomfortably warm, and on the sports model it used to wear out completely within a few hundred miles.

The Wilkinson Sword Company had experienced similar problems with their four-in-line TAC motor cycle of 1910, and in the later TMC models they switched over to a crownwheel and bevel drive. Sunbeam, on the other hand, just shrugged their shoulders and dropped the idea of building a sports version.

Delayed by the late arrival of bits and pieces from outside suppliers, production did not begin until December, 1946, and the first 25 machines off the assembly line were hurriedly shipped out to South Africa, where Pretoria Police were to provide a sovereign's escort for King George VI's tour.

Clang, again! The engines were bolted directly into the frames, and while this had worked well enough on the toolroom-built prototypes, the production models vibrated like nobody's business. The South African batch had to be shipped straight back to the BSA branch works at Redditch (where the Sunbeams were to be built) for rapid modification.

The modification took the form of mounting the engine on rubber, and to permit it to wobble within the frame a short length of flexible piping had to be inserted into the exhaust system. That makeshift solution was to remain to the end of the Sunbeam's production life.

To help spread the appeal of the Sunbeam to a wider public, the S8 was added from 1949 onward. Rather less of a lumbering elephant than the S7, it achieved a saving of 30 lb in weight, by adopting the front fork and wheels of the BSA A10 twin; it was also £30 cheaper than the S7.

Expert renovator Colin Wall, of Birmingham, rebuilt the Maudes Trophy BSA Star Twin featured elsewhere. An earlier exercise by Colin was this Americanised Sunbeam S7, a concours d'elegance winner at many rallies in the 1960s

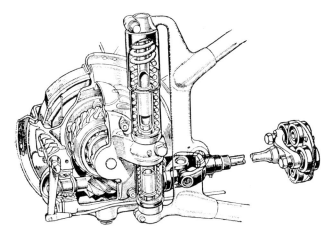

Use of an underslung worm drive to the rear wheel of the in-line Sunbeam twin was dictated by the low positioning of the gearbox output shaft. Unhappily, the worm drive was barely adequate for the power transmitted, and ruled out development of a sports version

Back at the factory, various Sunbeam experiments were put in hand, including a 250 cc single, and a 650 cc water-cooled four, but these never came to anything and, over the years, the amount of development devoted to the in-line twin was negligible. For 1950, Sunbeam dropped the antiquated inverted handlebar levers on the S7, and transferred the front fork springs to within the stanchions; a change in cam form was intended to lengthen the life of the rocker-arm pads.

Small changes in 1952 improved the camshaft-drive chain tensioner, and the oil-pressure switch, but one could sense that the BSA people had no real heart for the Sunbeam, and when it ceased production in 1956, nobody was really surprised. The tragedy was that the Sunbeam was intended for the gentleman tourist, and he just did not exist in sufficient numbers to make the exercise worthwhile.

487 c.c. Sunbeam

Luxury Tourer with Excellent Stee█

WHEN the first thrilling post-war Sunbeam was announced it was acclaimed as a mount embodying most of the features demanded by the cognocenti. With its in-line parallel twin-cylinder engine and gear box in unit, shaft drive, coil ignition, unique appearance and many ingenious features it represented a complete breakaway from current motor cycle design.

The Model S8, of course, is the lightened version of the original design. It is a machine which has so many praise-

Numerous detail features of the S8 Sunbeam make it easy to clean and maintain

worthy attributes that it is hardly possible to single out any one of them and say of it that therein lies the model's attraction. But if there is one feature that leaves an outstanding impression after experience with the S8 it is the smoothness of the engine and transmission, especially when the engine is revving in the higher ranges. The end of every run during the test, irrespective of length, and under all but the very worst of weather conditions, was reached with regret.

There was no pace above 30 m.p.h. which could be said with certainty to be the machine's happiest cruising speed. The engine gave the impression that it was working as well within its limits at 75-80 m.p.h. as it was at 45-50 m.p.h. It thrived on hard work and was a glutton for high revs.

A pronounced tendency to pinking on pool fuel was noted when the machine was being accelerated hard in top or in third gears. Therefore, on the occasions when it was wanted to reach B from A just as quickly as the machine could be urged, the engine had to be revved very hard in the indirect ratios. Peak r.p.m. in bottom and second gears, and almost as high r.p.m. as were available in third were frequently used—with the most pleasing results. Steering and road-holding were so good that the rider was encouraged to swing the bends with joie de vivre.

No oil leaks became apparent in the 600-odd miles of the test. The exhaust pipes did not even slightly discolour. Nothing vibrated loose. The toolkit was only removed from its box on one occasion—and that was out of sheer curiosity. Mechanical noise was no more apparent at the end of a hard ride than it was at the beginning. Except on the odd occasions when grit found its way into the jet block, engine idling was slow and certain. When the engine was running at idling speed or only slightly faster it rocked perceptibly on its rubber mounting. This rocking was transmitted to the handlebars in the form of slight vibration and was apparent up to speeds of just over 30 m.p.h. in top gear.

Above, say, 33 m.p.h., there was complete smoothness. Even when the engine was peaking in the indirect ratios the machine was smooth to a degree never hitherto experienced with motor cycles. The harder the engine was revved the smoother and more dynamo-like the machine apparently became. Only the inordinate exhaust noise tended to restrict the use of really high r.p.m.; the exhaust noise, it should perhaps be added, was never obtrusive to the rider.

Starting the engine from cold during the recent icy spell, or when it was already hot, was so easy that a child could do it. When the engine was cold it was necessary to close the carburettor air-slide by depressing the easily accessible spring-loaded plunger on top of the carburettor and lightly flood the carburettor; then, with the ignition switched off, to depress the kick-starter twice; switch on the ignition, and the engine would tick-tock quietly into life at the first kick. The air-slide could be opened almost immediately after a cold start.

Because of the combination of well-chosen kick-start gearing and relatively low compression ratio, so little physical effort is required to operate the kick-starter that it can be depressed easily by hand pressure. If there was ever such a thing as tickle-starting, the Sunbeam most certainly has it.

An outstandingly high standard of mechanical quietness was yet another of the Sunbeam's qualities. Only the pistons were audible after a cold start. As near as could be ascertained, the valve-gear was noiseless. Low-speed torque was very good, and the engine would pull away quite happily in top gear from 19-20 m.p.h.

From idling to full throttle the carburation was clean and the pick-up without any trace of hesitation. Acceleration was all that could be expected from a machine which falls into a "luxury fast-touring" rather

Notable features to be seen in this view include the unit-construction, pancake-type dynamo, streamlined air-cleaner, and rear-springing

S8 Twin

During the test, the unit remained free from oil leaks. Exceptional smoothness of running was a feature of the power unit

than a "sports" classification. When the mood was there, however, and the full engine performance was used in the indirect ratios, acceleration was markedly brisk.

Pressure required to operate the gear change was so light that the pedal could barely be felt under a bewadered foot. The range of movement of the pedal was delightfully short and allowed upward or downward gear changes to be made merely by pivoting the right foot on the footrest. Clean, delightful gear changing could be effortlessly achieved. Between bottom and second and second and third gears the pedal required a slow, deliberate movement. Between third and top gears the change was all that could be wished for—light and instantaneous. The clutch, too, was light in operation and smooth and positive in its take-up of the drive. It freed perfectly and continued to do so even after six standing-start "quarters." It required no adjustment during the course of the test.

Riding Position

For riders of all but unusually tall or short statures, a better riding position than that provided by the S8 could not be imagined. Saddle height is 30in. The footrests can be ideally situated (they are adjustable through 360 deg.) so that they provide a comfortable knee angle. Even at their lowest position of adjustment they are sufficiently high not to foul the road when the model is banked well over on sharp corners or fast bends, or when it is being turned round in the width of narrow lanes. The wrist angle provided by the handlebars was extremely comfortable.

Handling was at all times beyond criticism. There was no trace of whip from the duplex frame or of lack of lateral rigidity from the plunger-type rear suspension. With plunger-type suspension spring characteristics normally have to be rather "hard." Total movement was approximately 1¼in. The degree of cushioning is therefore not large. The hydraulically damped, telescopic front fork was very light round static load and behaved perfectly under all conditions.

Both brakes provided first-class stopping power. They were light to operate and smooth and progressive in action. They did not fade under conditions of abuse, never required adjustment

during the test, and were not adversely affected when the machine was driven hard through heavy rain and snow. The standard of mudguarding was very good. A long, road-width beam was provided by the 8in head lamp. Full lamp load was balanced by the 60-watt pancake generator at 30 m.p.h. in top gear.

Numerous detail features of the machine make it easy to clean and maintain. The ignition coil, voltage control regulator, ammeter and combined ignition and lighting switch are housed in a metal container below the saddle. Opposite to it the battery is housed in a lead-lined box of similar proportions and design. Both front and rear wheels are quickly detachable, the rear especially so. Ignition and oil warning lights are located in the head lamp, one on each side of the speedometer. The speedometer in this position was easily read when the rider was in a normally seated position. The instrument registered approximately seven per cent fast and ceased to function at 589 miles.

Finish of the test machine was black and chromium and the quality fully in keeping with the high engineering standards used on the machine.

Information Panel

SPECIFICATION

ENGINE: 487 c.c. (70 x 63.5 mm) in-line vertical-twin with chain-driven overhead camshaft. Valves set in single row at 22½ deg to vertical. Squish-type combustion chambers. One-piece aluminium-alloy cylinder head. Crankcase and cylinder block in one-piece aluminium-alloy casting with austenic cylinder liners. Light-alloy connecting rods with lead-bronze big-ends. Wet sump lubrication; sump capacity, 4 pints.

CARBURETTOR: Amal; twistgrip throttle control; air control on carburettor.

TRANSMISSION: Sunbeam four-speed gear box in unit with engine; positive-stop foot control. Bottom, 14.5 to 1. Second, 9 to 1. Third, 6.5 to 1. Fourth, 5.3 to 1. Sidecar ratios: Top, 6.13 to 1. Third, 7.4 to 1. Second, 10.3 to 1. Bottom, 16.6 to 1. Single-plate clutch. Final drive by shaft and underslung worm. R.p.m. in top gear at 30 m.p.h. (solo gearing), 2,034.

IGNITION AND LIGHTING: Lucas 60-watt "pancake" dynamo at front end of crankshaft. Coil ignition with auto-advance. 8in diameter head lamp.

FUEL CAPACITY: 3¼ gallons.

TYRES: Dunlop 4.00 x 18in rear; 3.25 x 19in front.

BRAKES: 8in x ⅞in rear. 8in x 1⅛in front.

SUSPENSION: Sunbeam telescopic fork with hydraulic damping. Plunger-type rear suspension.

WHEELBASE: 57in. Ground clearance, 5½in unladen.

SADDLE: Terry. Unladen height 30in.

WEIGHT: 423 lb with empty tanks and fully equipped.

PRICE: £179, plus Purchase Tax (in Britain only) £48 6s 8d. Price includes speedometer.

ROAD TAX: £3 15s a year; £1 0s 8d a quarter. Half-duty if only standard ration is used.

MAKERS: Sunbeam Cycles, Ltd., Birmingham, 11.

DESCRIPTION: The Motor Cycle, September 29, 1949.

PERFORMANCE DATA

MEAN MAXIMUM SPEEDS: First: *35 m.p.h.
Second: *58 m.p.h.
Third: 80 m.p.h.
Top: 83 m.p.h.
*Valve float just beginning.

MEAN ACCELERATION:	10-30 m.p.h.	20-40 m.p.h.	30-50 m.p.h.
Bottom	3 secs		
Second	5.2 secs.	4.2 secs.	4 secs.
Third	7.6 secs.	6.8 secs.	5.6 secs.
Top	—	9 secs.	7.2 secs.

Mean speed at end of quarter-mile from rest: 77 m.p.h.
Mean time to cover standing quarter-mile: 18.2 secs.

PETROL CONSUMPTION: At 30 m.p.h., 102 m.p.g. At 40 m.p.h., 92 m.p.g. At 50 m.p.h., 71 m.p.g. At 60 m.p.h., 62 m.p.g.

BRAKING: From 30 m.p.h. to rest, 25ft 6in (surface, coarse-textured tar-macadam).

TURNING CIRCLE: 15ft 9in.

MINIMUM NON-SNATCH SPEED: 12 m.p.h. in top gear.

WEIGHT PER C.C.: 0.91 lb.

Douglas
MARK III

Douglas flat-twins of pre-war days, with the solitary exception of the 1935 500 cc Endeavour, had always employed an engine with the cylinders disposed fore-and-aft in the frame. And anyway, the Endeavour scarcely counted; it was so much of a rush job that the engine unit was simply the Blue Chief turned around at right-angles, while the shaft final drive made use of a Morris 8 crownwheel and bevel (not even genuine Morris at that, but cheap 'pattern spares'). Reputedly, only about 50 Endeavours were ever sold.

But the machine announced in the motor cycle press of September, 1945, was a very different matter indeed. The engine was a transverse 348 cc overhead-valve flat-twin, direct coupled to a four-speed gearbox with final drive by chain. Full pivoted-fork rear suspension was incorporated, controlled by a longitudinal torsion-bar spring at each side, enclosed within the frame cradle tubes.

Each torsion bar was secured at the front end, but at the rear end was a short lever (mounted on splines, so that the springing could be adjusted to suit the load carried), with a linkage to the rear fork arm. Originally, the front springing, too, was to have been by torsion bar, with the spring rod housed in the fork stanchions and connected at the base to the short leading links carrying the wheel spindle. Before production began, however, this system was superseded by the Douglas Radiadraulic fork – similar in outward appearance, but embodying helical springs formed from square-section wire, and hydraulic damping.

To the public, the Douglas appeared to be a totally new design, one of the first such to appear on the post-war market. In fact, the engine was basically one that had been designed in wartime, to power portable generator plants. The designer was George Halliday (who, also, was the patentee of the torsion-bar springing system), but when the new Model T35 began to reach the showrooms (from July, 1946, onward) it was evident that all was far from well.

Not only was there considerable side-to-side shake at low engine speed, but quite often (especially in rain) one plug would cut out without warning – and cut in again, with interesting consequences, while the bike was being banked into a bend. Workmanship was poor, and in the first six months my own Model T35 suffered a split fuel tank, a stuck clutch mechanism (due to the case-hardening of the ramps wearing through), a collapsed front-wheel bearing and, finally, a frame break just above the gearbox on the left.

'Trouble is,' explained a Douglas service department foreman, 'no sooner do we train a lad up to a decent standard of workmanship, than off he goes to Bristol Aeroplane, for a much higher salary than we could ever afford!'

Obviously, something had to be done. Erling Poppe, the designer of the post-war in-line Sunbeam twin, had joined Douglas by this time as Technical Director, Walter Moore (designer of the CS1 Norton) was Works Superintendent, and for good measure the immortal Freddy Dixon, a Douglas designer and racer of the mid-1920s, was brought in as a consultant.

Dixon was mainly concerned with combustion chamber improvements, and the result of his work was the Mark III engine, with a new type of flat-top piston, a redesigned cylinder head and a kidney-shape rocker cover which no longer had the Douglas name cast into it. Cosmetic improvements included a restyled fuel tank (chromium plated, with blue side panels outlined in black and white).

Introduced for 1949, the standard Mark III retained the cast light-alloy woffle box silencer carried beneath the crankcase, and deeply valanced mudguards at front and rear. There was also a Mark III Sports, with exhaust pipes which swept up then straight back at each side, and this was possibly the prettiest of all the post-war Douglas machines.

The same season saw the introduction of yet another version, intended for trials work and with the transverse flat-twin engine mounted high in a frame which dispensed with rear springing entirely (for several years in the early 1950s the myth was prevalent that no rear-sprung model would ever make good in trials, because the springing did not permit the punch of the engine to be delivered, by way of the rear tyre, direct to the rockery).

The 1950 range included two very interesting newcomers, the 80 Plus and 90 Plus, the names being indicative of their maximum speeds. Based on the Mark III unit, their engines were specially tuned, had higher compression ratios than standard, and were capable of producing 25 bhp and 28 bhp, respectively, on the test bench. In practice, it was said that all the 'plus' engines were built to 90 Plus standard. If one reached 28 bhp on the brake (dynamometer), the bike was painted gold and called a 90 Plus; if it failed to reach this figure, the bike was painted maroon and termed an 80 Plus!

This pair, together with the rigid-frame trials model, the

The post-war transverse-flat-twin 348 cc Douglas was derived from a portable generator unit, and the first (Model T35) examples were disappointing in many ways. The legendary Freddy Dixon was brought in as a consultant and the engine, with redesigned cylinder head and piston, became the much more satisfactory Mark III

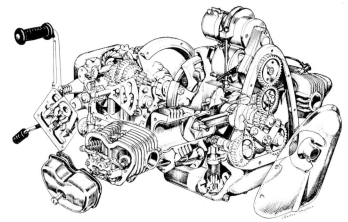

A flat-twin may seem totally unsuited for trials use. Nevertheless the Douglas factory made a serious attempt at producing a trials mount, and this 1951 example displays the special high-ground-clearance, unsprung frame devised for the model. Note the tremendous height of the saddle!

Mark III Sports, and the Mark III de Luxe of the road test which follows, made a total of five machines for the 1950 season. In addition, however, Douglas had come to an arrangement with Piaggio, of Italy, under which the standard 125 cc version of the Vespa scooter would be Bristol-built, also.

The 1950 Mark III de luxe was finished in new polychromatic light blue paintwork, and had discarded its woffle-box silencer in favour of long and rather tortuous exhaust pipes, on the ends of which sat tilted-up silencers. A new rear subframe structure of small-diameter tubing carried triangular tool boxes of cast light alloy. Finally, the big fixed front mudguard had been replaced by a guard which rose and fell with wheel movement.

For its day the Mark III was quite a potent job, and *Motor Cycle* must have been landed with a duff example, if all that they could obtain on road test was a mean maximum of 70 mph. Certainly the enthusiast-in-the-street regarded it as one of the quickest three-fifties around – even if it had been beaten out of sight in the Junior Clubman's TT Races by the BSA Gold Star.

It is one of the mysteries of Douglas production that there never was a Mark II, and the Mark IV had but a fleeting existence. Final development, therefore was the Mark V of 1951 to 1954. This was virtually the Mark III de luxe, but with straight, low-level exhaust pipes and a more sporty type of front mudguard; at first an optional extra, a dual seat was standard equipment on the later models.

During this period, the design and development departments had been at work on a new 348 cc transverse twin. This was the Dragonfly, revealed at the 1954 Earls Court Show, and featuring Earles pivoted front fork, rear suspension controlled for the first time by conventional Girling damper units, and a much sleeker-looking engine unit fed by a single carburettor and with an alternator to supply the electrics. Most notable feature,

Very much a one-off was this experimental 500 cc transverse-twin Douglas, a suprise exhibit at the 1951 Earls Court Show. Although the machine was never produced, the cylinder-head design was used in the later 348 cc Dragonfly

however, was a headlamp nacelle springing from the front of the fuel tank, much after the style of the old Wooler.

The Dragonfly was to be the Douglas factory's final fling. Already in the hands of the Official Receiver, the works were bought by Westinghouse Brake and Signal Company in 1956, and all two-wheeler production had ceased by the following spring.

<table>
<tr><td>

ROAD TESTS OF NEW MODELS

</td><td>

348 c.c. Mark III

A Very Comfortable Touring Machine for Solo or Pillio

</td></tr>
</table>

POST-WAR Douglas models have been available for about three years, and during that time have gained a following among those who prefer a machine with advanced features. These features are noteworthy, and include a horizontally opposed overhead-valve engine set transversely across the frame, a four-speed gear box in unit with the engine, and, specially interesting, pivoting-fork rear suspension controlled by torsion bars housed in the longitudinal cradle tubes of the frame.

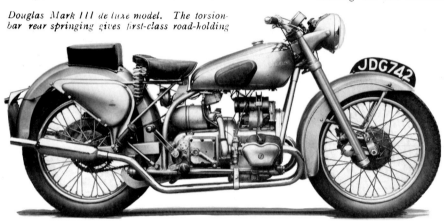

Douglas Mark III de luxe model. The torsion-bar rear springing gives first-class road-holding

The Mark III de luxe machine tested is the basic model of the range of five available for 1950 and is intended for touring purposes; riders interested in high-speed road-work, racing, trials, and scrambles are amply catered for by the four other models. The appeal of the Mark III de luxe lies in the fact that, while the absolute maximum speed available is not especially high, speeds of around 60 m.p.h. can be maintained indefinitely with a degree of mechanical and exhaust quietness, and of comfort, bettered by no other three-fifty on the market.

True to Douglas tradition, the machine under test started readily. Though the crankshaft is longitudinal, the kick-

starter crank operates in the normal fashion and is geared to spin the crankshaft adequately. Almost without exception the engine would respond to one depression of the pedal, on which no special effort had to be exerted; indeed, sometimes a negligent half-swing of the crank was all that was needed.

These observations apply to starting with the engine hot or cold; the only difference in technique was that for cold starting the two carburettors needed to be flooded. Each carburettor is fitted with a hand-operated plunger for the air slide, but in practice it was found that flooding alone gave a sufficiently rich cold-starting mixture. Carburettor intakes are connected to a large Vokes air-filter (an extra) mounted above the gear box, and intake hiss is eliminated.

Engine idling was satisfactory, provided the ignition control was not in the fully advanced position. Failure to retard the ignition meant that there was a chance that the engine would stall unless the throttle was opened slightly and, therefore, the running speed increased.

With the machine stationary and the engine idling, the clutch freed perfectly and bottom gear could be engaged noiselessly. Clutch control operation was slightly heavy and the take-up of the drive inclined to be quick. The take-up was, however, perfectly smooth and progressive. Gear changing was positive and clean provided the pedal was moved slowly; very rapid changes could be made with no loss of positiveness, but, in such cases, clashing of the gear pinions—which could be felt rather than heard—was unavoidable. Slight whine emanated from the indirect gears. Timing pinions, also, could be heard as a mild whine when the machine was delivered, but were, unquestionably, less audible after 1,000 miles had been covered.

The riding position is such that the footrests are farther to the rear in relation to the saddle than with the average British machine. Slightly unorthodox, also, is the handlebar, which is almost straight, mounted above the steering column, and clamped fractionally behind its axis. The rider has a sensation of being "over" the machine, well in command, and comfortable. In short, the riding position was adjudged first-class by a rider of average stature, and the only shortcoming was that the toe of a bewadered foot occasionally fouled a carburettor intake elbow casting.

With the machine's Radiadraulic bottom-link front fork and torsion-bar rear suspension, the road-holding and steering of the Douglas are far and away in advance of the majority of comparable machines. At all speeds, the road-holding is first-rate; this means that the suspensions absorb road shocks of the pot-hole variety encountered in built-up areas and on country lanes, and are equally effective on corrugations and other irregularities of fast main roads.

High-speed cornering could be indulged in with the comforting certainty that the front wheel would hold a precise line and that the

Efficient cylinder cooling is provided by the transverse engine mounting. The Radiadraulic fork features bottom links and hydraulic damping.

Douglas Twin

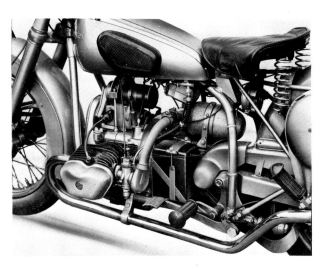

rear wheel would follow without any tendency to chop out. No traces of lateral whip in the frame were apparent and on no occasion did the rear springing or front fork bottom on maximum deflection. A steering damper is not fitted; if a damper were included in the specification, it would be completely superfluous.

As mentioned earlier, the Douglas is happy when cruising at speeds around a mile a minute and, of course, at lower speeds, though the engine is smoother from 40 m.p.h. up than at lower speeds in top gear. Below 40 m.p.h. a distinct hardness in power delivery can be felt. There is no vibration of the high-frequency type at any period of the engine-speed range, and torque reaction cannot be identified except when the engine is idling.

The engine responds to intelligent use of the ignition control. A quarter-retard setting was found the best for traffic work, with full retard for good idling at traffic stops. Pinking never occurs; there is, indeed, difficulty in provoking pinking by abuse.

Front and rear brakes, without being outstanding in efficiency, proved to be adequate for the performance of the machine. The rear-brake pedal is well placed for operation with a minimum of foot movement, and the front-brake lever can be grasped by an easy span of the fingers; front-brake operation was, however, inclined to be heavy.

Exhaust silencing was adequate at all engine speeds and mechanical noise did not obtrude. In over 1,000 miles of use, during which there were periods of high-speed open-road riding, the engine and gear box kept free from oil leaks. Valanced mudguards are fitted and give better-than-average protection. Instead of being attached to the fork legs, the latest design of front mudguard is retained on linkage connected to the wheel spindle. On the machine tested, play developed in the attachment bracket and could not be eliminated by tightening the pivot bolts. Eventually the brackets fractured.

A central stand with semi-circular feet is fitted. The machine could be rolled back on the stand with commendable ease, and rigid support for the machine is provided. The feet are spaced widely enough to be "safe" on cambered roads.

Each carburettor has a cast air intake elbow and an induction pipe leading to a large Vokes air-cleaner. The rear-brake pedal is adjustable for vertical position

Cast, light-alloy tool-boxes are fitted, one each side of the rear mudguard. These boxes are capacious and pleasing to the eye. The Lucas lighting set gave a good, properly focused driving beam; during the course of the test one tail lamp bulb distintegrated.

The speedometer was accurate at lowish speeds and not more than 2 per cent fast at 60 m.p.h. Finish of the machine tested was polychromatic light blue, with chromium plate for the exhaust system, handlebars, wheel rims, tank (except panels in blue), and incidental components. This blue finish is an alternative to black enamel at no extra charge.

The Douglas Mark III de luxe model is, as mentioned earlier, a touring mount which offers the tourist a reasonably high cruising speed in quietness and comfort. It is also a machine which will carry a passenger as well as the rider with consummate ease; during the test the pillion equipment was used and only a slight reduction in performance was apparent. It goes without saying, that the passenger spoke highly of the comfort given by the rear suspension.

Information Panel

SPECIFICATION

ENGINE : Douglas 348 c.c. (60.8 mm x 60 mm) horizontally opposed twin-cylinder o.h.v., mounted transversely in frame. Double-row ball bearing at crankshaft driving end, plain bearing at timing end ; gear-driven magneto. Dry-sump lubrication by vane-type pump ; 4 pt oil reservoir integral with crankcase.

CARBURETTORS : Twin Amal 27/4 ; twistgrip throttle control and independently operated air slides.

TRANSMISSION : Douglas gear box, four-speed, positive foot control ; in unit with engine. Bottom, 16.3 to 1. Second, 10.1 to 1. Third 7.24 to 1. Top, 5.86 to 1. Single-plate clutch ; secondary chain, ⅜in x ⅛in with guard over top run. R.p.m. at 30 m.p.h. in top gear, 2,300.

IGNITION AND LIGHTING : Lucas Magdyno with manual ignition control on handlebar. Lucas 7in head lamp with domed glass.

FUEL CAPACITY : 3¾ gallons.

TYRES : Firestone—3.25 x 19in front and rear.

BRAKES : 7in diameter front and rear.

SUSPENSION : Douglas Radiadraulic bottom link front fork with hydraulic rebound damping. Torsion-bar controlled pivoting-fork rear springing.

WHEELBASE : 54½in. Ground clearance, 5½in unladen.

SADDLE : Terry. Unladen height, 29½in.

WEIGHT : 408 lb with approximately ¼ gallon fuel, oil container full, and full equipment, including pillion seat and footrests.

PRICE : £135, plus Purchase Tax (in Great Britain only), £36 9s. Pillion equipment and air cleaner extra.

DESCRIPTION : October 14, 1948, and October 27, 1949.

MAKERS : Douglas (Sales and Service) Ltd., Kingswood, Bristol.

PERFORMANCE DATA

MEAN MAXIMUM SPEED : Bottom* : 31 m.p.h.
Second* : 50 m.p.h.
Third* : 64 m.p.h.
Top : 70 m.p.h.
* Valve float occurring.

MEAN ACCELERATION :	10-30 m.p.h.	20-40 m.p.h.	30-50 m.p.h.
Bottom	3.2 secs	—	—
Second	4.6 secs	5.2 secs	6.8 secs
Third	—	7.4 secs	7.5 secs
Top	—	10.2 secs	9.4 secs

Speed at end of quarter-mile from rest : 58 m.p.h.
Time taken to cover standing quarter-mile : 20.4 secs.

PETROL CONSUMPTION : At 30 m.p.h., 86 m.p.g. At 40 m.p.h., 82 m.p.g. At 50 m.p.h., 74 m.p.g. At 60 m.p.h., 61 m.p.g.

BRAKING : From 30 m.p.h. to rest, 31 feet. (Surface: bitumen-bonded, rolled granite chippings, wet.)

TURNING CIRCLE : 16ft 6in.

MINIMUM NON-SNATCH SPEED : 18 m.p.h. in top gear.

WEIGHT PER C.C. : 1.17 lb.

BSA
BANTAM DE LUXE

Although it may seem a trifle odd to include a cheap and cheerful little two-stroke in a collection of classic bikes of the 1950s, when that model is the BSA Bantam the choice can be justified. Used by everyone from Post Office telegram boys to gas-meter readers, and from missionaries in New Guinea to sheep-herders in the Australian outback, no bike had ever before gained such universal affection – unless, maybe, you count the BSA 'round tank' of the mid-1920s. Come to think of it, that one, too, was a product of the BSA branch works at Redditch, rather than of Small Heath itself.

It is no secret that the Bantam was only British by adoption, and its origin was the DKW RT125, built at the Zschopauer Motorradwerk, in Saxony. Plans of the DKW were acquired by the Allied forces as war reparations, and copies were passed to several factories, including Harley-Davidson. Also DKW-based, the 125 cc Royal Enfield 'Flying Flea' had been in production at Redditch since 1939, but the BSA technicians, unlike Royal Enfield, decided to make a 'mirror image' power unit, in which the various parts were not only converted from metric to inch dimensions but were 'opposite hand' to the German originals.

The first the British public knew of the scheme was a press announcement in March, 1948, that 'to meet a specific contract obtained from an overseas market' (actually, it was Sweden) BSA had evolved a new 123 cc (52 × 58 mm) two-stroke engine-gear unit. Details embraced concentric kick-starter and gear-lever shafts, a Wico-Pacy flywheel magneto, and a small Amal carburettor.

Two months later, it was announced that a complete lightweight motor cycle was on the stocks, the first BSA two-stroke since the abyssmal 175 cc two-speeder of 1928-29. This, too, was reserved for export only, and it featured an all-welded tubular frame, undamped telescopic spring forks, valanced mudguards (the front being fixed to the fork stanchions), direct lighting, and – nice touch, this – a bulb horn mounted through the steering head. Apart from cream tank panels the colour, like that of the Sunbeam S7 from the same Redditch works, was mist green.

Quantity production of the Model D1, which had yet to gain its Bantam name, began in July, 1948, and by the October had progressed well enough for some to be diverted at last to the home market. Now it was indeed the Bantam (a model name used also by Douglas in 1934), selling at a tax-inclusive price of £76 4s, plus a further £4 if a customer fancied a D-shaped Smiths speedometer.

Ironically, back in East Germany a small group of former DKW employees at about this time were struggling to get the Zschopauer Motorradwerk back into production. Their first product, too, was the RT125, initially under an IFA label. Later, they simply reversed the factory name so that it was Motorradwerk Zschopau or, in short, MZ.

Shortly after the first batch of Bantams reached Australia, the local racing lads began carving and hacking, welding lumps to the underside of the combustion chamber, and filing pieces out of the piston. Running at compression ratios of up to 15 to 1, they got 125 cc-class racing under way at minimal cost.

In Britain, too, enthusiasts such as John Hogan and Fron Purslow started to pit their modified Bantams against the sleeved-down pre-war Royal Enfield and New Imperial four-strokes in short-circuit racing. And Bantam owners were quick to take advantage of the newly-announced 125 cc Isle of Man TT of 1951.

By that time George Pickering, Reg Jackson and others were regularly picking up awards in trials, while Jackie Bodenham and Jimmy Bray kept the BSA flag flying in scrambles (where, it must be admitted, the Dot-Villiers had yet to make its formidable presence felt).

In fact, BSA had added a 'competitions' Bantam to the standard catalogue, although the description was warranted only by the fact that it had lowered gear ratios, a bigger rear tyre, and a tilted-up 'flat-fish' silencer.

The original D1 Bantam was augmented by the 148 cc (57 × 58 mm) D3 Bantam Major in 1954, with plunger-type rear springing (available also on the D1 de Luxe) and a more generous allowance of cylinder barrel and head finning. The 'flat-fish' silencer was replaced by a torpedo type with detachable baffle unit.

Mainly for institutional sales (Post Office, Forestry Commission, etc), the rigid-frame D1 123 cc model remained in production until 1956, when the plunger-sprung model only was marketed. In the same year, the Bantam Major fitted a pivoted rear fork, and a dual seat, and the competitions versions of the 123 and 148 cc models were dropped from the catalogue.

The last move was a bit surprising, because Brian Stonebridge

Simple but effective, that was the BSA Bantam. It originally had a 123 cc engine, but was complemented in 1954 by the Bantam Super with a 148 cc power unit, seen here in a sectioned drawing

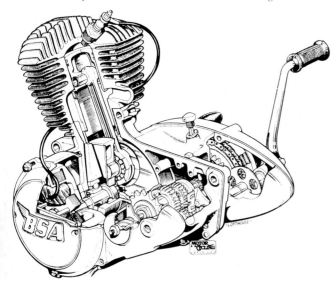

By 1960, when this 173 cc D7 Bantam Super was on offer, the little BSA had become slightly more sophisticated. The unusual lubrication system allowed the drive-side main bearing to be oiled by the primary chain, while the ignition-side main bearing was oiled from the gearbox

had joined the Small Heath competitions department in 1955 and, virtually for sheer devilment, had started to make Bantams fly a lot quicker than before. Brian himself scored a sensation at Shrubland Park, while John Draper with a Stonebridge-tuned 148 cc engine, won the lightweight class of the Experts Grand National scramble. Even more enterprising, Draper kept his Bantam Major on the 1956 Scottish Six Days Trial leader board all week, eventually tieing for sixth place with Sammy Miller (497 cc Ariel).

But it seemed that the BSA bosses just did not want to know, and the efforts of the competitions department received little encouragement from above.

The 173 cc (61·5 × 58 mm) D5 Bantam Super came upon the scene in 1958, evolving into the D7 of the same capacity from 1960 onwards. It was to gain still more power, becoming the

The Bantam in its almost final guise, as the 173 cc three-speed Bantam de Luxe of 1966, selling at £135. Last of the line was the four-speed D14/4 announced in 1968

D10 in 1967, the four-speed D13 a year later and, finally, the 14 bhp D14/4.

Even by May, 1951, 50,000 Bantams had been built, and the eventual tally must have been well over half a million. True, there were occasional mistakes – such as the time when the engineering department, without consulting the drawing office, put in hand a method of holding disc plates to the flywheel sides by light centre-punch peening; *that* caused a few wrecked engines before the trouble was rectified. But by and large, the Bantam did just what was expected of it. It was not glamorous, nor did the general public want it to be, but as the 1960s were coming to a close, so the whizz-kid brigade staffing the new BSA research establishment at Umberslade Hall tried to take it up-market.

But for all the extra potency of the D14/4, it was a harsher and less forgiving machine than its forbears.

It was during the winter of 1966-67 that the lads of the BSA competitions shop hatched another plot. By then, an off-road version of the Bantam was in production under the name of the Bushman, and while making a promotional film for Australia, world moto-cross champion Jeff Smith, and competitions manager Brian Martin, were struck by the Bushman's trials potential. They went into consultation with Michael Martin, who was involved with Bantam engine development, and with Mick Bowers.

Using a BSA C15 Trials front fork, a Triumph Tiger Cub rear fork, Victor Enduro air cleaner, and other bits from standard models, they built a small batch of experimental trials models, and on one of these Dave Rowland created a sensation by finishing second in the Scottish Six Days Trial (Sammy Miller was the winner).

'Not interested', said the BSA hierarchy. 'The trials market is too small to bother about.' And with indecent haste they killed off the Bantam, even putting a sledge-hammer through the jigs so that it could never be resurrected. But its ghost, at least, lives on – as the MZ TS150 Eagle.

B.S.A. 123 c.c. Bantam

High-performance Two-stroke with Excellent Front

SINCE the B.S.A. 123 c.c. Bantam was introduced three years ago, it has earned for itself a wide following among two-stroke enthusiasts. Now, with the A.C. generator available and probably more especially the addition of neat, plunger-type rear suspension, the model's appeal has been further enhanced.

The degree of comfort provided by the combination of the telescopic front fork and rear suspension is quite exceptional for a machine in the 125 c.c. class. Badly surfaced, cobbled roads and tram tracks can be traversed at speed without the wheel-

Rear springing gives the 123 c.c. B.S.A. Bantam de Luxe a high degree of comfort

hop sometimes experienced with lightweights. The rear suspension is commendably light round the static load position so that small road shocks—as well as severe ones—are satisfactorily absorbed.

More than this, however; because of the excellent build-up provided, bottoming on full-shock loading was never experienced with a 10½-stone rider in the saddle. Both front and rear suspensions occasionally could be made to bottom on rebound, but never seriously.

Steering and road holding were of the true confidence-instilling variety no matter what the speed and irrespective of

the conditions. The angle to which the model could be heeled over was limited only by the height of the footrests, but even that was sufficient not to cause concern except when heeling the model over rather farther than is strictly necessary under normal conditions.

Holding a chosen line on a corner or bend called for no effort and appeared to be all but automatic. On greasy cobbles and wood blocks the handling earned full marks. It was possible to ride the Bantam feet-up at the slowest crawl. Straight-ahead steering was very, very good.

Ignition on the A.C. generator model is, of course, by battery and coil, and the ignition switch is in the head lamp. To make a cold start the drill was to switch on the ignition, flood the carburettor and close the strangler and, with the throttle held rather more than one-third open, operate the kick-starter. Starting from cold generally needed two or perhaps three digs on the pedal. When started from cold the engine required only about a quarter of a mile to warm up. After the first few seconds the strangler could be opened the merest fraction; then, later, it could be fully opened. It was, incidentally, required for each cold start.

When the engine was hot, starting could be accomplished by making only a negligent half or quarter-swing on the kickstarter. Operating the kickstarter required little muscular effort, but it was necessary to finish the swing early so as not to come up against the footrest with one's foot.

Mechanical quietness of the engine was excellent and at no time at all were traces of two-stroke rattle identified. The standard of exhaust silencing, however, was not all it might have been both for the rider's and pedestrians' comfort.

Best fast cruising speed of the test machine was in the region of 40 m.p.h., though a maximum cruising speed of 45 m.p.h. could be held for hour after hour apparently without detriment to the engine. In fact, the engine just could not be made to tire. It was driven on full throttle, or nearly so, during 300-odd miles of the test and no ill-effects manifested themselves. At the bottom end of the r.p.m. scale the engine pulled very well indeed. It two-stroked smoothly and evenly at speeds down to 23 m.p.h. in top gear on a flat road where there was no appreciable head wind. The engine did not idle reliably at very low tick-over speeds.

Engine balance was very good and unimpaired at all normally used revs. Vibration was only apparent when the engine was screamed mercilessly in bottom and second gears. The transmission, too, was beautifully smooth and "taut," giving the impression, almost, that there was no rear chain there at all.

Acceleration and power on hills were probably rather better than those associated normally with small two-stroke machines. Similar praise might well be used in connection with the brakes. Both were smooth and

Concentric shafts for kick-start and foot gear-change levers are employed. The crankcase has a commendably neat exterior

powerful in operation and required only light pressure at the hand, or foot, control, as the case may be. During the course of the test the front brake cable required adjustment on one occasion.

The gear change operates on the up-for-upward changes and down-for-downward changes principle. Except for the fact that it was not possible to position the gear-change lever so that it could be operated without moving the right foot from its footrest, no criticism could be applied to the gear change; even this is a small criticism, since the pedal provides a short, light movement. Noiseless upward changes could be easily effected between any pair of gears, provided that the pedal was moved with a slow deliberate movement. If desired, upward changes could be made just as quickly as the controls could be operated and, though the gears with this treatment emitted a slight "click" as they engaged, there was no danger of missing a gear or, apparently, of causing harm.

Downward changes could always be executed quickly, lightly, easily. The clutch freed perfectly; it was smooth in its take-up of the drive and light in operation. Bottom gear could always be selected noiselessly from neutral notwithstanding a rather high idling speed. Neutral was easily located from either first or second gears.

A high standard of comfort was provided by the combination of a good riding position and controls that were smooth and light in operation and well placed. The handlebars are of the rather wide and flat variety and have the grips comfortably positioned in relation to the saddle. Probably an even greater standard of comfort would be provided if the footrests were mounted slightly farther forward.

Apart from the fact that the rear chain appeared to be receiving too much oil and, in delivery tune, the exhaust pipe joints became messy, the only oil which appeared outside the engine-gear unit was that resulting from flooding the carburettor. The petroil filler cap also had a tendency to leak slightly.

A Lucas A.C. generator, with battery and coil ignition, was fitted to the machine tested

A driving beam that allowed full-throttle riding after dark was provided by the 6in head lamp. The dipswitch was conveniently placed on the left handlebar, and the head-lamp switch itself had a sweet, positive action. The ammeter is illuminated when the lights are switched on. The lamp and coil load was balanced at 30 m.p.h. in top gear. An "emergency" position is provided in the combined light and ignition switch. This causes the battery and rectifier to be by-passed, the coil in this case being fed directly from the A.C. generator (so that the machine can be started even if the battery is flat). With the emergency position of the switch in use, sufficient current was available to provide easy starting on the kickstarter.

The tool-box provided is fitted on the seat pillar. It is large enough to accommodate comfortably the tool-kit, but not, in addition, a repair outfit. The colour scheme is green, cream and chromium and the general appearance very smart.

Information Panel

SPECIFICATION

ENGINE : B.S.A. 123 c.c. (52 x 58 mm) single-cylinder two-stroke with three-speed gear in unit. Roller-bearing big-end ; ball bearings supporting mainshafts. Domed crown, Lo-Ex, aluminium-alloy piston. Detachable aluminium-alloy cylinder head. Petroil lubrication.

CARBURETTOR : Amal needle-jet type with twistgrip throttle control. Air filter, with external lever for cold-starting strangler.

TRANSMISSION : B.S.A. three-speed gearbox in unit with engine. Positive-stop, fully enclosed, foot-change. Top, 7.0 to 1. Second, 11.7 to 1. Bottom, 22.0 to 1. Cork insert clutch running in oil. Primary chain ⅜ x 0.225in in oil-bath chain case. Secondary chain ½ x 0.305in with guard over top run.

IGNITION and LIGHTING : Coil. Lucas 45-watt A.C. generator, Westinghouse rectifier and Lucas 5-amp. battery. Twin filament, 24 w. main bulb.

PETROIL CAPACITY : 1¾ gallons.

TYRES : Dunlop, 2.75 x 19in front and rear.

BRAKES : 5in diameter internal expanding front and rear.

SUSPENSION : Telescopic front fork with a single helical spring in each leg. Plunger-type rear-springing.

WHEELBASE : 50½in. Ground clearance, 5in.

SADDLE : Mansfield. Height, 28in unladen.

WEIGHT : 171lb with dry tank and fully equipped.

PRICE : £74 3s. 6d., plus purchase tax (in Britain only), £20 0s. 7d.

ROAD TAX : £1 17s. 6d. a year ; 10s. 4d. a quarter. Half-rate if standard ration only.

MAKERS : B.S.A. Cycles, Ltd., Small Heath, Birmingham, 11.

DESCRIPTION : *The Motor Cycle,* October 6, 1949.

PERFORMANCE DATA

MEAN MAXIMUM SPEED : Bottom : 22 m.p.h.
Second : 40 m.p.h.
Top : 46 m.p.h.

MEAN ACCELERATION :	10-20 m.p.h.	15-25 m.p.h.	20-30 m.p.h.
Bottom	3.2 secs	—	—
Second	4.2 secs	4.4 secs	4.2 secs
Top	8.4 secs	8.4 secs	8.0 secs

Mean speed at end of quarter-mile from rest : maximum.
Mean time taken from rest to 30 m.p.h. : 7.8 secs.

PETROIL CONSUMPTION : At 20 m.p.h., 160 m.p.g. At 30 m.p.h., 144 m.p.g. At 40 m.p.h., 112 m.p.g.

BRAKING : From 30 m.p.h. to rest, 32 feet. (Surface, dry tar-macadam.)

TURNING CIRCLE : 11 feet.

MINIMUM NON-SNATCH SPEED : 13 m.p.h. in top gear.

WEIGHT PER C.C. : 1.4 lb.

ROYAL ENFIELD
BULLET

'It seems to me there has been more rubbish talked, and criticism made, about Enfields than about any other marque. I'm glad I have managed to turn a few heads by showing just what a Bullet can do!' So says Bedfordshire nurseryman Steve Linsdell, whose performances with a home-tuned 346 cc Royal Enfield Bullet in Vintage MCC meetings of the late 1970s have been little short of astounding. Steve's Bullet, a village hack purchased for just £10, began life as a 1950 model exactly as road-tested here.

Subsequent modifications included regrinding the cams (basically to BSA Gold Star profiles), opening up the inlet port and fitting a bigger inlet valve and, perhaps the major significant change, substituting a caged-roller big-end bearing for the admittedly archaic white-metalled free-floating big-end bush first adopted by Royal Enfield in the 1930s and used throughout the Second World War in the thousands of 346 cc Model WD/CO ohv singles supplied to the British Army.

The origin of the Bullet name is older still, and dates from September, 1932, when three new sports models (respectively of 248, 346, and 499 cc) were added to the Royal Enfield range.

The depth to which the cylinder barrel of the Bullet engine was spigoted into the crankcase mouth is seen clearly in this exploded view of a 1952 power unit. The semi-unit-construction, four-speed Albion gearbox was bolted directly to a facing at the rear of the crankcase

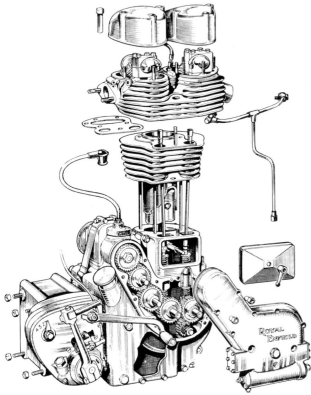

Common to all three, even at that remote period, were foot-change four-speed gearboxes which embodied an external gear-position indicator, an oil compartment integral with the crankcase, dry-sump lubrication and, naturally, the rubber-block cush-drive rear hub pioneered by Royal Enfield in the mists of history. Chilled-iron valve guides, and nitrided valve stems, were features very much in advance of contemporary motor cycle engineering.

That 1932 Bullet, however, had an inclined engine, exposed valve gear, Pilgrim oil pump, and chain-driven magneto, and for the true ancestor of the post-war model we turn to the 346 cc (70 × 90 mm) Model G, first revealed to the public in August, 1935.

Features of the new Model G included vertical cylinder, cast-in pushrod tunnel, totally-enclosed valve gear, magneto driven by train of gears, and a unique double-ended eccentric oil pump. This was the unit which was eventually to form the basis of the military machine and, indeed, the Model G was to continue into peacetime production – little changed except for the now almost obligatory telescopic front fork.

But in February, 1948, the Royal Enfield works trials team of Charlie Rogers, George Holdsworth, and Jack Plowright made a surprise appearance at the Colmore Cup Trial on three brand-new models equipped with oil-damped, pivoted fork rear suspension. These were the first prototypes of what was to be the new 346 cc Bullet, and although their Colmore Cup Trial debut was only modestly successful (Rogers and Plowright each won first-class awards, Holdsworth a second-class), the machine was to cover itself with glory in the International Six Days Trial that same autumn, when Charlie Rogers and Vic Brittain, both on Bullets, were members of the victorious British Trophy squad.

Although the layout of the Bullet engine was, obviously, inspired by the Model G unit, and the famous floating big-end bush was retained, in many other respects it was a complete redesign. Notably, the barrel was spigoted into the somewhat higher crankcase mouth by almost half its length, and the cylinder head was of light-alloy instead of cast-iron. Internals included a light-alloy connecting rod in RR56 material, and an oval-turned piston in low-expansion alloy. Power output was 18 bhp at 5,750 rpm.

The four-speed gearbox was bolted directly to a facing on the rear of the crankcase in semi-unit-construction style, and this permitted the use of a duplex primary chain tensioned by a slipper. The model joined the range for the 1949 season, priced at £171, as against the £146 asked for the standard (and still rigid-framed) Model G.

Not unexpectedly, the Bullet was tried in the Isle of Man Clubman's TT, where five models were entered for the Junior race, two of them ridden by Bill Lomas, and Sam Seston (who was later to become better known as a trials sidecar ace). Sad to say, only one of the five machines finished, although for the first two laps Bill Lomas had kept his Bullet up among the leading dozen.

Indeed, it was in the trials field, rather than as a speedster, that

the Bullet was to make its mark. At first, though, it had considerable prejudice to overcome. Trials machines, said the pundits, had to have rigid rear ends, otherwise they would be unable to find grip. With Royal Enfield's own rear spring units, the Bullet offered no more than 2 in rear wheel movement, but at least it was a start, and with teenager Johnny Brittain demonstrating just how well a springer could perform, the machine gained acceptance.

Gradually, a whole family of 346 cc Bullets came into being; trials, scrambles, and roadster. By the mid-1950s, Armstrong rear damper units had supplanted Enfield's own (and incidentally, now offered 3 in of wheel travel), and the coming of branded, higher-octane fuels had allowed the manufacturers to raise compression ratio to 7·25 to 1; this, in conjunction with new cam profiles, brought a welcome increase in performance.

For 1956, a completely new all-welded frame was introduced, as also was a crankshaft-mounted alternator, but the latter was reserved for lighting and battery-charging purposes, and an independent ignition supply was provided by a Lucas rotating-magnet magneto. By this time the 692 cc Super Meteor vertical twin (which was just a double-up of the 346 cc single) had had the benefit of a year's development, and in turn the Bullet was able to enjoy the development feedback of a modified combustion chamber and larger-diameter inlet valve.

The older-type frame was still fitted to the 346 cc cast-iron engined Clipper (in effect, the old Model G), but eventually the new frame was standardised and the old frame jigs were shipped out to the Enfield India subsidiary – where, ironically, they are still in use, although the Redditch works where they had originated has long disappeared.

On the competitions side, the trials Bullet evolved into the 346 cc Trials Works Replica, before being superseded by a 248 cc unit-construction trials mount derived from the Crusader. Meanwhile the roadster version soldiered on, with no more major changes, until the end of 1963 when a new 346 cc Bullet found its way into the Royal Enfield catalogue. But this, too, was a Crusader derivative owing nothing to the earlier Bullet and so, at last, the floating big-end bush had been laid to rest.

Above: *best-known exponent of the 346 cc Trials Bullet was Wolverhampton's Johnny Brittain. He is seen making a feet-up climb of Foyers, on the shores of Loch Ness, during the 1960 Scottish Six Days Trial, in which he was destined to finish fifth with 30 marks lost*

Above, left: *close-up of a classic trials unit of the 1950s, the 346 cc Bullet in 1951 form. Use of the crankcase castings to incorporate an oil tank was typical Royal Enfield practice. Unusually, the big-end bearing was a floating bronze bush, white-metal coated inside and out, operating in a forged light-alloy connecting rod*

41

ROAD TESTS OF NEW MODELS

346 c.c. Royal Enfield

Overhead-valve Three-fifty With Sporting Performance a

BEFORE the war there were several sports three-fifties on the market. Their engines thrived on revs and could withstand full-throttle driving all day long; they had manual ignition control, full-blooded exhausts, and slick gear changes. The performance approached that available from a 500 c.c. machine. In short, they were "enthusiasts mounts," which paid dividends when handled by an expert rider.

The Royal Enfield 346 c.c. Bullet revives the spirit of the type and has the advantage over its predecessors of

Front and rear suspension systems of the Bullet provided a high standard of riding comfort

ten years' research. With its excellent telescopic front fork and pivot-action rear suspension, the machine is endowed with handling qualities that are second to none. At the bottom end of the scale, the engine will pull uncommonly well, with a degree of smoothness surpassing that of many a modern parallel twin.

Minimum non-snatch speed of the Royal Enfield was a genuine 15-16 m.p.h. in top gear. From this speed the machine would accelerate quite happily, assuming intelli-

gent, co-ordinated handling of ignition lever and throttle. Above 20 m.p.h. in top gear, the ignition lever was required only if very hard acceleration was wanted. Above 25 m.p.h. in top, the ignition control was not called for at all. It was next to impossible to make the engine pink.

In restricted areas, on gradients that are sufficient of a drag to demand third gear from several five-hundred twins, the Bullet would climb effortlessly and smoothly in top gear, and it was even possible to shut off and open up again without the need to change down. Outstandingly good flexibility was one of the machine's most endearing characteristics. At the opposite end of the range, there was no limit that need be imposed to save the engine from being overdriven. Fifty m.p.h. averages were obtained without fuss or bother. If desired, the model would cruise in the upper sixties, and it was apparently as happy and effortless at that gait as it was at 45 m.p.h.

Engine characteristics were of the most pleasing kind. Use of small throttle openings and changing up at comparatively low revs gave a performance of the most gentlemanly character; the machine was then as docile as the most genteel tourer. In traffic, top gear was generally engaged at between 22 and 25 m.p.h. Out of restricted areas, with the machine given its head, the engine came into its own. Affection for the machine built up into high admiration.

The power comes in with a surge when the engine is revving in the higher ranges. Full performance in the gears results in remarkably good acceleration. During fast road work on the test machine, upward gear changes from second and third respectively were best made at about 48 m.p.h. and 65 m.p.h. The exhaust was loud with this type of riding and, though having a note that was stirring to the enthusiast, was probably objectionable to non-motor cyclists.

An aid to brisk acceleration was the excellent gear change. Upward or downward changes could be achieved by making an easy, short, light movement of the right foot. The change was entirely positive and it appeared to be impossible to "scrunch" a change or to miss a gear.

Starting from cold was generally accomplished at the third or fourth dig on the kick-starter, assuming a fairly accurate control setting and no flooding. It was necessary to close the air lever, set the ignition at three-quarters advance, and open the throttle fractionally. The correct throttle setting was very important

A neutral selector operated by a separate pedal on the end of the gear box is a feature of the machine

Bullet

A sturdy centre stand as well as a prop stand is fitted. The tool-box is of ample size

if an easy start was to be achieved with certainty. The Bullet is fitted with a special compression-release valve in place of the more usual exhaust-valve lifter. The valve has the same effect as an exhaust-lifter; the control was well placed for ease of operation.

The same cannot be said of the front brake and clutch controls, which required considerably too great a hand reach. The clutch was rather heavy in operation. It freed perfectly at all times and did not appear to be adversely affected by abuse. It was sweet and smooth in its take-up of the drive. Bottom gear could be effortlessly selected from neutral when the engine was running and the machine stationary. The Royal Enfield is, of course, fitted with a neutral selector. This is operated by a separate pedal on the end of the gear box. To select neutral from any gear except bottom it is only necessary to lift the clutch and depress the pedal to the limit of its travel.

The engine was moderately quiet mechanically. There was a fair amount of noise from the valve gear. The piston was audible just after a cold start. Towards the end of the 600-mile test, a slight oil-leak appeared at the cylinder-head joint and there was oil seepage, too, from the oil-filler cap. Apart from this, the engine—and, indeed, the whole machine—remained remarkably clean.

No praise is too high for the steering and road-holding. The telescopic fork has a long, easy movement that suits the characteristics of the pivot-action rear-springing—which itself provides a higher standard of comfort than the majority of spring-frames available today. Whether the machine was being ridden slowly or at high speeds, the suspension absorbed road shocks most satisfactorily.

This excellent suspension has great advantages during bend-swinging or cornering at speed. Wavy- or bumpy-surfaced bends could be taken fast with the knowledge that the rear wheel would follow the front one with unerring accuracy. Excellent comfort was provided over cobbled, city streets. Low-speed steering was first-class, allowing the rider to raise his feet to the rests the instant the clutch began to bite and to keep them there at the slowest crawl without resort to body lean or other balancing tricks.

Fitted as standard is a neat air cleaner. There are sturdy centre and prop stands, both of which are easy to use and both of which, when in use, ensure that the machine is absolutely safe from falling. The tool-box is of sensible proportions. The speedometer in its light-alloy forged housing is neatly mounted and easily read. Pillion footrests are fitted as standard.

Probably most outstanding of all is the machine's smart appearance coupled with its complete "functionality." Finish of the frame and mudguards is battleship grey; the tank is chrome and silver, and the usual parts are chromium-plated.

Information Panel

346 c.c. Royal Enfield Bullet

ENGINE: 346 c.c. (70 x 90 mm) single-cylinder o.h.v. Fully enclosed valve-gear operated by push-rods. Plain big-end bearing. Double-ball bearing on drive-side of mainshaft. Large-diameter plain bearing on timing side. Compression ratio, 6.5 to 1. Dry-sump lubrication. Oil-tank cast integral with crankcase; capacity, 4 pints.

CARBURETTOR: Amal: twistgrip throttle control; air slide operated by handlebar control.

IGNITION AND LIGHTING: Lucas Magdyno with manual ignition control. 7in head lamp with pre-focus light unit.

TRANSMISSION: Royal Enfield four-speed gear box with positive-stop foot-change incorporating patented neutral finder. Bottom, 15.8 to 1. Second, 10.2 to 1. Third, 7.37 to 1. Top, 5.67 to 1. Multi-plate clutch with bonded and cork inserts. Primary chain, ⅜in duplex, with hard-chromed slipper-type adjuster. Secondary chain, ⅝ x ⅜in, with guard over top run. R.p.m. at 30 m.p.h. in top gear, 2,250.

FUEL CAPACITY: 3¼ gallons.

TYRES: Dunlop, 3.25 x 19in. Ribbed front; Universal rear.

BRAKES: 6in diameter front and rear.

SUSPENSION: Royal Enfield hydraulically damped front fork. Swinging-fork rear suspension with hydraulic damping.

WHEELBASE: 54in. Ground clearance, 6¼in unladen.

SADDLE: Terry. Unladen height, 29½in.

WEIGHT: 351 lb, with empty fuel tank (oil-tank full) and fully equipped.

PRICE: £140, plus Purchase Tax (in Britain only), £37 16s 0d.

ROAD TAX: £3 15s a year. £1 0s 8d a quarter. Half-duty only if standard ration is used.

MAKERS: Enfield Cycle Co., Ltd., Redditch, Worcs.

DESCRIPTION: *The Motor Cycle,* 11 March, 1943.

PERFORMANCE DATA

MEAN MAXIMUM SPEED:		
Bottom:	34 m.p.h.*	
Second:	54 m.p.h.*	
Third:	68 m.p.h.	
Top:	73 m.p.h.	

* Valve float starting.

MEAN ACCELERATION:	10-30 m.p.h.	20-40 m.p.h.	30-50 m.p.h.
Bottom	4 secs.		
Second	5 secs.	5.2 secs.	5.0 secs.
Third	8.2 secs.	6.4 secs.	6.6 secs.
Top		8.8 secs.	8.2 secs.

Mean speed at end of quarter-mile from rest: 68 m.p.h.
Mean time to cover standing quarter mile: 20.4 secs.

PETROL CONSUMPTION: At 30 m.p.h., 102.4 m.p.g. At 40 m.p.h., 96 m.p.g. At 50 m.p.h., 80 m.p.g. At 60 m.p.h., 64 m.p.g.

BRAKING: From 30 m.p.h. to rest, 32ft 6in (surface, dry tar macadam).

TURNING CIRCLE: 12ft 9in.

MINIMUM NON-SNATCH SPEED: 15-16 m.p.h. in top gear with ignition fully retarded.

WEIGHT PER C.C.: 1.01 lb.

ROYAL ENFIELD TWIN

Of all the 500 cc vertical twins on the British market in the 1950s, the Royal Enfield must surely rank among the most ruggedly handsome. It had, too, an internationally proved sporting character (although, surprisingly, as an off-roadster rather than as a roadburner). And yet, with all that was going for it, the model never did achieve a very large following.

Based in Redditch, Worcestershire, the old-established Enfield Cycle Company rarely brought out a new design without incorporating as many existing parts as practicable. This policy applied to the 496 cc twin (first introduced in November, 1948) as much as to any other model in the range, and with bore and stroke dimensions of 64×77 mm it was, to some extent, a double-up of the 248 cc Model S single.

Designed and developed by Ted Pardoe and Tony Wilson-Jones, the machine made use of the familiar double-ended plunger oil pump employed on Enfield four-strokes since the early 1930s. Familiar, too, was the practice of embodying a half-gallon oil reservoir with the crankcase castings. And by housing the new engine in the pivoted-rear-fork frame already proved successful on the 346 cc Bullet single, production was certainly facilitated.

However, in other respects the twin broke new ground, for in conception and construction it was unlike its competitors from other British factories. Mounted on a common crankcase were two independent cast-iron cylinder barrels, each carrying its own light-alloy head with integral rocker box. The exhaust camshaft was carried along the front of the engine, the inlet camshaft at the rear, but the short pushrods were located at the outer ends of each camshaft (so that there would be an uninterrupted flow of cooling air between the cylinders, claimed the manufacturers).

Unlike most other British vertical twins, Ted Pardoe's 496 cc Royal Enfield employed two independent cylinder barrels, each with its own cylinder head. The camshaft drive chain was tensioned by means of a jockey sprocket carried on a moveable quadrant

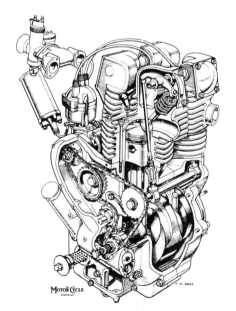

The camshafts were driven by chain, which was tensioned by a jockey pulley mounted on an adjustable quadrant. The crankshaft, carried on one timing-side ball bearing and one drive-side roller bearing, was a hollow, one-piece casting in alloy iron, with integral central flywheel, and was both statically and dynamically balanced before assembly (a practice carried out on Royal Enfield twin crankshafts right to the end of Interceptor production in the early 1970s).

Catalogued as a gentle tourer, the 496 cc Twin had a compression ratio of 6·5 to 1 in 1948 (which permitted it to run on the equivalent of present-day two-star fuel) and a leisurely power output of only 25 bhp at 5,500 rpm. No tearaway was this, but a top-gear slogger of immense charm and almost totally devoid of vibration.

Prototype testing had been carried out in the Swiss Alps, yet in a way that was an omen, because in the not too far distant future the model was to carry the British flag proudly in similarly mountainous terrain.

Throughout its production run, the Twin was to be dressed in various shades of grey with, for its first season, a most attractive battleship grey causing it to stand out from the pack. A change to silver grey came in 1950, for which season, also, a new cast-light-alloy front fork yoke incorporating the speedometer mounting was fitted.

It was in 1951, though, that the 496 cc Twin (it never did carry any other model designation) came into the headlines. That year, the strenuous International Six Days Trial was to be held in the mountains of Northern Italy, and greatly to the surprise of enthusiasts everywhere, the British team selectors invited the Royal Enfield works to prepare three twins for the tests to be held in mid-Wales.

The tests were successful, and when the teams were announced it was seen that 'Jolly Jack' Stocker, on one of the twins, was included in Britain's Trophy squad (which, in fact, was entirely vertical-twin mounted). In the trial itself, not only did Britain gain the International Trophy, but the Enfield works team which, in addition to Stocker, comprised Johnny Brittain and Stan Holmes on two more twins, collected a maker's team award with no marks lost.

True, there had been an anxious moment during the final day's speed test when Stan Holmes' model blew a cylinder head gasket, but because the design made use of separate heads, he was able to continue and retain his gold medal.

The ISDT twins had featured new die-cast crankcases, forged front-fork ends, and front mudguards which rose and fell with the wheel. These improvements were transferred to the production models for 1952, and it may be noted that the new crankcases brought the dry weight down to a very commendable 390 lb.

Again, Enfield twins were included in the British ISDT effort for the 1952 trial, located in the Bad Aussee district of Austria, but by then a 692 cc twin – a virtual double-up of the 346 cc Bullet – had joined the range, and two of the bigger twins were prepared for Trophy teamster Jack Stocker, and for one-legged sidecar driver Harold Taylor. The 496 cc version was not forgotten, and while Don Evans had one for the Vase 'A' team, Johnny Brittain used another as a Vase 'B' team member.

Alas, the event was tough, wet, and muddy. Don Evans came off heavily on the third day, suffering concussion which led to his retirement a day later, and Johnny Brittain dropped out of the fifth day with engine failure.

Nevertheless, the trial did bring a benefit to the standard twin which, thereafter, blossomed out with die-cast cylinder heads, a redesigned crankcase breather, and new low-expansion pistons. Less happily, due to a world shortage of chromium the handsome plated fuel tank was now painted all over and adorned with an embossed flash as still exhibited on Enfield India three-fifties.

To this point, the standard road going twins had employed a direct current dynamo and coil ignition, but a surprise change for 1954 was to a Lucas Magdyno system – at first as an optional extra, but later as original equipment.

Gradually, the 496 cc Royal Enfield twin slipped into the background. It still remained in the programme, but the factory gave more prominence to the 692 cc twin, which developed from the mildly-tuned Meteor into the Super Meteor, and then into the quite potent Constellation. With other models in the range, the small twin was given a cast-light-alloy fork-top headlamp mounting known as a Casquette, and for 1957 there was a considerable rejig whereby it gained, at last, a crankshaft-mounted alternator, and a new all-welded frame similar to that designed for the latest singles.

For all that, the good old 496 cc Twin was on its way out, and after just one more year of production it was supplanted by a newcomer of the same 496 cc capacity, but of rather different aspect. This was the Meteor Minor, in essence a double-up of the 248 cc Crusader and employing the Crusader's 70 × 64·5 mm dimensions, 8 to 1 compression ratio, pistons, and so on. Very much more livelier in performance than the older twin, the Meteor Minor was, perhaps, more in tune with the times. The general public no longer wanted a soft, chuffy stroller of a machine. But that, surely, was their loss.

Above: Motor Cycle's *Midland editor in 1951 was George Wilson, who made good use of a 500 cc Royal Enfield twin in reporting that September's International Six Days Trial, held at Varese in Northern Italy*

Below: *in addition to supplying a 500 cc Twin to British ISDT teamster Jack Stocker, the Royal Enfield factory also prepared three models for Sweden's 1951 Silver Vase squad. They are here seen preparing for the weigh-in at the start of the trial*

ROAD TESTS OF NEW MODELS

496 c.c. Royal

High Performance Allied to Excellent Handlin

WHEN deciding as to whether this machine or that meets one's requirements it is usual to assess good and bad features and make comparisons. In the main—where five-hundreds are considered—the features mostly concerned in the check-up are: handling, braking, gear change, highest comfortable cruising speed, acceleration and smoothness. In all of these, with possibly one exception, the 496 c.c. Royal Enfield Twin gains full marks; which makes it all the more disappointing that, because of problems of supply

The Royal Enfield Twin is a good-looker. Finish is in light grey

and export demands, delivery to the home market is still severely restricted.

So good are the majority of the Royal Enfield's features that it is difficult to select one and say of it that herein lies the model's most magnetic attribute. The engine started easily from hot or cold, requiring no particularly meticulous setting of the controls. To start from cold it was merely necessary to flood lightly, close the air lever, switch on the ignition and give a gentle prod on the kickstarter. The

air lever could be opened almost immediately the engine had started. The engine would idle as slowly and reliably after a cold start as it would after its normal working temperature had been reached. Mechanical noises were not marked and were inaudible to the rider when he was astride the machine.

From idling right up the throttle scale the pick-up was clean-cut and lively. Bottom gear could be selected effortlessly and noiselessly when the machine was stationary with the engine idling. At all times the clutch freed perfectly and it was silky smooth throughout the engagement period. The gear change proved to be perfect. No delay in pedal-movement was necessary when making upward or downward changes between any pair of gears. All that was required was a quick, light flick of the right toe. Neutral could be selected easily from bottom or second gears by means of the gear lever. The neutral selector could not be readily operated by a bewildered foot, because of its height and proximity to the kickstarter

At traffic speeds the Royal Enfield proved to be tractable to an extent not hitherto experienced with a modern parallel twin. It would trickle happily at 15 m.p.h. in top gear—and indeed at an even lower speed if care was used in the manipulation of the twistgrip. From 20 m.p.h. in top gear, acceleration was all that was required under normal driving conditions. At such low speeds the combination of the engine's smooth power delivery and the famous Enfield cush-hub in the rear wheel eliminated any suggestion of roughness. Vibration was negligible throughout the speed range.

Acceleration through the gears was such as to give a favourable impression of the engine's capabilities. Cruising speeds of 60, 70 and 75 m.p.h. were commonplace throughout the test. There was at no time the slightest indication of excessive heat. The engine remained free from oil leaks until the performance data were being obtained; then cylinder-head seepage occurred. When the maximum-speed figures were being recorded there was a hindering diagonal wind.

Another factor contributing to the high average speeds obtainable was the good standard of the exhaust silencing. Only when the engine was revving at high r.p.m., such as when the road speed was in the region of 55-60 m.p.h. in third gear, was it felt that the exhaust noise might prove objectionable to pedestrians. Be-

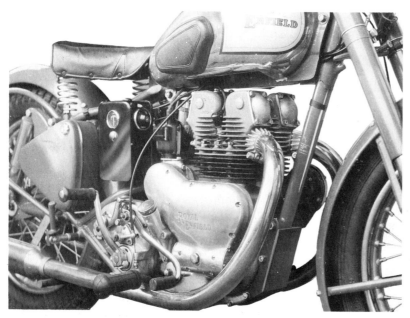

Power unit is up-to-the-minute in design. Cylinder heads and cylinders are separate castings

Enfield Twin

Machine With Numerous Attractive Features

Coil ignition is employed. The high-output dynamo is chain driven

cause of the engine's excellent low-speed torque, acceleration in the higher gears is particularly good.

It is widely held in these days that the best rear suspension is achieved with the oil-damped, pivot-fork design. The excellence of the Royal Enfield suspension bears this out in every respect; a high standard of comfort is provided and high speeds are possible on the worst of surfaces. The test machine was driven over the time-section used in the British Experts' Trial and the time taken was within minutes only of that of the faster five-hundreds competing in the event. Corners and bends could be taken stylishly at speed, the wheels hugging the chosen line in the highest, confidence-instilling manner. The machine cornered with the effortless ease of a lightweight. Low-speed steering was equally good; the model could be ridden feet-up, slowly, and to a standstill. Handling on greasy surfaces was markedly good. The worst of road shocks were well cushioned from the rider—to such an extent, indeed, that there was a deliberate tendency between to ride over broken road edges, and seek out sunken man-hole covers.

Both brakes proved to be rather spongy. The front brake lacked real power, no matter how hard it was applied.

A comfortable riding position, as well as one which provided excellent control of the machine at high or low speeds, was furnished by the relationship between saddle, footrests and handlebar. The handlebar is mounted to the rear of the facia and has an orthodox bend, providing a sensible wrist angle. The reach was such that the rider naturally adopted a straight-arm posture. Relationship between the saddle and footrest was such that an angle of more than 90 deg was formed at the knee; but a disadvantage was that, in their optimum position, the footrests were not sufficiently high from the road and were often grounded during fast cornering or when the machine was being turned in narrow lanes. Riding comfort, it was felt, would have been enhanced had the tank width been less across the kneegrips.

The controls were reasonably well positioned for ease of operation. More hand reach than is desirable for easy and rapid manipulation was required to operate the clutch and front-brake controls. Throttle, rear-brake and gear controls were all light in operation; both rear-brake and gear pedals are readily adjustable relative to the footrests.

Two stands are fitted, a prop and a centre stand. The propstand leg was too long for easy manipulation and general machine safety. Moreover, it was weak at the hinge, the welding fracturing during the test. Operation of the centre stand required knack plus considerable effort.

Finish of the machine is a smart battleship grey and chromium. The combination of an attractive colour scheme and trim lines make the machine æsthetically right. More important, however, is that with its good all-round performance and excellent handling the Royal Enfield Twin takes its place proudly among the foremost machines in its capacity class.

Information Panel

SPECIFICATION

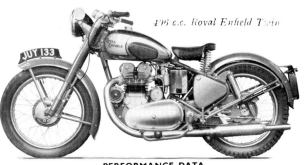

496 c.c. Royal Enfield Twin

ENGINE : 496 c.c. (64 x 76 mm) parallel twin o.h.v. with separate cylinders and heads. Fully enclosed valve-gear. Ball and roller bearings supporting one-piece alloy-iron cast crankshaft. Plain, split big-end bearings. Light-alloy connecting rods. Slightly-domed aluminium-alloy pistons. Standard compression ratio, 6.5 to 1. Dry-sump lubrication with the oil compartment cast integral with, and at rear of crankcase : capacity, 4 pints.
CARBURETTOR : Amal, twistgrip throttle control and handlebar-mounted air lever.
IGNITION AND LIGHTING : Coil through vertical distributor incorporating auto-advance and retard. Lucas 3½in dia. dynamo. Switch, ammeter, voltage control and ignition warning light carried in box alongside seat tube. Lucas 7in headlamp.
TRANSMISSION : Royal Enfield four-speed gear box with positive-stop foot-change incorporating neutral-finder. Bottom, 13.9 to 1. Second 9.0 to 1. Third, 6.5 to 1. Top, 5.0 to 1. Multi-plate clutch with bonded and cork inserts. Primary chain, ⅜in duplex with hard-chromed, slipper-type adjuster. Secondary chain, ⅝ x ¼in with guard over top run. R.p.m. at 30 m.p.h. in top gear, 1,950.
FUEL CAPACITY : 3¼ gallons.
TYRES : Both Dunlop. Front, 3.25 x 19in ribbed. Rear, 3.50 x 19in Universal.
BRAKES : 6in diameter front and rear.
SUSPENSION : Royal Enfield hydraulically damped front fork. Swinging-arm rear suspension with hydraulic damping.
WHEELBASE : 54in.
SADDLE : Terry. Unladen height, 29½in.
WEIGHT : 410lb fully equipped and with full fuel and oil tanks.
PRICE : £167 10s plus Purchase Tax (in Great Britain only), £45 4s 6d.
ROAD TAX : £3 15s a year ; £1 0s 8d a quarter.
MAKERS : Enfield Cycle Company Ltd., Redditch, Worcs.
DESCRIPTION : *The Motor Cycle*, 4 November, 1948.

PERFORMANCE DATA

MEAN MAXIMUM SPEED :

Bottom	: *35 m.p.h.
Second	: *56 m.p.h.
Third	: *75 m.p.h.
Top	: *85 m.p.h.

*Valve float starting

MEAN ACCELERATION :

	10-30 m.p.h.	20-40 m.p.h.	30-50 m.p.h.
Bottom	2·4 secs	—	—
Second	4 secs	3·2 secs	3·8 secs
Third	6·2 secs	5 secs	4·8 secs
Top	—	6·8 secs	6·4 secs

Mean speed at end of quarter-mile from rest : 75 m.p.h.
Mean time to cover standing quarter mile : 16·2 secs.
PETROL CONSUMPTION : At 30 m.p.h., 81 m.p.g. At 40 m.p.h. 74 m.p.g. At 50 m.p.h., 65 m.p.g. At 60 m.p.h., 57 m.p.g.
BRAKING : From 30 m.p.h. to rest, 38ft (surface, damp tar macadam).
TURNING CIRCLE : 13ft.
MINIMUM NON-SNATCH SPEED : 12 m.p.h. in top gear.
WEIGHT PER C.C. : 0.83 lb.

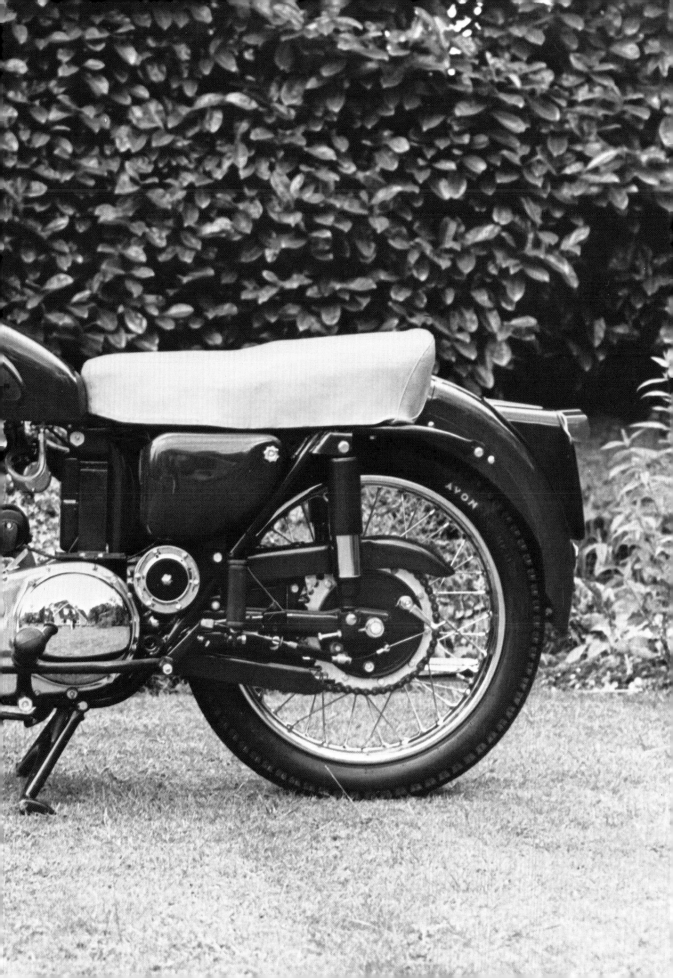

ARIEL
RED HUNTER

Credit for that much-loved single from Selly Oak, the 497 cc Ariel Red Hunter, lies at the door of two famous designers. Certainly it was Edward Turner who, for 1933, evolved the first red-and-chrome-tank beauties to carry the Red Hunter name; but the engine on which he based the exercise was a Val Page product – in much the same way that, three years later, Turner was to take Page's Triumph range of Mark V singles and, with the touch of the expert cosmetician, transform them into the handsome Tiger series.

As a preliminary to the story, however, let us start with the 1931 Ariels. This was the last year of Page's upright-engined 497 cc single, because the main emphasis had switched to a pair of duplex-frame 497 cc machines respectively two-valve and four-valve ohv, in which the engines sloped so much as to be near horizontal.

For 1932, the two-valver was dropped, in favour of a new short-stroke 499 cc four-valve unit, mounted upright in a single-down-tube frame. The new engine looked most impressive, but big trouble was looming on the horizon. Britain was entering a deep financial depression, and before 1932 was out, the Ariel company was bankrupt.

Jack Sangster, the managing director, threw in his personal fortune, and managed to save enough from the wreckage to keep the Ariel name alive, although operations were on a more restricted scale, carried out in one small part of the former Ariel premises. To emphasise Jack Sangster's faith, the new firm took the title of Ariel Works (JS) Ltd.

Obviously, there was no hope now of continuing the full eight-model range as had been listed for 1932, with its multiplicity of types and frame designs. Economy of production was the watchword and, accordingly, Edward Turner proposed a 1933 range, still of eight models but all employing the same frame, even though they extended from a 350 cc single to the 600 cc Square Four.

In truth the range was slightly less extensive than it seemed, because there were three 348 cc singles (three-speed standard, four-speed standard, and Red Hunter), two versions of the 557 cc side-valve, and *four* 497 cc models comprising three-speed standard, four-speed standard, four-speed de luxe, and Red Hunter.

Essentially, the three-fifties were smaller-bore versions of the five-hundred, and so it all boiled down to just *one* basic two-valve ohv engine. For that, Turner took the 1931 Val Page design, but gave it the crankcase and timing-chest assembly of the 1932 four-valve.

Top-of-the-range singles were the 348 (72 × 85 mm) and 497 (86·4 × 85 mm) Red Hunters, a catchy name, but rather more than that because they each had a shapely new chromium-plated fuel tank with bright red top and side panels lined with gold paint, while a big triangular tank-top panel served to display the speedometer, ammeter, filler cap, and panel lamp.

For the larger-capacity mount (but not the smaller), each customer was provided with two pistons; the 7 to 1 compression ratio piston was for road use, and with it the engine developed a claimed 28 bhp. The alternative high-compression piston was for racing, and although no power output was quoted, it was reputed to give the Red Hunter a maximum in excess of 90 mph.

Probably it did, but although Hartley-tuned Ariels were to do very well in the less-important racing events, it has to be said that the only Senior TT Ariel victory was cinematic, when George Formby, riding a Red Hunter thinly disguised as a 'Rainbow', took the laurels in the 1935 film, *No Limit*.

Trials and scrambles, though, were something else, and in the off-road type of competition such riders as Len and Joe Heath, Monty Banks, Alfie West, Jack White, and many more were to take the Red Hunter right to the top of the tree. Indeed, an October, 1936, Ariel advertisement could trumpet the fact that Red Hunter models had won no fewer than 32 important trials during the 1936 season, and that did not take into account the lesser events, class cups, and first-class awards.

Possibly the most elegant British single of all, the 497 cc Ariel Red Hunter is seen here in 1955 form. Colour was claret, with a light tan dual seat

Gradually, the trials versions of the Red Hunters evolved into models in their own right, with lighter, higher-ground-clearance frames, and it is an interesting fact that the 350 cc W/NG ohv machines built for the British Army during the Second World War were really detuned Red Hunter engines, fitted into Ariel trials frames. The point was certainly appreciated by the troops to which the machines were issued!

As intimated in the opening paragraph of our 1951 road test, actual changes in engine specification were remarkably few over the years, which speaks volumes for the 'rightness' of the original design. The type of cylinder head seen here, with separate light-alloy rocker boxes, had been introduced as far back as 1938, and the compensated-link plunger rear springing was an optional extra in the 1939 programme.

In post-war years the 497 cc engine was to gain still greater trials fame, because it formed the heart of GOV132, almost certainly the most illustrious trials machine of all time and the bike on which Sammy Miller made his reputation. Right up to the two-stroke invasion of the 1970s, too, the Ariel was an absolute must for sidecar trials work, as Ron Langston, Alan Morewood, Peter Wraith, Roger Martin, and Roy Bradley demonstrated, week after week throughout the muddy winter months.

Of course, these were competition variants on the original Red Hunter theme, but there were variants in the roadster range, also. By 1954 pivoted rear-fork suspension was in use, with the fork arms formed from box-section pressings, and a new cylinder barrel with integral pushrod tunnels had been adopted. For the following year, there was a light-alloy cylinder head on the 497 cc model (but not the 348 cc) and, eventually an all-alloy engine – as used in the trials and scrambles Ariels – could be specified for the roadster.

Possibly the most handsome Red Hunters of all, although this is a personal opinion, were those from 1956 onward. By that time a new duplex tubular frame was in use, and the headlamp

At one time, the 497 cc Ariel was used almost universally for sidecar trials work. The outfit used by Frank and Kay Wilkins was typical of the 1950s

was housed in a somewhat ecclesiastical cowl. There were full-width hubs, automatic rear chain lubrication, full rear chain enclosure if required, and a gorgeous finish of claret, set off by the lovely light tan of the dual seat.

On the competitions side, the award-gathering continued – led, of course, by Sammy Miller, but not forgetting the efforts of Gordon Blakeway, Ron Langston, Bob Ray (out of retirement to win the 1957 Beggars Roost Trial with only one mark lost) and, across in Ireland, Benny Crawford.

By the time Miller's HT5 trials mount reached the zenith of its development, it weighed under 250 lb. That was the good news. The bad news was that the road-going Red Hunter from which the HT5 had been derived was dead – mortally wounded in 1959 (or so it was said) by an Arrow.

No individual trials machine ever achieved such fame as GOV132, Sammy Miller's highly-special 497 cc Ariel, which won nearly 600 awards in events such as this 1959 national Bemrose Trial

497 c.c. Ariel Re

Famous Overhead-valve Sports Model Tes

FOR nearly twenty years Ariels have listed a 497 c.c. Red Hunter. Since the original two-valve model was introduced in 1933, very few changes in the engine design have taken place, though detail modifications such as total valve-gear enclosure and telescopic forks have become part of the general scheme of things to keep the model in step with current trends.

As all who study design practice well know, when few changes are made to any machine it means that (a) the manufacturer concerned is not suffering mechanical bothers, and (b) that

A straightforward and robust single — the Red Hunter Ariel

the model is proving popular with the public. And so far as the Ariel Red Hunter is concerned, the reasons behind these twin facts are simple ones: the design is straightforward and the construction robust; and, considered in its particular "type classification," the Red Hunter's all-round performance is most satisfying.

Cold or hot, engine starting was always easily accomplished: when cold on the second or third kick-starter depression, and when hot, invariably on the first. A certain cold start required only that the carburettor was flooded lightly, then, provided the

throttle was barely open, the engine would fire, as has been mentioned, on the second or third prod on the kick-starter. With the exhaust-valve lifter operated in the approved manner, kick-starting called for no physical effort of any consequence. The air lever was at no time required during the test.

For the remaining starts after the first of the day, very light flooding was again sufficient to provide the required mixture strength. As soon as the engine had started, the twistgrip could be rolled right back against its closed stop with the certain assurance that a reliable tickover would result. At idling speeds, valve-gear and piston were audible if the ignition was fully advanced. On full retard, however, at which ignition setting the slowest and most reliable idling resulted, the piston was all but silent.

On the road with the Red Hunter, engine noises—piston slap chiefly—were apparent only as an undertone, which was barely heard above the sounds of the wind, and, at high engine r.p.m., the exhaust. Exhaust noise was not obtrusive in open country, but it was too reverberant when the machine was being driven in average-width city streets.

From idling speeds right up through the speed range the pick-up was clean-cut and brisk. Though the tendency to pinking was not particularly marked—even when the sidecar was fitted—it was necessary to use the ignition control in close conjunction with the throttle if the best results were to be obtained. Low-speed torque is particularly good; good to a degree, indeed, that gives one the initial impression that the engine falls into the "woofly" big-single class. Minimum non-snatch speed in top (solo) gear was 17 m.p.h., and the transmission at speeds above that was entirely free from harshness. Transmission smoothness, in fact, proved to be one of the Red Hunter's superior features.

Acceleration from 20 m.p.h. could be satisfactorily brisk in either top or third gears without fuss, provided the ignition control was used judiciously. However, if the right grip was twisted in earnest, and the full performance used in the indirect gears, the Red Hunter was transformed from a single definitely possessing those characteristics which are called "gentlemanly" into one in the famous big-single tradition: a tradition that will assuredly never die so long as there are motor cyclists.

In this case, acceleration was all that the majority of avid sports riders are ever likely to require. Peak r.p.m. in the indirect gears is achieved remarkably quickly. The gear change is utterly positive, and the pedal may be operated by pivoting the right foot in a short arc about the footrest. Snap changes could be made if desired, there being no doubt about certain engagement, though the change would be accompanied by a scrunch from the pinions. Snap upward gear changes, however, are rarely, if ever, required outside

Excellent low-speed torque was a feature of the 497 c.c. overhead-valve engine

Hunter Single

Solo and Sidecar Forms

the sphere of competitive events, and the Red Hunter gear change was clean and sweet provided one caused the pedal to pause in mid-travel, or moved the pedal with a leisurely, deliberate movement. Pedal movement was pleasantly short and light. All the indirect gears were silent on both drive and overrun.

The clutch freed perfectly, and it was light in operation and sweet in its take-up of the drive. It required no adjustment or other attention throughout the test. As with all other hand-operated controls, that for the clutch was well placed in relation to its respective grip. The grips, in turn, go to provide, in conjunction with the footrest and saddle position, what is probably one of the most comfortable riding postures of the present day. The handlebar is of the flat, nearly straight pattern with the grips turned slightly to the rear.

Supreme comfort, however, was not the only attribute of the Ariel's riding position. In addition, it proved to be one which automatically sets the rider in a posture which means much in terms of maximum control—whether the speed be a traffic-crawl or a 70 m.p.h. bat on a fast dual-carriageway. Speeds in the 70 m.p.h. category were commonplace during the test, and were in no way considered excessive so far as the engine's capabilities were concerned. At 40 m.p.h. to 50 m.p.h. the engine was at its best, developing sufficient power to deal with steep gradients without a slackening in speed, and turning over with delightful smoothness. Above 60 m.p.h. there was high-frequency vibration which was not apparent lower down the scale.

If the machine had proved an attractive solo, it was found to be even more likeable as a sidecar mount. When fully laden with a complement of three males (scaling *in toto* some 30-stone), it would cruise quite comfortably at speeds in the region of

The Watsonian Albion coupé sidecar was found to be roomy and comfortable

50-55 m.p.h. The speedometer fitted, incidentally, proved to have an error of rather more than 10 per cent. Acceleration was apparently little impaired by full loading, and neither was handling affected. Although there was sometimes, at high speeds on irregular surfaces, an impression of more than desired lightness in the fork and rear-springing characteristics, neither suspension was found to bottom even on cross-country going.

The Watsonian Albion coupé sidecar gave satisfaction in nearly every direction. Six-foot adults found it roomy, there being plenty of leg space whether the legs were stretched out or bent at the knees. A greater than average stature male—5ft 10in tall—could wear a hat inside and still have adequate clearance below the hood. But, in any case, the hood was seldom required—thanks to the adequate side panels, there are no draughts and all but the heaviest rain was deflected overhead.

Information Panel

The 497 c.c. Ariel Red Hunter single

SPECIFICATION

ENGINE : 497 c.c. (81.8 95 mm) single-cylinder o.h.v. Fully-enclosed valve gear operated by push-rods from a single cam. Double-row roller bearing big-end. Roller and ball main bearings supporting drive-side of mainshaft, ball bearing on timing side Compression ratio, 6.8 to 1. Dry-sump lubrication with double-plunger pump ; tank capacity, 6 pints.

CARBURETTOR : Amal ; twistgrip throttle control. Air slide operated by handlebar lever.

IGNITION and LIGHTING : Lucas Magdyno with manual ignition control. Long 5in 45w dynamo. 7½in headlamp, with 30/30w main bulb controlled by handlebar switch.

TRANSMISSION : Burman four-speed gear box with positive foot control. Bottom, 12.6 to 1. Second, 8 to 1. Third, 6 to 1. Top 4.7 to 1. Sidecar ratios : Bottom, 15.3 to 1. Second, 9.7 to 1. Third, 7.2 to 1. Top, 5.7 to 1. Multi-plate clutch with cork inserts. Primary chain, ⅜ 0.305in in cast-aluminium oil-bath case. Secondary chain, ⅝ ¼in with guard over both runs.

FUEL CAPACITY : 3½ gallons.

TYRES : Dunlop. Front, 3.00 20in ribbed ; rear, 3.25 19in studded.

BRAKES : Both 7in diameter 1⅛in wide ; fulcrum adjusters

SUSPENSION : Ariel telescopic front fork. Ariel link-type rear-springing, with springs for compression and rebound.

WHEELBASE : 56in. Ground clearance, 5in unladen.

SADDLE : Lycett. Unladen height, 30in.

WEIGHT : 385lb, with one gallon of fuel and fully equipped.

PRICE : £146 ; with Purchase Tax (in Britain only), £185 8s 5d. Spring-frame extra, £16 ; with P.T., £20 6s 5d.

ROAD TAX : Solo £3 15s a year ; £1 0s 8d a quarter. Sidecar, £5 a year ; £1 7s 7d a quarter.

MAKERS : Ariel Motors; Selly Oak, Birmingham, 29.

DESCRIPTION : *The Motor Cycle*, 28 November, 1950.

SIDECAR

MODEL : Watsonian Albion single-seater coupé.

CHASSIS : Tubular construction with Silentbloc wheel mounting. Silco-manganese, 1⅛ wide seven-leaf quarter-eliptic rear springs ; eyes and shackles fitted with grease nipples. Front suspension by four coil springs. Taper-roller bearing wheel hubs. Wheel fitted with 3.25 19in tyre. Four-point chassis attachment with adjustable rise lug to allow correct fitting to different makes of machine.

WEIGHT : 90lb approx.

BODY : Ash framework panelled in sheet steel. Dimensions : Overall length, 85in ; squab to nose, 54in ; width inside at shoulder level, 21½in ; height from cushion to roof, 34in ; squab, 23in high × 21½in wide ; seat, 20 20in ; luggage boot, 15in deep × 22in wide × 29in long. Weight, approximately 110lb. Luggage grid and bumper bar standard.

PRICE : Complete, £57 10s 0d ; with P.T. (in Britain only) £72 16s 8d.

DESCRIPTION : *The Motor Cycle*, 6 October, 1949 ; 9 November, 1950.

PERFORMANCE DATA
(Sidecar figures in brackets)

MEAN MAXIMUM SPEED : Bottom :* 40 (30) m.p.h.
Second :* 62 (49) m.p.h.
Third : 77 (62) m.p.h.
Top : 85 (63) m.p.h.
* Valve float occurring

MEAN ACCELERATION :

	10-30 m.p.h.	20-40 m.p.h.	30-50 m.p.h.
Bottom	3.2 (3.8) secs	3.4 (—) secs	— (—) secs
Second	5.2 (5.8) secs	4 (7.2) secs	4 (7.4) secs
Third	— (—) secs	5.4 (8.4) secs	5.8 (9.4) secs
Top	— (—) secs	6.8 (11.4) secs	6.8 (13.4) secs

Mean speed at end of quarter mile from rest : 71 (54) m.p.h.
Mean time to cover standing quarter-mile : 13 (22.2) secs.

PETROL CONSUMPTION : At 30 m.p.h. 112 (70) m.p.g. At 40 m.p.h 84 (53) m.p.g. At 50 m.p.h., 67 (40) m.p.g. At 60 m.p.h. 53 (32) m.p.g.

BRAKING : From 30 m.p.h. to rest, 29ft 6in (52ft) (surface, dry tar mac-adam).

TURNING CIRCLE : 14ft 4in.

MINIMUM NON-SNATCH SPEED : 16 (13) m.p.h. in top gear with ignition fully retarded.

WEIGHT Per C.C. : 0.77 (1.18) lb.

BSA
STAR TWIN

One line in the road test of the 1952 497 cc BSA Star Twin says it all; '. . . the Star Twin has few equals as a machine for sustained, high-speed road work.' Just how incontrovertibly true was that observation, the events of September of the same year were to prove, because BSA embarked on what just has to be the most audacious test ever carried out in the full glare of the spotlight.

The idea was simple enough. An official observer from the ACU would be invited to visit the BSA factory at Small Heath, Birmingham, and there select at random from the batch currently under construction, three perfectly ordinary Star Twins. The three machines would then be put through a demonstration ride, every move being logged by the observer to ensure that there was no cheating.

But *what* a demonstration ride! It was to be no less than a 5,000-mile tour of Europe, taking in the International Six Days Trial on the way. Three riders were selected (Norman Vanhouse, Fred Rist, and Brian Martin), and in view of the stiff task ahead, the three chosen machines were each equipped with such ISDT necessities as competitions-style number plates, tank-top map case and toolbag, ex-RAF clock, and 49-tooth, instead of 45-tooth, rear sprockets.

In due course the trio reached Vienna, where the addition of more ISDT equipment (air bottle, extra tyre security bolts, sump undershield, etc) was permitted. It is a matter of historical record that all three completed the event with clean sheets, earning BSA a manufacturer's team award and also, for Birmingham MCC, a club team prize.

Then it was on with the tour, through Germany, Denmark, Sweden, and Norway, and so to a tumultuous welcome on their return to Birmingham. The ride earned for BSA the coveted Maudes Trophy, presented for the most meritorious demonstration ever carried out in a particular year, and never was the cup more justly earned.

The three Star Twins had been registered as MOL 301, MOL 302, and MOL 303, and nobody really knows what happened to them after they had been returned to the factory. Possibly, as was usual BSA practice, they were sold off cheaply to employees. Certainly MOL 301 and MOL 302 seem to have departed to that motorway in the sky, but many years later MOL 303 was to come to light again in curious circumstances.

There it was, partly cannibalised, and at some stage in its past life half-heartedly converted to a chopper, sitting forlornly on a scrapheap at the rear of a small Birmingham motor cycle shop, just about to close its doors for ever.

At that point it was rescued by Birmingham vintage enthusiast Colin Wall and, over a considerable period, gradually restored to the condition in which it had originally left Small Heath for its ISDT exploit, 26 years before. It was the model which Norman Vanhouse had ridden through the test, and man and machine were at last reunited when Norman rode the reborn MOL 303 in the Mallory Park 'Parade of the Greats', in the spring of 1978.

Resembling the Val Page 650 cc Triumph twin of the early 1930s in employing a single camshaft at the rear, and with the gearbox bolted to the crankcase in semi-unit-construction style, the original 495 cc (62 × 82 mm) Model A7 BSA was intended for introduction in 1940, but the Second World War put the mockers on that scheme, and it was not until 1946 that it was at last produced. First example off the post-war assembly track was flown straight to Paris for display at the first Motor Cycle Show held since the return of peace.

It is likely that Val Page, in his spell at BSA immediately before the war, had laid down the basic lines of the twin, but the actual detail design work was by Herbert Perkins. However, the Model A7, as first made, did have a number of built-in bothers. In particular, the combustion chamber shape did not cope very well with the 75-octane pool petrol of the day, the engine used to overheat in consequence, and would 'run on' for several seconds after the ignition was switched off.

Meanwhile Bert Hopwood had been recruited on to the design staff, and the 646 cc (70 × 84 mm) Model A10 Golden Flash which joined the range for 1950 was from his drawing board. Ostensibly, it was an enlarged version of the A7, but in fact the resemblance was only superficial. Major difference was

Big brother of the BSA Star Twin was the 650 cc BSA Golden Flash, designed by Bert Hopwood. Internal construction of both engines was similar, and each featured a rear-mounted camshaft and sloping pushrods.

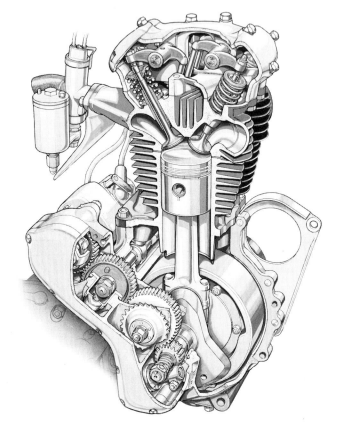

Above: *(left to right) Norman Vanhouse, Fred Rist and Brian Martin on their BSA A7 Star Twins, before setting out on their victorious 1952 Maudes Trophy test. As part of the test, all three machines won gold medals in that year's ISDT.*

Right: *Norman Vanhouse, Brian Martin, and former BSA competitions manager, Bert Perrigo are reunited with MOL303, one of the three Maudes Trophy machines, at Mallory Park's 1978 Vintage Race of the Year. On the left is Colin Wall, who restored the bike from scrap condition.*

in cylinder-head design, the bigger unit employing narrow angle valves, a shallower combustion chamber, and more generous head finning.

The first A7 Star Twin, with high-compression pistons, twin carburettors, and plunger-type rear suspension had been added to the range for 1949, but both this model and its more humdrum A7 forebear were given an entirely new engine from 1951 onward. Bert Hopwood had been at work, and the new unit was shorter in stroke but larger in bore and, as might be expected, had 95 per cent of its parts interchangeable with those of the 646 cc A10 Golden Flash. The latest cylinder head, too, was A10 pattern, and incorporated inlet and exhaust valves in austenitic steel. Capacity was now 497 cc. The sports version, the A7 Star Twin, reverted to a single Amal carburettor.

And so to 1952, the momentous year in which the trio of Star Twins captured the Maudes Trophy. But that was not the only remarkable Star Twin achievement of the year, because in the United States, the BSA distributor for the West Coast, Hap Alzina, got to work on a model with which Gene Thiessen was to make a bid for the American Class C (standard catalogue machine) speed record.

No major changes to the bike were permitted, but by careful workbench attention Hap Alzina got the unit to turn out 40 bhp, using 80 octane fuel and a compression ratio of 8 to 1. The result was an outstanding success, with Thiessen taking the record with a two-way flying-mile speed of 123·69 mph.

For the past season or so, the finish of the Star Twin had been uninspiring. The world nickel shortage had accounted for the dropping of the chromium plated tank and, instead, the tank finish had been all-silver enamel, with embossed metal badges. But the finish improved for 1953 when chromium-plated tank side panels returned, and the Star Twin adopted its most handsome livery yet, with a frame of dark green, tank and mudguards in polychromatic light green, and large three-dimensional name badges in Diakon clear plastic. Mechanical details were unchanged, except that the front brake drum diameter was increased to 8 in.

Nevertheless, the model was nearing the end of its run, and when the 1955 BSA programme was revealed, the Star Twin was missing. In its place came a slightly more sophisticated 497 cc sports twin, equipped for the first time with pivoted instead of plunger rear suspension, and with high-lift cams, high-compression pistons, and a one-piece light-alloy cylinder head. The two-tone green finish was retained, but the name had changed to the Shooting Star.

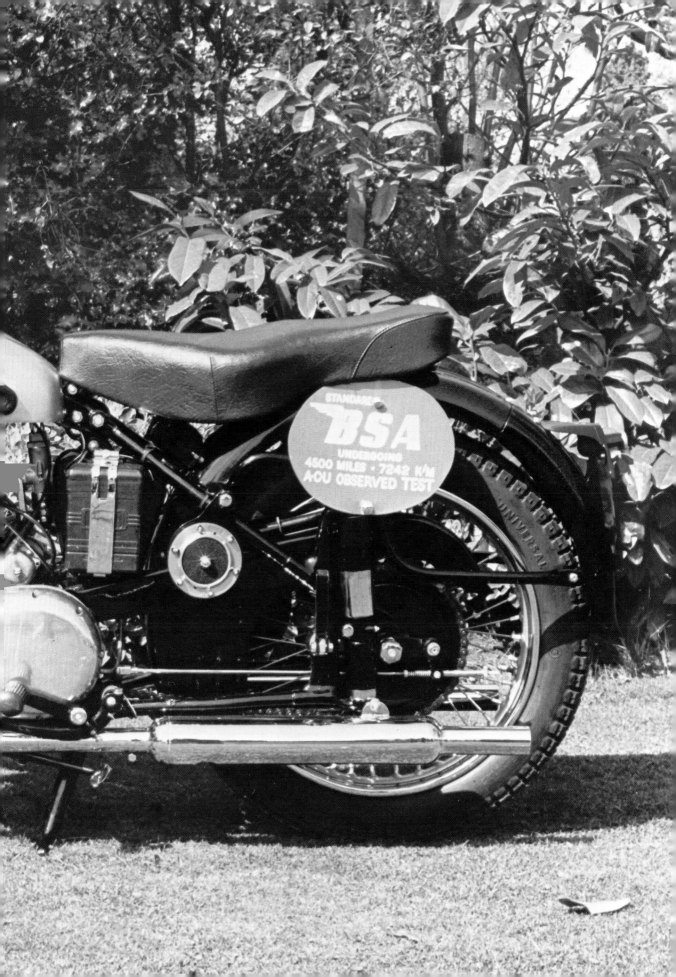

ROAD TESTS OF NEW MODELS

The 497 c.c. B.S.A

A High-performance Model in the

ZESTFUL acceleration, excellent road holding, and the ability to devour the miles in unobtrusive fashion, are but a few of the attributes of the 497 c.c. B.S.A. Star Twin. Fitted with the compact, semi-unit construction B.S.A. engine and gear box, the machine is the sports version of the now celebrated A7. A redesigned engine was employed for 1951. Good as the pre-1951 Star Twin was, the present model is decidedly better. There is now only one carburettor instead

The Star Twin now has a single carburettor and an 8in-diameter front brake

of two; and carburation, once the engine is warm, is as clean as could be desired. With the present B.S.A. gear box, the gear-change is among the best encountered on present-day machines.

A sports machine in the true tradition, the Star Twin requires "knowing" if it is to give of its best on Pool-quality fuel. The throttle must be used intelligently in conjunction with the manual ignition control; engine revolutions must be maintained in the higher ranges; in short, there must be knowledgeable understanding of the engine's characteristics. These requirements fulfilled, the Star Twin has few equals as a machine for sustained, high-speed road work.

Used to the full in conjunction with the indirect gear ratios, the twin-cylinder engine provides acceleration of no mean order. In bottom and second gears the speed can be stepped up with exhilarating rapidity; and even in third or top gears the build-up from medium to peak r.p.m. is shatteringly quick. At 70 m.p.h. in top gear, the machine noticeably surged forward in response to a tweak of the twistgrip. Vibration was negligible. No matter how hard the engine was driven or for how long, there was at no time any indication that it was being over-driven.

During the test, cruising speeds in the seventies were used as often as road conditions permitted; 70 m.p.h., indeed, was felt to be the machine's happiest cruising speed. The engine turned over smoothly and sweetly, and with no more fuss than there was in the fifties. That it would cruise without being over-driven at higher speeds, say, 75-80 m.p.h., there is little doubt; but, at speeds of over 70 m.p.h., wind pressure became tiring to the rider's arms. At a true road speed of 65 m.p.h., the speedometer registered approximately 5 m.p.h. fast.

An idea of the Star Twin's performance may be gained from the fact that on several (admittedly favourable) occasions during the course of the 700-mile test, 20 miles were covered in as many minutes. Notwithstanding such usage, no engine oil leaks were apparent at the end of the test. A small seepage of oil appeared at the oil-tank filler-cap, and some messiness resulted through excessive oil issuing through the oil-tank breather if the tank was over-filled.

Engine performance is but one of the ultimate factors in the attainment of high road averages. Steering and road-holding are equally important; as far as the B.S.A. was concerned, these characteristics were fully up to desirable standards. The long, soft action of the B.S.A. telescopic front fork dealt adequately with every type of going encountered. Steering was of the hair-line variety. A steering damper is fitted; during most of the test it was set just barely biting.

The action of the plunger-type rear springing was pleasantly soft around the static-load position and it proved to be equally effective whether the machine was ridden one- or two-up. A criticism is that the suspension clashed on the occasions when deep road irregularities (such as sunken manhole covers) were encountered. Steering was good whether the machine was on greasy city surfaces, or ridden at speed on the open road.

For a person of average height, the riding position could hardly be bettered. Seat height is 30in—a height which permitted a comfortable knee angle while allowing easy straddling of the machine for kick-starting. The position of the brake-pedal pad was such that the brake could be applied without the foot being taken off the rest; an adjustable brake-pedal stop—a new feature—allows the pedal to be set in the optimum position relative to the footrest. Some discomfort to the rider's knees resulted from contact with the angular edge of the tank knee-grips.

That the Star Twin is a sports machine has been amply illustrated, and it might be thought

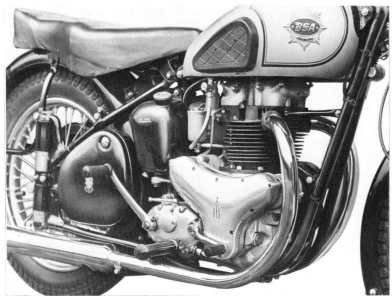

Though endowed with zestful performance characteristics, the 497 c.c. engine was found to be pleasantly flexible

from this that the engine would prove intractable under slow-running conditions. Yet the reverse is true. During town riding the machine proved to be pleasantly flexible. As intimated earlier, knowledgeable handling of the ignition control was called for; the long ignition lever fitted to the left handlebar is pleasant to use and, because of its length, greatly facilitates accurate settings.

Upward or downward gear changes could be effortlessly achieved by lightly pivoting the right foot on the footrest. Pedal movement was short and feather-light, and clean, precise upward or downward gear changes called for no special care. Racing-type upward gear changes were accompanied by a slight click from the gear box as the pinions engaged—a click which could be heard rather than felt. Clean, noiseless downward changes could be made as rapidly as the clutch and gear pedal could be operated.

Both front and rear brakes were smooth and progressive and, applied in unison, provided satisfactory stopping power, even for a machine in the Star Twin's performance class. The 8in front brake was very good, yet did not provide quite all the power of which this type of brake is known to be capable. During the course of several hundred miles of fast road work, both brakes came in for hard usage. In spite of this, no fade was experienced, and only slight adjustment was called for.

Little effort was required to operate the kick-starter. With the temperature below freezing point, the engine would start from cold at the second or third kick—this provided that the carburettor was lightly flooded and normal cold-starting procedure followed. The air lever could be fully opened after the engine had been running for about a minute.

The degree of exhaust and mechanical quietness was commendably high. With the machine stationary and the engine idling on full retard, no individual source of mechanical noise could be indentified. Slight piston-slap could just be detected when the ignition was set at full advance. Induction hiss is eliminated by the built-in air-cleaner. Effective at all speeds,

A picture showing the compactness of the semi-unit construction of engine and gear box

the silencers produced a pleasant yet unobtrusive exhaust note.

Mudguarding on the Star Twin was only reasonably effective. Operation of the centre-stand called for a fair amount of muscular effort until the knack had been mastered. Its use is facilitated by the lifting handle on the left side and a curved, "roll-on" extension piece on the left leg of the stand. Adjustment of the primary chain is by moving the slipper-tensioner inside the chain case; the adjusting screw protrudes through the bottom of the case. Another commendable feature is that the guard for the rear chain has a deep back plate which effectively shields the chain from much of the road grit shed by the rear tyre. Other notable features are the B.S.A. really quickly detachable wheels; and the use of heavy-gauge clutch and front brake control cables. A comprehensive set of tools is provided.

The standard of finish on the Star Twin is extremely high. A general colour scheme of black and silver is employed; the tank is finished in matt-silver, lined in red, and it bears a handsome "Star Twin" insignia.

Information Panel

SPECIFICATION

ENGINE : 497 c.c. (66 x 72.6 mm) o.h.v. vertical twin. Fully enclosed valve gear operated by push-rods from a single camshaft. Plain-bearing big-ends. Mainshaft supported by roller and plain bearings. Compression ratio, 7.2 to 1. Dry-sump lubrication ; tank capacity, 4 pints.

CARBURETTOR : Amal ; twistgrip throttle control ; air-slide operated by handlebar lever. Built-in air cleaner.

IGNITION and LIGHTING : Lucas magneto with manual ignition control on left side of handlebar. Separate, 3in diameter Lucas dynamo ; 7in headlamp ; 30 24w headlamp bulb.

TRANSMISSION : B.S.A. four-speed gear box with positive-stop foot control. Bottom, 12.9 to 1. Second, 8.8 to 1. Third, 6.05 to 1. Top, 5.0 to 1. Multi-plate clutch with fabric inserts. Primary chain, ⅜in duplex running in cast-aluminium, oil-bath case. Rear chain, ⅝ x ⅜in, lubricated by breather from oil tank. R.p.m. at 30 m.p.h. in top gear, approximately 1,950.

FUEL CAPACITY : 3½ gallons.

TYRES : Dunlop ; front 3.25 x 19in ; rear, 3.50 x 19in ; both studded tread.

BRAKES : 8in diameter front, 7in diameter rear ; finger-operated adjusters.

SUSPENSION : B.S.A. telescopic front fork with hydraulic damping ; plunger-type rear springing.

WHEELBASE : 54¾in. Ground clearance, 4½in. unladen.

SEAT : B.S.A. dual-seat. Unladen height, 30in.

WEIGHT : 423 lb fully equipped and with one gallon of fuel.

PRICE : £174, with Purchase Tax (in Great Britain only), £222 6s 8d. Extras : dual-seat in lieu of saddle, £3 (P.T., 16s 8d) ; prop-stand, 15s (P.T., 4s 8d).

ROAD TAX : £3 15s a year ; £1 0s 8d a quarter.

DESCRIPTION : *The Motor Cycle,* 19 October, 1950.

MAKERS : B.S.A. Cycles, Ltd., Small Heath, Birmingham, 11.

PERFORMANCE DATA

MEAN MAXIMUM SPEED : Bottom : 37 m.p.h.*
Second : 55 m.p.h.*
Third : 86 m.p.h.
Top : 92 m.p.h.
* Valve float just starting.

MEAN ACCELERATION :

	10-30 m.p.h.	20-40 m.p.h.	30-50 m.p.h.
Bottom	3 secs	2.4 secs	—
Second	4.2 secs	3.2 secs	3.2 secs
Third	6 secs	5.4 secs	4.8 secs
Top	—	7.2 secs	6.8 secs

Mean speed at end of quarter-mile from rest : 84 m.p.h.
Mean time to cover standing quarter-mile : 16.8 secs.

PETROL CONSUMPTION : At 30 m.p.h., 89 m.p.g. At 40 m.p.h., 75 m.p.g. At 50 m.p.h., 70 m.p.g. At 60 m.p.h., 64 m.p.g.

BRAKING : From 30 m.p.h. to rest, 30ft 6in (surface, dry tar macadam).

TURNING CIRCLE : 13ft 6in.

MINIMUM NON-SNATCH SPEED : 22 m.p.h. in top gear.

WEIGHT per C.C. : 0.73 lb.

Excelsior
TALISMAN

Excelsior, who were the first firm in Britain to take up motor cycle manufacture on a commercial scale ('Founded 1874' ran the legend on the tank transfer; but in fact their earliest powered machines dated from 1897), led something of a Jekyll-and-Hyde existence in pre-Second World War days. At the bottom end of the scale were the cheap Villiers-engined lightweights, starting with the fully-equipped 98 cc two-speed Universal at only 14 guineas (£14.70). But the same factory produced the very up-market overhead-camshaft Manxman models, in 250, 350 and 500 cc sizes and listed as super-sports roadsters or as outright road racers.

The Manxman was designed by H. J. Hatch and Eric Walker, and was an exclusive Excelsior product, although at the time the works in Kings Road, Tyseley, Birmingham had no engine-building facilities and so engine production had to be farmed out – initially to Blackburnes, but later to Beans Industries.

Expansion of the factory to meet War Department contracts meant that Excelsior could return to peacetime trading in 1945 with the benefit of a well-equipped machine shop and so, for the first time, Excelsior engines could actually be made on the premises. However, the prestige Manxman failed to return to the market, although it can now be disclosed that a post-war prototype was indeed built and tested on the road.

Instead, the new facilities were employed on two-stroke engine production, notably of the 98 cc Excelsior Spryt and Goblin engines used in Excelsior's own autocycles (forerunners of the moped) and in the Brockhouse Corgi mini-scooter derived from the wartime Excelsior Welbike paratrooper's machine.

A 149 cc two-stroke unit was added and then, in October, 1949, came a 244 cc (50 × 62 mm) two-stroke parallel twin

No fewer than five ball and roller races supported the built-up crankshaft of the 244 cc (50 × 62 mm) Excelsior Talisman two-stroke twin. Current for lighting and ignition was supplied by a Wico-Pacy flywheel alternator mounted on the left-hand end of the crankshaft

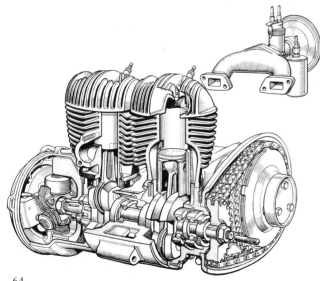

known as the Talisman. It was, apart from the water-cooled Scott, the only unit of this layout in British production, and its appearance on the company's stand at the London Show attracted a great deal of attention.

The specification included a five-bearing mainshaft, three-piece crankcase construction with vertical joints, and separate cast-iron cylinders and light-alloy heads. An Albion four-speed gearbox was bolted to the rear face of the crankcase in semi-unit-construction style, and ignition was by a Wico-Pacy 36-watt flywheel magneto-generator housed in a compartment on the right of the crankcase assembly.

Plunger-type rear springing of an unusual kind, in which the spring boxes themselves travelled up and down fixed rods, afforded 1·75 in rear wheel movement, and undamped front forks with two-rate internal springs looked after the front wheel.

Smartly finished in maroon, with cream panels to the fuel tank sides, the Talisman was a very fetching little machine. It weighed 220 lb, handled well (as one might expect from a factory with a racing background), and if the performance was a little less than world-shattering, at least the power delivery was smoother than anything the unsophisticated motor cyclist of the day had experienced hitherto. The rear springing, although offering the barest minimum of movement, was better than the rigid frames still very much in evidence, while the undamped spring front forks were an improvement over the old girder type.

The original Talisman, listed as Model TT1, was joined for the 1952 season by a twin-carburettor version known as the Sports Talisman, or STT1. This was distinguished by a rather pleasant all-over finish of beige, with red striping, by gaiters on the front fork, and by a distinctly ugly dual seat in place of the TT1's single saddle. Performance had gone up, too, and the 'Sports' was able to achieve a mean speed of 64 mph, not at all bad by the standards of the day.

Sales of the Talisman Twin did not break any records, though (which was a pity, because on the whole it was a nice little bike) and the firm began to look elsewhere for sales outlets for their engines. That is how they made contact with a very peculiar little three-wheeler, built at Seymour Wharf, Totnes, Devon, which carried the absolutely appalling name of The Worker's Playtime. Two prototypes, powered by 244 cc Talisman engines, were built but that was about all.

Excelsior had a shade better luck with some of the other three-wheeler projects which seemed to proliferate in the 1950s, notably the London-built Powerdrive and Coronet (which used a 328 cc Talisman twin). There was, too, the Wolverhampton-made Frisky, which managed to reach limited production – and, finally, the Berkeley, which had such an important part to play in the Excelsior story that a paragraph or two must be reserved for this alone.

Meanwhile, back to the bikes, and to the introduction for the 1953 season of a pair of Talisman twins (TT2 standard, and STT2 sports) with pivoted-fork rear suspension and a redesigned frame incorporating an engine cradle. Other features included a fork-top instrument facia, and a much more elegant

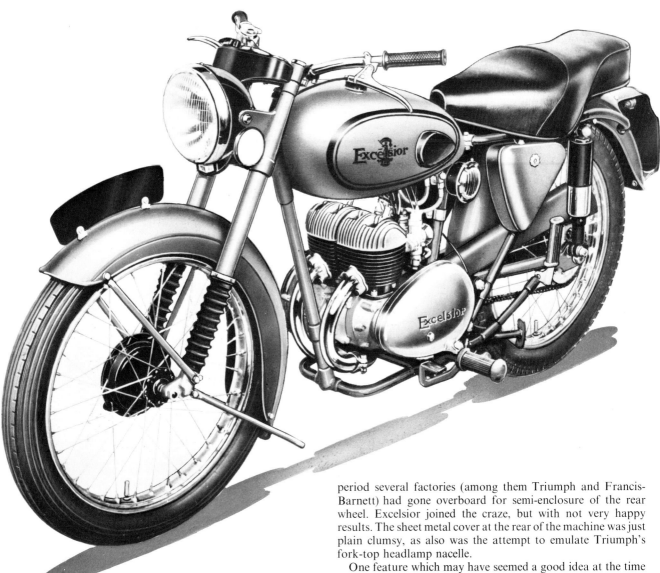

By 1955 the Excelsior Talisman Sports STT2 had progressed from plunger springing to a conventional pivoted rear fork. The new frame incorporated, also, a tubular cradle, but traditional brazed-lug construction was still being employed

dual seat. The plunger-sprung TT1, still with single saddle, and STT1 sports were continued (although these were just unsold stock).

The following year saw the introduction of full-width wheel hubs, and in subsequent seasons there was a revised cylinder head design with hemispherical combustion chamber and very much deeper finning, and a number of styling and colour-scheme changes.

The next major step was the production of a 328 cc twin for the Coronet three-wheeler and the new 1958 Super Talisman. The autumn of the same year saw Excelsior in production with yet another version, the 328 cc S9 Special Talisman, of which the power unit differed mainly in that it now had a 60-watt Miller alternator instead of the Wico-Pacy unit. At this particular

period several factories (among them Triumph and Francis-Barnett) had gone overboard for semi-enclosure of the rear wheel. Excelsior joined the craze, but with not very happy results. The sheet metal cover at the rear of the machine was just plain clumsy, as also was the attempt to emulate Triumph's fork-top headlamp nacelle.

One feature which may have seemed a good idea at the time was the inclusion of a tool cavity in the top face of the tank. The lid, secured by a pair of Oddie snap fasteners, was supposed also to serve as the fuel tank filler cap. It leaked.

But at this stage we must return to the Berkeley three-wheeler mentioned a few paragraphs ago. Designed by Laurie Bond (who was responsible also for the design of the Bond three-wheeler), this was a sporty little two-seater with a glass-fibre body, produced in Biggleswade, Bedfordshire, by a well known firm of caravan manufacturers.

To power the Berkeley, the Excelsior company evolved a 492 cc three-cylinder engine, which was really three of the cylinders of the 328 cc Talisman (58 × 62 mm) arranged on a seven-bearing crankshaft with the throws at 120 degrees. A Siba Dynastart unit served to provide electric current and, also, gave the little car electric starting.

Another version of the Berkeley used the 328 cc engine. It was a good little vehicle, but an unfortunate experience on the American market led to the collapse of Berkeley and, not having been paid for engines supplied, Excelsior folded, too. The company was bought by Britax, and still forms part of that group, but is now concerned solely with making car and motor cycle accessories.

ROAD TESTS OF NEW MODELS

244 c.c. Excelsior

A Vertical Twin Two-stroke Lightweight w

SINCE its introduction late in 1949, the 244 c.c. Excelsior parallel twin two-stroke, the Talisman, has achieved no small measure of popularity. The Talisman Sports, which made its bow at last year's London Show and which recently came into production, embodies modifications that are mainly

Luxury features include plunger-type rear springing, twin carburettors and a special twin-seat adjustable for height

in the nature of " gilding the lily "—except that the " gilding " process has included functional as well as ornamental features. Among the refinements are twin Amal carburettors. As a result, increased maximum speed has been obtained.

Salient characteristics of the twin two-stroke engine are its " four-cylinder " torque and well-nigh perfect balance. Almost throughout the entire speed range the engine delivers its power in a turbine-like flow, without fuss or vibration. Only at one small period (a period bracketed by a bare 2 m.p.h.) could the slightest of vibration tremors be detected; this was at 40-42 m.p.h. in top gear. No palpable vibration was apparent at the handlebars.

Like most two-strokes. the Excelsior would not fire evenly

with the engine on light load. For instance, at a steady 30 m.p.h. along a level road, with no headwind, the twistgrip had to be eased off fractionally, then opened again if a tendency to four-stroking was to be avoided. Under such conditions, the minimum speed in top gear (on a fixed throttle opening) required to avoid four-stroking was approximately 34 m.p.h. This does not mean, of course, that there was not good two-stroking at low speeds. On the contrary, due to the exceptionally good low-speed torque, the engine was so flexible that it would pull evenly away from speeds as low as 12 m.p.h. in top gear. At any speed between 15 and 50 m.p.h. in top gear, the throttle could be wound open without any protest from the engine, and immediate results were forthcoming.

Acceleration through the indirect ratios, as well as in top gear, was extremely lively for a 250 c.c. machine. A comfortable cruising speed for both engine and rider was adjudged to be 50 m.p.h., though even when the engine was held on full throttle for long periods, it gave the impression that it would hum on tirelessly for as long as the rider wished. Under these conditions there was not the slightest sign of overheating; the cylinder head and barrel fins remained relatively cool, and the exhaust pipes did not become even slightly discoloured. The power unit remained absolutely oil-tight, but burnt oil leaked from the joint between silencer and exhaust pipe.

When the maximum speed, acceleration and fuel consumption figures were taken, a stiffish breeze was blowing which had some adverse effect. It should be mentioned that the engine just failed to reach its ultimate peak revs in second gear, because of a period of four-stroking occurring high up in the r.p.m. range. When the engine was held on full throttle in bottom gear, the revs climbed slowly through, and clear of, this four-stroking period and attained absolute maximum.

It is an axiom that the smaller the engine, the greater should be the number of gears. In hilly country, four carefully chosen gear ratios enable a small-capacity engine to be kept turning over happily, as distinct from slogging hard or over-revving. However, such was the flexibility of the Excelsior that it tended to make the four-speed gear box appear something of a luxury rather than a necessity. There were occasions, of course, such as when overtaking slower traffic on hills, on which the four-speed gear box was a valuable asset.

Only slight effort was required to operate the gear-change pedal, which has a short arc of travel. Quick-action gear changes, both upward and downward, could be made without fear of " scrunching." Some deliberation had to be exercised when engaging neutral; otherwise there was a tendency to overshoot the neutral position.

It was felt that the gear pedal was a little too low, in relation to the most desirable footrest position, for maximum ease of operation when making downward gear changes, i.e., moving the pedal upward. Though the pedal is located on serrations, and is therefore adjustable, its adjustment for height is limited by the position of the mag-generator case. The clutch was exceptionally light to operate; it was smooth and progressive in taking up the drive.

Starting the engine from cold, even after it had been standing all night, was invariably accomplished

Impressive twin power unit. Note also the pivoted crank of the kick-starter pedal and the rectifier mounted below the tank

ˈalisman Sports

Attractive Performance

first kick provided the following simple preliminaries were observed: the float chamber tickler was depressed until the fuel just began to appear at the base of the mixing chambers; the air lever was fully closed and the twistgrip was set one-third open. After the engine had been running for a few minutes, the air control could be opened fully. Starting with the engine warm could usually be effected by a leisurely prod on the kick-starter, with the throttle set one-third open. The kick-starter crank is mounted concentrically with the gear pedal; if the ball of the foot was used when operating the kick-starter, the crank could be moved through its full arc of travel without the foot-rest obstructing it.

For its exhaust silencing and quiet running, the Excelsior gained full marks. Even under conditions of brisk acceleration, the exhaust note was little more than an unobtrusive buzz. At cruising speeds on the open road, especially when there was a slight breeze, the rider could not hear a sound from the machine unless his head was turned sideways—then the pleasant thrum of the exhaust could be heard, but no more. At maximum speed, very slight piston rattle ("two-stroke rattle") was audible.

Both steering and road-holding are first class. The machine could be whistled round bends and corners without deviating a fraction from the desired line. Handling was equally good at high or low speeds. All road shocks were cushioned, and an appreciated degree of comfort was provided by the telescopic front fork and the plunger-type rear springing. It was felt that a softer action of the front fork would have further enhanced the riding comfort.

An excellent riding position is furnished by the relationship between dual-seat (adjustable for height), handlebar and foot-rests. The split handlebar is accommodated in sockets which lie one on each side of the top fork bridge. By swivelling the bars in their sockets, adjustment for both height and angle of the grips is obtainable. The handlebar control levers are of the clip-on type and are therefore adjustable; they fell easily to hand. The twin-rotor twistgrip throttle control for the two carburettors was inordinately stiff in operation, and no amount of lubrication of the cables resulted in much improvement.

Perfectly positioned in relation to the footrest, the brake pedal

Both exhaust pipes are led into one pipe which feeds into a silencer on the left side of the machine

pad could be depressed merely by swivelling the foot lightly on the rest. An adjustable stop for the brake pedal is provided. Though subjected to hard usage, both front and rear brakes retained their efficiency. Applied in unison, they provided commendable stopping power.

The driving light provided by the Lucas pre-focus lamp unit was considered adequate for the full performance of the machine to be used at night. The total lamp load was balanced on the ammeter at 38-40 m.p.h. in top gear. Mounted on top of the fork bridge, the speedometer was easily read by day or by night; it registered accurately at 30 m.p.h. and was $2\frac{1}{2}$ m.p.h. fast at 50 m.p.h.

Parking equipment consists of a spring-up central stand; even after much practice this proved difficult to operate. Embodied in the gear box is a dip-stick; an excellent feature in itself, it nevertheless proved awkward to read as, during extraction, it fouled the right-hand carburettor. Two spacious tool boxes, provide good facilities for carrying tool-kit, repair outfit and spares. The Talisman Sports is finished in beige enamel, with the fuel tank lined red and bearing the Excelsior motif.

Information Panel

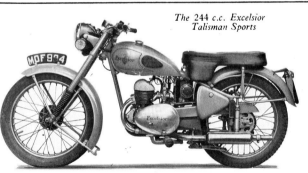

The 244 c.c. Excelsior Talisman Sports

SPECIFICATION

ENGINE : 244 c.c. (50 x 62 mm) two-stroke parallel twin. Separate cast-iron cylinder barrels and light-alloy heads ; crank throws at 180 deg ; crankshaft supported on four ball bearings and one roller bearing ; roller-bearing big-ends ; aluminium-alloy, flat-top pistons. Compression ratio 7.8 to 1. Petroil lubrication.

CARBURETTORS : Amal ; twistgrip throttle control ; air-slides operated by handlebar lever.

IGNITION AND LIGHTING : Wico-Pacy flywheel mag-generator, with rectifier and battery. 7in headlamp with pre-focus light unit. 24-24 w headlamp bulb.

TRANSMISSION : Four-speed gear box with positive-stop foot control. Bottom, 17.78 to 1. Second, 10.86 to 1. Third, 9.22 to 1. Top, 6.09 to 1. Two-plate cork-insert clutch running in oil. Shock absorber incorporated in clutch. Primary chain, duplex ⅜ x ⁷⁄₁₆in in cast-aluminium case. Rear chain, ½ x ⅜in with guard over top run. Engine r.p.m. at 30 m.p.h. in top gear, 2,380.

FUEL CAPACITY : 2¾ gallons.

TYRES : Dunlop, 3.00 x 19in front and rear.

BRAKES : 5in-diameter front, 6in rear.

SUSPENSION : Excelsior undamped telescopic front fork. Plunger-type rear springing.

WHEELBASE : 50½in. Ground clearance, 5in unladen.

SEAT : Excelsior twin seat. Unladen height, 30in.

WEIGHT : 250lb fully equipped and with one gallon of fuel.

PRICE : £136, plus Purchase Tax (in Britain only), £173 15s 7d.

ROAD TAX : £1 17s 6d a year : 10s 4d a quarter.

MAKERS : Excelsior Motor Co., Ltd., King's Road, Tyseley, Birmingham, 11.

DESCRIPTION : *The Motor Cycle*, 15 November, 1951.

PERFORMANCE DATA

MEAN MAXIMUM SPEED : Bottom : 30 m.p.h.
Second : 45 m.p.h.
Third : 55 m.p.h.
Top : 64 m.p.h.

MEAN ACCELERATION :

	10-30 m.p.h.	20-40 m.p.h.	30-50 m.p.h.
Second	4.6 secs	5.4 secs	—
Third	5.6 secs	6.4 secs	9.0 secs
Top	8.2 secs	7.6 secs	10.0 secs

Mean Speed at end of quarter-mile from rest : 57 m.p.h.
Mean time to cover standing quarter-mile : 23 secs.

PETROIL CONSUMPTION : At 30 m.p.h., 96 m.p.g. At 40 m.p.h., 88 m.p.g. At 50 m.p.h., 67 m.p.g. At 55-60 m.p.h., 60 m.p.g.

BRAKING : From 30 m.p.h. to rest, 29ft 11in (surface, dry tar macadam).

TURNING CIRCLE : 13ft.

MINIMUM NON-SNATCH SPEED : 12 m.p.h. in top gear.

WEIGHT PER C.C. : 1.02 lb.

TRIUMPH
TIGER 100

Edward Turner was a crafty kind of character, but still, when a man is wearing two hats – that of chief designer, *and* that of managing director of Triumph Engineering Co Ltd – crafty is what he has to be. Good husbandry and the economic use of raw materials is the province of the managing director, and so no part had to be any heavier than necessary. Many minor lightnesses add up to a general major lightness, and such was Turner's skill as a designer, that the 498 cc Triumph Speed Twin which startled the motor cycle world of 1937, was in fact lighter than the 500 cc single it replaced.

And Edward Turner was crafty in another direction, because it was his policy never to introduce a sports model until its touring counterpart had been given at least a year's production run, during which any bugs could be eliminated. The early Speed Twin did have a few bugs. For example, the six-stud fixing of the cylinder block to the crankcase was a weakness, overcome by the mid-season introduction of a thicker base flange, and an eight-stud fixing.

The Tiger 100, unveiled in the weekly press in late August, 1938, created almost as much of a sensation as the Speed Twin had done, a year before. It was, of course, a hotted-up edition of the touring model with, from the start, the benefit of the beefier cylinder-base fixing. But there was, also, a whole lot more to whet the enthusiast's appetite.

Polished flywheels and con-rods, for instance; forged, flat-top pistons with valve cutaways in the crown; a compression ratio of 8 to 1; a gas-flowed cylinder head, and the ability to rev to 7,000 rpm.

One feature greatly appreciated by the sportier type of motor cyclist was a patented silencer of which the tail pipe, end cap and baffle could be detached, to leave a pukka racing megaphone. In fact, the Tiger 100 was intended primarily for clubman racing, while for those who wanted to tackle the more serious stuff, a bronze cylinder head was on offer at £5 extra.

As with the Tiger singles, the sports twin was finished in silver sheen, outlined in black and with die-cast name badges.

Triumph decided to have a go at collecting the Maudes Trophy and so, in February, 1939, two machines – a Speed Twin and a Tiger 100 – were selected from stock then, under ACU observation, were ridden up to John O'Groats, down to Land's End, and then to Brooklands, where they were subjected to a six-hour speed test. Freddie Clarke and Allan Jefferies shared the Speed Twin in 1½-hour spells, and Ivan Wicksteed and David Whitworth alternated as the Tiger 100 pilots.

The test was successful, with the Tiger 100 averaging 78·50 mph for six hours, and putting in a last lap at 88·46 mph. That year, several other factories were making determined efforts to win the Maudes Trophy (BSA were indulging in a Round Britain ride, and Panther were scorching up and down the Great North Road on a big sloper), but the ACU judged the Triumph test to be the more meritorious, and so the Maudes came to Coventry.

Clubman racers were not slow to put the Tiger 100 to the track test, and there were literally dozens of Tigers at the Brooklands Clubmans Day in April, 1939, and at Donington Park a month later (where, incidentally, T100s finished first, second, third and fifth in the Clubmans 500 cc event).

Not many 1940 models were produced before the wartime halt to civilian production, but it is worth noting that the changes included a new full-skirt piston, check springs on the girder front fork, and a speedometer dial with concentric rpm scales for each gear.

Under the heading 'First of the New', the Triumph company, now located at Meriden, announced their post-war range on 1 March 1945, before the shooting had actually stopped. The T100 was there, much as before except that a telescopic front fork was fitted, and the crankcase had adopted a new and soon to be familiar appearance because, instead of the pre-war Magdyno electrics, there were now separate magneto and dynamo, respectively at rear and front. The megaphone silencer was dropped, but with each T100 a certified test card would be issued.

As peacetime motor cycling got under way, so the demand for rear springing grew. Even to add plunger suspension would have meant making new, or at least modified, frame jigs, but the canny Edward Turner had another solution. In the late 1930s he had patented a large-diameter rear hub which contained its own springing system; now he brought the drawings out of storage and put the Sprung Hub into production, at £20 extra to the standard rigid-frame models.

First major change was for 1949, when the tank-top instrument panel current since 1939 was dropped in favour of a fork-top headlamp nacelle. The chromium-plated fuel tank was discontinued a year later, and replaced by a painted-all-over silver tank with chrome-plated horizontal styling bands along the sides; another familiar Triumph feature to make its appearance that year was the tank-top parcel grid.

Next significant date was 1951, when the Tiger 100 blossomed out in a new die-cast light-alloy cylinder block with close-pitched finning. Nor was that all, because the rather disappointing Grand Prix racing model had been deleted from the range and, instead, a complete racing kit was listed for the T100 at £35. This embraced a racing camshaft, high-compression pistons, stronger valve springs, twin carburettor mixing chambers, a rev counter, etc, all of which boosted the 33 bhp output of the Tiger 100 to something over 40 bhp.

The racing kit remained available until 1954, when the T100, in common with other Triumphs, discarded the sprung hub and at last went over to a pivoted rear fork. The semi-racing T100C variant, equipped with twin carburettors, was discontinued but a twin-carburettor head was included in the list of optional extras for the standard model.

In listing the technical changes of the Tiger 100, we are slightly ahead of the competitions story, but in spite of a 1952 Clubmans Senior TT victory by Bernard Hargreaves, in this type of racing the Triumph usually came off second-best by comparison with the BSA Gold Star. Still, there was more cheerful news for Triumph owners from America, where Johnny Allen, in 1955,

To avoid expensive frame jigs, the Triumph company devised an intriguing suspension system in which the springs were concealed within the rear hub itself. This allowed the firm to provide rear springing for a rigid-framed machine. The photograph shows a 1948 Tiger 100 with spring wheel

broke the AMA national Class C stock-machine record with a two-way speed of 123·952 mph.

By 1957 the pre-unit-construction Triumph engine was nearing the end of its production life, but there was one last change for the Tiger 100; the fitting, for the 1957 season, of a new light-alloy cylinder head with splayed instead of parallel inlet tracts. Enthusiasts liked the new 8 in front brake, with cast-in air scoop, but they were much less happy about the new die-cast tank badge – a futuristic effort known derisively as the 'space rocket', or 'five-bar gate'.

The Triumph Engineering Company Ltd had taken over from the older company in 1936 and so, to mark the 21st anniversary of TEC, the name 'Twenty-One' was given to the 1957 350 cc Model 3TA, harbinger of a new policy of unit-construction. In the next year or two there would be a 490 cc version (the 5TA Speed Twin) plus a sports model carrying on the old Tiger 100 name, but these were complete redesigns, and their relationship to the original Tiger 100 had grown remote.

The small chromium-plated cover just forward of the kickstart spindle shows that this 1958 Triumph Tiger 100 has the patented 'Slikshift', introduced that year. Initial movement of the gear pedal operated the clutch. Customers disliked the idea, which was hastily dropped

Announced in 1957 at an extra cost of almost £12 was this special cylinder head for the Tiger 100, with widely-splayed inlet tracts and a pair of Amal Monobloc carburettors

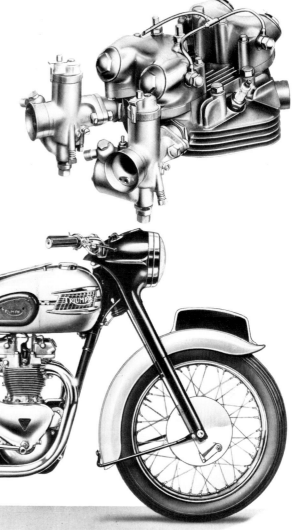

<table>
<tr><td>

ROAD TESTS OF NEW MODELS

</td></tr>
</table>

498 c.c. Triumph

Outstanding Sports Twin with a Scintillating Performa

FOR a number of years the 498 c.c. Triumph Tiger 100 has enjoyed an enviable reputation as a super-sports mount with a Jekyll and Hyde personality, docile and gentle when the occasion demands, such as in heavy traffic, yet possessed of truly tigerish characteristics when given its head on the open road. In 1951 its appeal was widened by the introduction of a light-alloy cylinder block and head and, as an extra, a conversion kit for transforming the model into a pukka racing machine. The model's success in the competition sphere was

Finish of the Tiger 100 is silver, black and chromium

recently underlined by victory in the 1952 Senior Clubman's T.T.

It is on the open road, as "Mr. Hyde," that the Tiger 100 really comes into its own. Acceleration up to speeds in the seventies is vivid yet smooth. The engine seems to revel in the continued use of full throttle, and high average speeds are not difficult to maintain. The rapidity with which the speedometer needle could be sent round to the 80 m.p.h. mark in third gear, and held between 80 and 85 m.p.h. in top for as long as road and traffic conditions permitted, made averages of over 50 m.p.h. commonplace.

Twice in one day the 102-mile journey between the Midlands and a London suburb was covered in an hour and three-quarters, in spite of the usual volume of week-day traffic. On these trips the speedometer frequently read 87 m.p.h. for some miles, though the rider was normally seated and clad in a stormcoat and waders. Long main road hills pulled the needle back no farther than the 80 m.p.h. mark. Checked electrically, the speedometer was found to register 2½ m.p.h. fast at 30 m.p.h. and approximately 5 m.p.h. fast at all speeds between 40 and 80 m.p.h.

In spite of the hardest of driving methods, there was never the slightest sign of engine tiredness, nor was there any tendency for the engine to "run on" when the ignition cut-out was operated after prolonged use of the maximum speed performance. At the conclusion of one particular day's riding, which comprised some 300 miles—many of them on full throttle—the only visible signs of hard riding were discoloration of the exhaust pipes for a few inches from the ports, an oil leak from the cylinder head joint, a faint smear at the base of the push-rod tubes and a slight oil deposit on the rear-wheel rim.

Except at high engine r.p.m. there was no vibration. At no speed, indeed, was vibration sufficient to warrant criticism. Provided normal use was made of the gear box and engine to pink, even though the fuel employed throughout the test was the usual low-octane Pool petrol.

The exhaust note was pleasant and inoffensive whether the Tiger 100 was trickling through towns and villages or being driven hard. Mechanically, as is to be expected with light-alloy cylinders and heads, the engine was slightly noisy, though this ceased to be apparent to the rider when the road speed rose above 35 m.p.h. Most of the mechanical noise was from the pistons, and it was emphasized mainly by the complete absence of induction noise; responsible for this last condition is a large Vokes air filter incorporated as a standard fitting.

Top gear maximum speed figures were taken, on a 1,650-yard straight, both with and without the air filter. Downwind speeds were identical (97.06 m.p.h.) in each case; upwind, without the filter and using the same 170 main jet, there was a speed increase of 1.79 m.p.h. compared with that obtained with the filter in position.

Engine starting, whether the unit was hot or cold, was invariably accomplished at the first kick. The air control, which is situated beneath the left-hand side of the twinseat, was never required during the course of the test. When the engine was cold, the only pre-starting drill was flooding of the carburettor. Provided a small throttle opening was used, there was no need to retard the ignition. As would be expected, the tick-over was rather "lumpy" on full advance, but the idling was improved when the ignition was one-third retarded; however, for complete reliability, the tick-over had to be set faster than some consider desirable.

As to "Dr. Jekyll," though a certain amount of docility and low-speed flexibility is inevitably sacrificed in the interests of top-end performance the Tiger 100 is nevertheless very well-mannered

The high-efficiency power unit has impressive and pleasing lines

Tiger 100

Fast Road Work or Racing

The light-alloy cylinders and heads are die-cast and are characterized by their close-pitch fins

It could be driven unobtrusively at speeds in the region of 30 m.p.h. in top gear. Fuel consumption under these conditions was markedly good. Oil consumption was negligible throughout the test.

The relationship between the handlebar, with its distinctive, rearward sweep, the footrests and the twinseat provided a comfortable riding position for all normal conditions. For prolonged, ultra high-speed work, a slightly more rearward footrest mounting or a raised support on the twinseat would have been appreciated —these solely to relieve the arms of tension caused by wind pressure. Much appreciated was the slenderness of that part of the tank which lies between the rider's knees; the width was just right for maximum comfort and controllability.

Located on a serrated shaft, the gear pedal was adjustable to a position which gave easy operation without removing the foot from its rest. The rear brake pedal came conveniently under the ball of the left foot. The reach from the handlebar to the clutch and front-brake levers was felt to be a trifle too great. Horn button and dipswitch were excellently positioned for left and right thumb operation respectively. The twistgrip, which incorporates a knurled, self-locking friction adjuster, was slightly heavy in operation. The pillion footrests were well positioned for passenger comfort and the twinseat provided comfortable accommodation for two. Riders of large build, dressed for long-distance travel, might desire slightly greater length in the seat.

Pleasantly close, top and third gear ratios are well-chosen in relation to engine characteristics; in fact, the gear change between them was so slick as to encourage more frequent changes than was necessary—just for the sheer pleasure of it. In order to achieve silent changes between bottom and second, and second and third gears, a leisurely movement of the pedal was called for. Owing to slight clutch drag on the machine tested, bottom gear could not be engaged silently when the machine was stationary with the engine idling. Neutral selection was easy from either bottom or second gears. The clutch was delightfully sweet in taking up the drive. It was light in operation and appeared to be impervious to abuse.

Both brakes were smooth, reasonably powerful, and progressive in action. The front brake by itself was good but required somewhat heavy pressure. Rear-brake pedal travel was rather too long to permit maximum braking effort.

The Triumph front fork has a soft action around the static-load position; it absorbed road shocks in an exemplary manner. Occasionally, with the added weight of a pillion passenger, it was made to bottom under conditions of heavy braking. The sprung rear hub provided reasonable comfort at touring speeds but rather more movement would have been preferred at high speeds.

On corners and bends the Tiger 100 could be heeled over confidently and stylishly. On very bumpy bends taken at speed there was a slight tendency to roll. Straight-ahead steering was first class. Bumpy surfaces and gusty winds produced an impression of lightness, which could be curbed by a turn of the steering-damper knob.

With its fine blending of silver, black and chromium, the finish of the machine is a credit to the manufacturers. To sum up, the Tiger 100 is a thoroughbred sporting five-hundred, calculated to inspire pride of ownership both on account of its magnificent all-round performance and its handsome appearance.

Information Panel

SPECIFICATION

ENGINE : 498 c.c. (63 × 80 mm) vertical twin o.h.v.; fully enclosed valve gear. Die-cast aluminium-alloy cylinder block and head ; Hiduminium alloy connecting rods ; Duralumin push rods ; plain bearing big-ends ; mainshafts mounted on ball and roller bearings. Dry-sump lubrication ; oil tank capacity, 6 pints.

CARBURETTOR : Amal ; twistgrip throttle control ; air slide operated by Bowden cable with lever situated under seat. Large Vokes air filter included.

TRANSMISSION : Triumph four-speed gear box with positive-stop foot control. Bottom, 12.2 to 1. Second, 8.45 to 1. Third, 5.95 to 1. Top, 5. to 1. Multi-plate clutch with cork inserts operating in oil. Primary chain ⅜ × 0.305in, in oil-bath case. Rear chain, ⅝ × ⅜in, lubricated by bleed from primary chain case. Guards over both runs of rear chain. R.p.m. at 30 m.p.h. in top gear, 1,938.

IGNITION AND LIGHTING : Lucas magneto with manual control. Separate Lucas 60-watt dynamo. 7in-diameter headlamp.

FUEL CAPACITY : 4 gallons.

TYRES : Dunlop. Front, 3.25 × 19in ribbed. Rear, 3.50 × 19in Universal.

BRAKES : Triumph 6⅞ × 1⅛in front : 8 × 1⅛in rear ; hand adjusters.

SUSPENSION : Triumph telescopic front fork with hydraulic damping. Triumph spring hub in rear wheel.

WHEELBASE : 55in. Ground clearance, 6in unladen.

SADDLE : Triumph Twinseat ; unladen height, 31in.

WEIGHT : 383 lb with approximately one gallon of fuel, full oil tank, and fully equipped (including pillion footrests and prop stand).

PRICE : £175, plus Purchase Tax (in Britain), £48 12s 3d. Spring hub extra, £16, plus £4 8s 11d P.T. Pillion footrests and prop stand extra.

MAKERS : Triumph Engineering Co. Ltd., Meriden Works, Allesley, Coventry.

DESCRIPTION : The Motor Cycle, 9 November, 1950.

498 c.c. Triumph Tiger 100

PERFORMANCE DATA

MEAN MAXIMUM SPEED : Bottom : *41 m.p.h.
Second : *60 m.p.h.
Third : 85 m.p.h.
Top : 92 m.p.h.
* Valve float occurring.

MEAN ACCELERATION :

	10-30 m.p.h.	20-40 m.p.h.	30-50 m.p.h.
Bottom	2.3 secs	2.2 secs	—
Second	3.0 secs	3.0 secs	2.6 secs
Third	—	4.6 secs	4.6 secs
Top	—	5.6 secs	5.8 secs

Mean speed at end of quarter-mile from rest : 79 m.p.h.
Mean time to cover standing quarter-mile : 16.6 secs.

PETROL CONSUMPTION : At 30 m.p.h., 101.6 m.p.g. At 40 m.p.h., 83.2 m.p.g. At 50 m.p.h., 70.4 m.p.g. At 60 m.p.h., 59.2 m.p.g.

BRAKING : From 30 m.p.h. to rest 28ft 6in (surface, dry tar macadam).

TURNING CIRCLE : 16ft.

MINIMUM NON-SNATCH SPEED : 17 m.p.h. in top gear.

WEIGHT PER C.C. : 0.8 lb.

BSA
B31

If one motor cycle had to be chosen to represent the solidly reliable British overhead-valve medium-weight single of the 1950s, then high on the list of candidates for the honour must be the 348 cc BSA B31. The B31 was a workaday relative of the glamour-puss Gold Star, and did not hit many headlines during its long lifetime; but even today, in the industrial areas of the country, many a B31 can be seen giving the same sterling service it produced when new. And many another, relegated to the depths of the garage when family needs meant the purchase of a car, is now being brought back to life as second-string transport.

Entirely a post-war product, the B31 was a member of BSA's first civilian programme, announced in August, 1945. Most handsome it looked, too, with the silvered panels of its chromium-plated fuel tank set off by black striping. It had a rigid frame, of course, but front suspension was by BSA's recently-patented hydraulically-damped telescopic fork.

The BSA people described the new three-fifty as a sports unit with excellent slogging power (which, indeed, it was). On 73 octane pool petrol and a compression ratio of only 6.8 to 1, it could whip up to just over 70 mph.

But of course, new designs rarely come out of the blue, and for the true ancestry of the B31 we must go back to the 1940 Small Heath catalogue. Surprisingly, the 499 cc M24 Gold Star was an absentee from that year's range, but there was an interesting newcomer, the 348 cc B29 Silver Sports, which employed the early Goldie's robust bottom-end assembly, plus a cast-iron

cylinder head with integral rocker boxes housing hairpin valve springs.

Only a handful of B29 Silver Sports models were ever built, due to the war (and most of those were requisitioned by the Army). However, a military version of the B29 had been under evaluation for some time and, early in 1940, the factory received an urgent order for a thousand, to replace machines lost in the Dunkirk evacuation. The order was never put in hand, because the British Army had hasty second thoughts and, instead, settled for yet another batch of side-valve M20s.

Nevertheless, the B29 Silver Sports had not been forgotten, and in the immediate post-war period it was to sire an entire brood of three-fifties. First of these was the B31, still with the hairpin-valve-spring type of integral rocker box, but employing coil-spring valve operation. By January, 1946, the first B32 had come upon the scene – in effect a trials job, and fettled by competitions manager Bert Perrigo; features were a high-level exhaust pipe, greater ground clearance, lower gear ratios, and narrower, chromium-plated mudguards. Price of the B32 Competitions was exactly £100, although purchase tax of £47 had to be added.

A third version of the design, announced for the 1949 season, was a clubman racer known as the B32 Special. This was first of the group to be given a plunger-type rear suspension and it had, also, a light-alloy cylinder barrel and head, plus the option of a close-ratio gearbox. Development of this model had included the entry in the 1947 Junior Manx Grand Prix of an experimental BSA with B29-type engine (including hairpin valve springs), magnesium crankcase and light-alloy cylinder head. Inevitably, the B32 Special was to grow into the B32GS

This is how the 348 cc BSA B31 looked when first produced in 1945. The speedometer, mounted in the top of the fuel tank, is an echo of pre-war practice. Tank panels were silver, with black lining

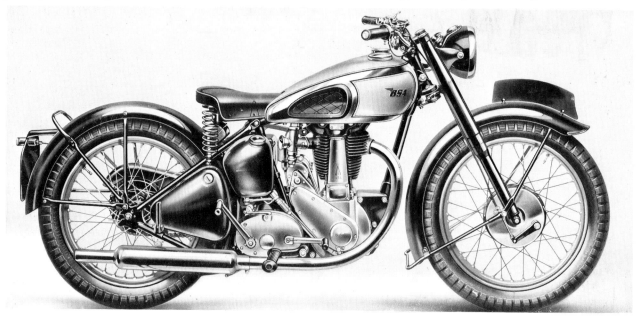

A 1955 BSA catalogue picture of the B31. At this time three versions of the machine were on sale: rigid frame (£131 plus £26.4s tax); spring or plunger frame (£140 plus £28 tax); and swinging arm (£150 plus £30 tax) as shown here

Gold Star before very long. But let us not become side-tracked . . .

For 1948 the standard B31 had exchanged its original silver-painted tank for one of mid-green lined in gold, possibly the most handsome livery the model was ever to wear, and one that will be well-remembered by those who were on the roads at this period. A rather stronger frame (still rigid, though) was adopted for the following season, recognisable by the forged steel rear-wheel lugs.

As time went by, it appeared to the general public that while development of the B32 Gold Star proceeded apace, its country cousin, the B31, had been left to vegitate. Thus while the Goldie had been fitted with a light-alloy cylinder and head with cast-in pushrod tunnels, the B31 still retained its now elderly engine arrangement of separate pushrod tower, connected to the underside of the integral rocker-box head by a castellated ring nut. In fact the only notable change for 1953 was to the fuel tank which was given chromium-plated side panels and a red instead of green paint finish. The frame still had no rear springing in standard trim but, eventually, plunger-type suspension could be supplied at extra cost. There was even one interim period when the model was listed in rigid, plunger-sprung, and pivoted-fork versions.

Power output was only mediocre, remaining at around 18 bhp, but at least this had the virtue of leaving the working parts to do their job unhurriedly and without fuss or frenzy. In consequence, the machine seemed to have the ability to go on for ever, with little more attention than adding oil and petrol when necessary.

The coming of three-dimensional plastic tank badges, in place of the rather horrid pressed-steel flashes of 1953, and the fitting of a headlamp semi-cowl, restored to the B31 a little of the style it had lost. It was not until 1956 that major changes were made.

The B31 now emerged with a full duplex-tube frame, pivoted rear springing, deep valanced guards at front and rear, and Ariel brakes in full-width hubs. An optional extra, well worth specifying, was total enclosure of the rear chain.

All this was really an extension of the BSA Group policy of gradual rationalisation. In fact, in everything but cylinder bore, the B31 was the same machine as its B33 499 cc sister, and that accounted for the 420 lb weight quoted in the specification panel of the accompanying road test.

Cylinder head of the 1945 BSA B31, showing the integral rocker boxes. In this engine the ohv pushrods were housed in an external, tapered tower (the later Gold Star version had integral pushrod tunnels in the cylinder and head)

From its introduction, the B31 had been capable of a little over 70 mph flat-out, and the 1956 model, with its two-way maximum of 72 mph, carried on the Small Heath tradition.

As the 1950s progressed, BSA felt that there was still a small corner of the market for the B31 and, accordingly, for 1958 the image was updated by abandoning, at last, magdyno electrics and adopting a crankshaft-mounted alternator. They also enhanced the good looks of the model further by fitting a deeper and more graceful fuel tank, and new-style headlamp mounted integral with the fork upper shrouds. The Ariel brakes were superseded by Triumph pattern. There was a new paint finish, too, of polychromatic almond green, although this was not to everybody's fancy.

Alas, the new-look B31 was destined for a production life of only two seasons, and as the 1950s closed, so the model was dropped from the Small Heath programme. The 1960 range still included the 499 cc B33, plus 348 and 499 cc Gold Star singles, but the B31 was gone.

In due course there would be another 350 cc BSA ohv single, a much lighter affair evolved from the 250 cc unit-construction C15 and no doubt a very worthy model, too. But the newcomer never did achieve the same measure of universal affection as that afforded the old, original slogger.

The B31 is admirably proportioned and smartly finished in maroon and chromium. Front and rear mudguards are of deep section.

THE question as to the most suitable type of motor cycle for all-round purposes is almost as old as the industry. Though riders' decisions are inevitably influenced by personal preferences, the three-fifty has long enjoyed a large following as an all-purpose mount. Generally speaking, the attractions of the type are comparatively low initial outlay and running costs, light handling and an engine which blends docility for town work with brisk, open-road performance.

Road Tests of New Models

348 c.c. B.S.A. B31 A Most Economical Single, Comfortable
and Fast for Long-distance Touring, Handy in Heavy Traffic : Excellent Steering and Brakes

Rear-suspension units are provided with three-position adjustment for load. Adjustment is effected with a C-spanner. Neat in appearance, the rear chaincase proved most effective.

Scaling more than 400 lb, the 348 c.c. B.S.A. B31 is no lightweight; yet it is not heavy to handle. It combines adequate tractability for dense city traffic with a mile-a-minute cruising speed. But probably the brightest of the model's attractions is its fuel economy. As shown by the performance data in the information panel, petrol consumption at 30 m.p.h. was about average for a 350 c.c. machine but the figures obtained at 40, 50 and 60 m.p.h. were remarkably good. In conjunction with a fuel capacity of four gallons, the low consumption rate endows the B31 with an unusually long range.

The model tested was equipped with a rear chaincase (an optional extra). So worth while was this enclosure of the drive in enhancing both the cleanliness of the machine and the condition of the chain that it is reasonable to suppose the chaincase will become a standard item of specification before long.

The B31 engine has manual ignition control and no great skill was called for in its use. A three-fifty cannot be made to slog on a retarded ignition setting as can a machine of 500 c.c. or more. Hence, apart from engine starting, the ignition on the B31 was retarded only for two purposes, namely, to give a slow and regular tickover and to obviate the need for clutch slipping when trickling along at 4 or 5 m.p.h. in heavy traffic. For both conditions a setting of one-half to two-thirds retard was found to be suitable. But for normal running it was best to employ full advance and keep the engine spinning happily by correct use of the gear box.

Engine starting was almost invariably achieved at the first swing of the kick-starter and the preliminary drill was simple. When the engine was cold the air lever was closed, the ignition partially retarded, the carburettor lightly flooded and the throttle set as for fast idling. It was then necessary to ease the piston over compression by using the exhaust-valve lifter before thrusting the kick-starter down smartly. When the engine was warm the only prerequisite for a first-kick start was to ease the piston over compression. If required the engine could be started on full advance but in that case care was needed to employ only a minute throttle opening to avoid a kick back.

The air lever could be opened to its full extent very soon after a cold start and, as implied earlier, a slow, even tickover could be obtained on half retard. When moving off from a standstill, however, it was best to have the ignition at full advance; that pre-

Left: Valve-clearance adjusters are situated at the lower ends of the pushrods. Right: Contact-breaker points are readily accessible

sented no problem for it was easy to thumb the ignition lever forward before releasing the clutch lever.

At low and medium speeds the engine functioned smoothly and reasonably quietly. Mechanical noise was about average for a single, slight piston slap and valve-gear clack being audible, while the exhaust had a full, mellow tone. Use of large throttle openings resulted in a harsher exhaust note but it was not difficult to ride the B31 fast and unobtrusively. At indicated speeds of 53 to 63 m.p.h. in top gear (and corresponding speeds in the indirect gears) engine vibration was perceptible through the dual-seat.

When used for serious touring, the B31 proved capable of maintaining sufficiently fast average speeds to permit large daily mileages to be covered without boredom. Under average conditions, use of half throttle gave an indicated speed of 60 to 65 m.p.h. in top gear. At that throttle setting the engine was working happily but not unduly hard and up to 50 miles could be covered in each hour on fast roads. A similar speed could be sustained up the majority of main-road hills by increasing the throttle opening. Speedometer flattery increased progressively from 1 m.p.h. at 30 m.p.h. to 5 m.p.h. at maximum speed.

Light to operate, the clutch freed completely and took up the drive smoothly and firmly. With the engine idling slowly, only a negligible click accompanied the engagement of bottom gear. Once the initial stiffness in the gear-control mechanism had worn off, clean gear changes could be effected by gentle, synchronized operation of clutch, throttle and gear pedal without any appreciable pause in pedal movement. On the model tested selection of neutral from second gear was frequently stiff and remained so throughout the test.

Riders of various statures found the riding position uncramped and such as to afford maximum control. Even when a period of several hours was spent awheel no discomfort was felt. The pillion position, too, was comfortable and the dual-seat long enough for two medium-size riders. With the exception of the rear-brake

Information Panel

348 c.c. B.S.A. B31

SPECIFICATION

ENGINE: B.S.A. 348 c.c. (71 x 88 mm) overhead-valve single with fully enclosed valve gear. Crankshaft supported in ball and roller bearings on drive side and in roller and plain bearings on timing side. Roller big-end bearing. Compression ratio, 6.5 to 1. Dry-sump lubrication; oil-tank capacity, 5¼ pints.

CARBURETTOR: Amal Monobloc with twistgrip throttle control; air slide operated by handlebar lever.

IGNITION and LIGHTING: Lucas Magdyno with manual ignition control. Lucas 6-volt, 12-ampere-hour battery. Lucas 7in-diameter headlamp with pre-focus light unit.

TRANSMISSION: B.S.A. four-speed gear box with positive-stop foot control. Gear ratios: bottom, 14.42 to 1; second, 9.82 to 1; third, 6.77 to 1; top, 5.6 to 1. Multi-plate clutch with fabric and cork inserts. Primary chain, ½ x 0.305in in oil-bath case. Rear chain, ⅝ x ¼in enclosed in pressed-steel case. Engine r.p.m. at 30 m.p.h. in top gear, 2,200.

FUEL CAPACITY: 4 gallons.

TYRES: Dunlop 3.25 x 19in; rear, Universal; front, ribbed.

BRAKES: Both 7in diameter x 1⅛in wide; fulcrum adjusters.

SUSPENSION: B.S.A. telescopic front fork with hydraulic damping. Pivoted-fork rear springing employing coil springs and hydraulic damping; three-position adjustment for load.

WHEELBASE: 56in unladen. Ground clearance, 5in unladen.

SEAT: B.S.A. dual-seat; unladen height, 31¼in.

WEIGHT: 420 lb fully equipped, with full oil tank and approximately one gallon of petrol.

PRICE: £162. With purchase tax (in Great Britain only), £200 17s 8d. Extras: rear chaincase, £2 10s (p.t., 12s); prop stand, 15s (p.t., 3s 8d).

ROAD TAX: £3 15s a year; £1 0s 8d a quarter.

MAKERS: B.S.A. Motor Cycles, Ltd., Small Heath, Birmingham, 11.

DESCRIPTION: *The Motor Cycle,* 13 October 1955.

PERFORMANCE DATA

MEAN MAXIMUM SPEED: Bottom: *32 m.p.h.
Second: *47 m.p.h.
Third: *68 m.p.h.
Top: 72 m.p.h.
*Valve float occurring.

HIGHEST ONE-WAY SPEED: 73 m.p.h. (conditions: still air; rider wearing two-piece plastic suit and overboots).

MEAN ACCELERATION:

	10-30 m.p.h.	20-40 m.p.h.	30-50 m.p.h.
Bottom	4.2 sec	—	—
Second	5 sec	5 sec	—
Third	—	7.4 sec	8.6 sec
Top	—	9.2 sec	9.8 sec

Mean speed at end of quarter-mile from rest: 63 m.p.h.
Mean time to cover standing quarter-mile: 20.4 sec.

PETROL CONSUMPTION: At 30 m.p.h., 110 m.p.g.; at 40 m.p.h., 105 m.p.g.; at 50 m.p.h., 90 m.p.g.; at 60 m.p.h., 68 m.p.g.

BRAKING: From 30 m.p.h. to rest, 32ft (surface, dry tarmac).

TURNING CIRCLE: 14ft 3in.

MINIMUM NON-SNATCH SPEED: 14 m.p.h. in top gear with ignition fully retarded.

WEIGHT PER C.C.: 1.21 lb.

pedal all controls are adjustable for position and can be well set for convenient manipulation. The left footrest rubber forms a stop for the brake pedal which is set a trifle high.

Both front and rear springing allowed an ample range of wheel deflection and combined to take the sting out of the majority of road shocks. The three settings on the Girling rear shock absorbers were ample for all normal loads though a manual adjustment, without the need for using a spanner, would be preferred for casual passenger carrying. The front fork on the model tested was sufficiently damped to prevent undue pitching, with the result that movement around the static-load position was a little firm

Equipped with a ribbed front tyre and endowed with steering geometry similar to that of the successful Gold Star clubman-racing models, the B31 possesses excellent steering qualities.

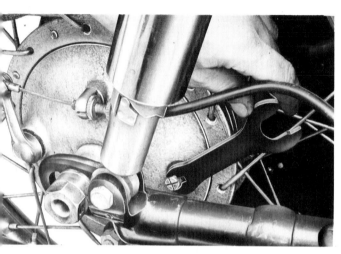

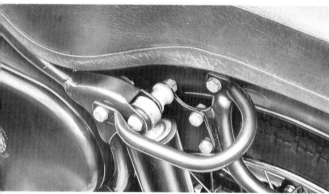

Whether the model was following a straight course or being swung stylishly through fast or slow bends it followed the intended path precisely. Heeling the model over required little effort and stability at steep angles of lean was such as to engender every confidence. Though the prop stand could be caused to scrape the road surface lightly by spirited left-hand cornering, the fault was very rarely apparent provided the rear springing was set correctly for the load carried.

Braking efficiency matched the general high standard of the machine. Both brakes are contained in smart, full-width, light-alloy hubs and have generous friction areas. Consequently the need for adjustment (made at the shoe fulcrum and not at the cable adjuster) was infrequent in spite of extensive hard use. Power of the brakes was such that either tyre could be made to squeal loudly and the model could be arrested in a short enough distance to cope with any emergency. There was no significant lessening of braking power when the B.S.A. was ridden for a period of two hours in torrential rain.

The brightness of the main headlamp beam was sufficient to make a mile-a-minute speed quite safe on unlit main roads after dark. But, as is sometimes found with the B.S.A. headlamp cowl, the best setting of the beam required removal of the rubber beading from the front edge of the cowl except when a pillion passenger was carried (which naturally results in a slight raising of the beam).

Considering that the test involved over 1,000 miles of hard riding, external cleanliness of the B31 at the finish was commendable. With the exception of some messiness around the drain pipe from the cylinder head to the crankcase, oil seepage was almost negligible. Leakage past the oil-tank filler cap was not entirely absent when the model was ridden fast. As already implied the rear chaincase made a considerable contribution towards keeping the rear portion of the model free from filth in addition to protecting the chain and thus minimizing wear. By the time the test was concluded the exhaust pipe had blued for a length of seven or eight inches at the cylinder-head end.

Apart from difficulty in removing the high-tension pick-up brush holder, routine maintenance presented no problems. Lifting the model on to its centre stand, however, required appreciable physical effort. Setting the valve clearances did not entail removal of the petrol tank: the two adjusters are incorporated in the tappets and are accessible on removal of the cover at the lower end of the pushrod tunnel. The adjusters for the contact-breaker points, front and rear chains, clutch and brakes are also accessible. Though the battery is concealed beneath the dual-seat, topping-up required only the prior removal of the two bolts holding the seat in place. The standard tool kit proved adequate for making all adjustments. When it becomes necessary to remove the petrol tank, such as for decarbonizing the engine, only one retaining bolt has to be withdrawn after disconnecting the fuel pipe and detaching the bracing strap from the base of the tank.

To sum up, the B31 B.S.A. with rear chain enclosure is an attractive model for the rider who wants a lively, economical, easy-to-handle all-rounder but who is not insistent on an ultra-high maximum speed. Finish is in the customary B.S.A. maroon enamel, with chromium plating for the tank sides as well as for the more usual parts.

Top: Brake adjustment, made at the shoe fulcrum, was rarely necessary and easily carried out by means of a short spanner.

Above: A lifting handle is conveniently mounted to the left of the seat.

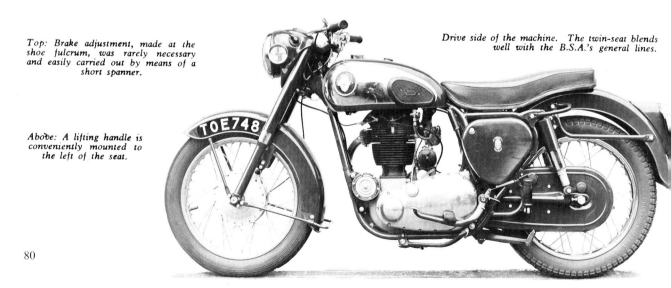

Drive side of the machine. The twin-seat blends well with the B.S.A.'s general lines.

ARIEL
SQUARE FOUR MARK II

Probably one of the best-known legends of motor cycling tells of how a Dulwich (South London) dealer named Edward Turner, who had been building an overhead-camshaft 350 cc single of his own design, thought of a way to build a particularly compact four-cylinder engine, by mounting the cylinders two by two.

That way, the overheating problems that affected an in-line four were bypassed, and at the same time the width problem of an across-the-frame four did not arise. Jotting down the bones of his idea on the back of a cigarette packet – a Wild Woodbine cigarette packet, confirmed Mr. Turner, in later years – he travelled to the Midlands and tried to get first one factory, then another, interested. For a while, it looked as though the AJS firm might be interested; but AJS, in the mid-1920s, were already pretty well extended with recent ventures into the light car, bus chassis, and even radio fields.

At last Turner tackled Jack Sangster, boss of the Ariel factory at Selly Oak, Birmingham. Sangster liked the idea, but refused to commit himself until he had had the chance to study some rather more workmanlike drawings. To that end, though, he was willing to instal Turner in a quiet office away from the bustle of the works and, what is more, he would provide a young assistant draughtsman to help with the detailing. That young man turned out to be Bert Hopwood who, nearly two decades later, would be designing such all-time classics as the Norton Dominator and BSA Golden Flash.

What emerged was an extremely light and lively overhead-camshaft 500 cc four, essentially a pair of vertical twins mounted one behind the other and with their crankshafts geared together in the middle. The design embraced unit-construction, with a three-speed gearbox, with the crankcase split horizontally. It was so light that for development test purposes the engine was mounted in the frame of a 250 cc single.

However, prudency and expediency meant that the Square Four in production form was rather more sedate and weighty. For a start, the Ariel range standardised on Burman gearboxes – so unit construction was out and a separate, heavier gearbox was in. For economy reasons, it had to use the duplex frame already in production for the Val Page single-cylinder sloper (which was fair enough, because although the 250 cc frame could serve for development, it would have been too flimsy to let loose upon the ham-fisted populace at large).

The first, 1931, five-hundred was followed by a 600 cc overhead-camshaft version. Naturally enough, racing types wanted to get rather more performance out of the design, and both Howard Somerville Sikes, and Ben Bickell tried the effect of adding a supercharger. But the curse of the early Square Four was a weak and insufficiently cooled cylinder head which tended to warp and blow a gasket when put under duress. Ben Bickell managed to get his 500 cc four to lap Brooklands at 100 mph – but three laps was about the limit before the head blew once again.

Edward Turner was aware of the drawbacks and so, for 1936, he evolved a totally new engine which retained the Square Four name and cylinder layout, but that was about all. The newcomer was a 997 cc pushrod overhead-valve model, with a chain-driven central camshaft running across the unit between the two pairs of cylinders. The crankshafts were still geared together, but now the gears were located on the left-hand end of each shaft, instead of in the middle.

The maker's advertising claimed '10 to 100 mph in top gear', and that the engine would require only light servicing at 10,000-mile intervals. Very elegant was the 1936 Square Four, for Edward Turner was not only a designer but a stylist with a sure touch, and the flowing lines of the valanced front mudguard, handsome chromium-plated tank with instrument panel in its top face, and lozenge-and-fishtail silencers, made for an harmonious whole. Amazingly, the all-up weight was only 410 lb. Power output was 38 bhp which, for the day and age, was quite something.

Initially, the 600 cc ohc four was continued alongside, but in reality this was just to use up existing stocks of parts, and before 1936 was out the 'cammy' had been replaced by a pushrod ohv model of the same dimensions. There, though, Selly Oak had miscalculated. There was but little demand for the 600 cc, and it was dropped after only one season, while the Mark I iron-engine Model 4G 997 cc continued alone.

First major post-war change for the 998 cc Ariel Square Four came in 1949, when employment of light-alloy cylinder block and head castings reduced overall weight by over 100 lb. This drawing shows the 'two-pipe' light-alloy engine, replaced for 1953 by the final 'four-pipe' model

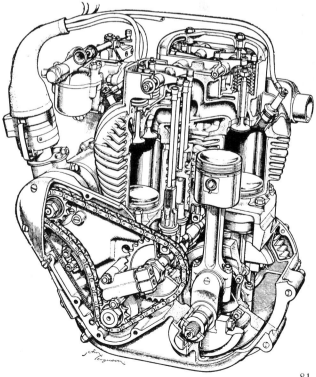

Unusual role for a 'four-pipe' Square Four was this sprinter, built in 1955 by Peter Peters, of the Avon Tyre company. Another Ariel four was sprinted by the Healey brothers at a slightly later period

Compensated-link plunger rear springing, designed to keep the rear chain in constant tension, was available for 1939 (in which year, by the way, the 600 made a surprise re-appearance), and this was again featured when the 4G made its post-war re-appearance – now graced with Ariel's own telescopic front fork – late in 1946.

It could be, of course, that Selly Oak felt that the addition of a pivoted rear fork would lengthen the wheelbase, but in truth the

Another unfamiliar Square Four was this road-racing sidecar outfit, used in 1966 by its constructor, Stan Nightingale. The Ariel, however, is a difficult engine to tune for speed and tends to suffer from camshaft whip which restricts the usable rpm band

production Square Four was to retain compensated-link plunger springing to the end of its day. A prototype with a pivoted fork was indeed built, and is at present in a private collection, but it did not reach the assembly line.

In the next few years, the Square Four found particular favour among USA enthusiasts. Through the efforts of an energetic West Coast importer, some even found their way to local Californian Police Departments (as at Monterey, for example). Police in Australia, too, added the Square Four to their strength.

Nevertheless, there had been very little engine development since the pushrod four was first announced and, in the meantime, the machine had undoubtedly put on a lot of excess weight. So the redesign of late 1948 was well timed.

The bottom-end assembly was hardly altered, but now there was a light-alloy cylinder block and head. Weight-saving was carried on in other directions, too, and as a result the 1949 Square Four (still listed as the 4G Mark I) had shed over 100 lb. That was not all, because the use of the light-alloy block served also to lower the centre of gravity and therefore improve the handling.

The old trouble of overheating was still prevalent, and so a further redesign was undertaken for 1953, resulting in the famous four-pipe Mark II model. Again the cylinder block and head were of light alloy, but in the new model the exhaust manifolds (also light-alloy castings) were bolted to each side of the head instead of being cast integrally, and there was a separate exhaust pipe for each cylinder. Inlet porting was revised and enlarged and, on the 73 octane fuel available at the time, power output was raised to 40 bhp at 5,600 rpm.

Possibly to celebrate the launch of the Mark II model, there was a complete departure from the earlier colour schemes, and the Square Four was presented in a delicate shade of light Wedgwood blue. The colour change was of short duration, for by 1954 it was back to maroon. A few minor changes were yet to come – a one-gallon oil tank, a full-width front hub, a headlamp cowl – but in general the Square Four had served its time, and by 1959 it had gone.

The Square Four was to achieve a kind of posthumous popularity, with Americans, especially, combing the backyards of Britain for examples to ship back to the States. But there cannot be many left now.

ROAD TESTS OF NEW MODELS

997 c.c. Mark II Ariel Square Four

SINCE only two British manufacturers market machines in the 1,000 c.c. class, it might be asserted that the thousand, as a type, has a limited appeal—an appeal restricted to fastidious connoisseurs. However, the latest version of the long-established Ariel Square Four—the 997 c.c. Mark II—by the enhanced versatility of its performance over that of its predecessors, extends the appeal of the 1,000 c.c. machine to the widest possible range of tastes. An outstanding trait of the model is the smoothness and flexibility of its engine torque over an unusually large range of r.p.m. The outcome of more than

The lines of the latest Ariel Four are distinctly sleek and well proportioned. Chromium-plated flashes enhance the appearance of the five-gallon fuel tank

20 years' development of the original concept, the 4G Mark II combines, in large measure, the docility for which Ariel Fours have always been renowned with an open-road potential capable of satisfying the most hardened road burner.

The Ariel's repertoire contains a type of performance to suit a rider's every mood. It may be ridden in top gear at speeds below 20 m.p.h. Alternatively, full use may be made of the engine's high power output in all gears. In either case, acceleration is exceptionally smooth, quiet and unhesitant; if the full performance is used, acceleration has an urgency matched by few road-going vehicles. Intermediately, the Square Four will

cruise quietly and unostentatiously at 50, 60 or 70 m.p.h. on a mere "whiff" of throttle.

For long or short journeys, the Ariel was easy and pleasant to ride. Factors contributing to this characteristic were comfortable wheel suspension, excellent riding position and control layout, a large reserve of engine power, good brakes and—not least in importance—a high degree of exhaust and mechanical quietness. At no period in the performance range does the exhaust note rise above a pleasant, subdued hum. Mechanical noise, except when the engine was idling, was reminiscent of that of a well-oiled sewing machine. On tickover, the only audible noises were in the form of a rumble from the crankshaft coupling gears, and a slight rustle from the valve-gear.

In spite of its weight, the 4G Mark II has a high degree of handleability. On slow and medium-pace corners it could be heeled over confidently until the prop stand or silencers grounded — which could occur readily when the suspension was loaded by the added weight of a pillion passenger. This ease of handling, coupled with the machine's zestful but unobtrusive acceleration, made the Ariel a commendably safe and pleasant machine to use under traffic conditions.

The riding position is a fine compromise between an "armchair" layout for maximum comfort at town speeds, and a slight crouch for fatigue resistance at high speeds—with, perhaps, a slight bias towards the former. Relationship of seat and footrests resulted in an agreeably wide knee angle. The shape of the handlebar provided a natural position for the grips. Seat height was such as to enable a rider of average height easily to place his feet on the ground at traffic halts. All controls could be well placed for ease of operation and were silky to use. Those on the handlebar are reduced to a minimum number. The twistgrip has a somewhat longer than usual rotary travel, a feature providing a delicacy of throttle control which enhances the already outstanding sweetness of the engine.

Starting the four-cylinder engine was always simple. No great muscular effort was required to operate the kick-starter, even when the machine had been standing outdoors overnight in the cold weather experienced in March. Under such conditions, three depressions of the starter pedal were normally sufficient to start the engine with the carburettor bi-starter control in operation. This control could be moved to its intermediate stop after a few seconds' running, and moved to its normal-running position when the machine had covered about a quarter of a mile. When warm, the engine could be brought to life by no more than a leisurely movement of the kick-starter. Carburation at very small throttle openings was uneven, particularly when the engine was cold.

With the engine idling, bottom gear could be engaged noiselessly from neutral. Occasionally, partial release of the clutch was required for gear selection. Neutral was at all times easy to locate from either bottom or second gears. Clutch operation was reasonably light and entirely positive. Gear changes, both upward and downward, could be effected with great rapidity. Owing to the engine's unusually quick response to throttle opening and

Close-up view of the massive, yet compact, four-cylinder engine. The distributor is seen in front of the oil tank

A Unique High-performance Mount
with Gentle Manners
and Outstanding Acceleration

closing, it was found that a fast gear-changing technique achieved the best results. Partial clutch and throttle operation, with a simultaneous, light depression of the gear pedal, produced excellent upward changes, though sometimes second and top gear engagement could be felt slightly. Second to third was a particularly sweet change. Clean and ultra-rapid downward changes were easily made.

Both front and rear wheel suspensions possessed an adequate range of movement and worked well at all speeds. A reasonably soft response around the static-load position and a progressively increasing resistance to deflection brought both small and large surface irregularities within the compass of the springing. Only at ultra-high speeds, on surfaces which were not smooth, did a certain amount of pitching set in. Steering was first class, being both light and positive; bend-swinging was quite effortless. A slight tendency to weave was apparent only when travelling at very high velocities on bad surfaces. The top hamper of a full, five-gallon fuel tank was virtually unnoticeable, except under extreme conditions.

Both brakes were pleasantly light to operate, smooth and extremely powerful. Though their hard use incurred frequent need for adjustment in the early stages of the test, the adjustment took only a matter of seconds.

In the matter of ultimate road performance, the figures shown in the panel speak for themselves. In fact, these data were obtained after the machine had been ridden exceptionally hard for 1,500 miles with little attention, and when a gusty, 15-20 m.p.h. three-quarter wind prevailed. There can be little doubt that, under more favourable conditions, a mean maximum speed of 100 m.p.h. would have been recorded. The fastest one-way run in top gear was at 107 m.p.h.

Under suitable road and traffic conditions, speeds of 80-85 m.p.h. could be maintained for as long as required. In a deliberate attempt to tire the engine, the machine was ridden for many miles with the speedometer needle hovering between 90 and 95 m.p.h., but the engine betrayed not the least sign of distress. Its reserve of power enabled high cruising speeds to be sustained against headwinds and up long gradients, thus making high average speeds commonplace. A slight vibration period

Noteworthy features are the neatness of the power unit and the 20-amp-hour battery. The ignition coil and voltage regulator are mounted beneath the seat

sets in between 50 and 55 m.p.h., but is not felt above 60 m.p.h.

The minimum non-snatch speed is of more than academic interest in the case of the Ariel. In the normal course of town riding, it was frequently throttled back below 20 m.p.h. in top gear and accelerated away sweetly.

The speedometer fitted to the test machine had a high standard of accuracy up to 60 m.p.h. There was virtually no error up to 50 m.p.h.; from 60 to 90 m.p.h. the instrument registered four to five m.p.h. fast. Failure of the ammeter necessitated a replacement during the test. When riding on flooded roads, there was a tendency for one sparking plug to cut out.

The main head lamp bulb provided an adequate beam for fast night riding. The dynamo balanced the full ignition and lamp load at 30 m.p.h. in top gear.

The discerning Ariel Four owner will appreciate the 20-amp-hour battery and its accessibility for topping-up purposes. Another praiseworthy feature is the fuel-tank capacity, which enables 200-250 miles to be covered at high cruising speeds without refuelling. In spite of the machine's weight, it is a relatively easy matter to place it on its rear stand. The accessible prop stand is excellent for use on cambered roads.

Information Panel

997 c.c. Ariel Square Four Mark II

SPECIFICATION

ENGINE : 997 c.c. (65×75 mm) four-cylinder o.h.v. Aluminium-alloy cylinders cast *en bloc* in square formation. Detachable light-alloy cylinder head embodying cruciform induction manifold ; totally enclosed and positively lubricated valve gear, with push-rod operation ; separate exhaust manifolds. Twin crankshafts coupled by hardened and ground gears. Light-alloy connecting rods with plain, shell-type big-end bearings. Compression ratio, 7.2 to 1. Dry sump lubrication ; oil-tank capacity, 6 pints.
CARBURETTOR : Solex, Bi-starter type ; twistgrip throttle control.
IGNITION and LIGHTING : Coil ignition. 70-watt, voltage-controlled Lucas dynamo incorporating distributor with automatic timing variation. 7 in-diameter headlamp with sealed-beam light unit. 6-volt, 20-amp-hour Lucas battery.
TRANSMISSION : Burman four-speed gear box with positive-stop foot control. Bottom, 11.07 to 1. Second, 7.1 to 1. Third, 5.46 to 1. Top, 4.18 to 1. Multi-plate clutch with Neoprene inserts, operating in remote case. Primary chain, $\frac{1}{2} \times 0.305$ in. oil-bath case. Secondary chain, $\frac{5}{8} \times \frac{3}{8}$ in, lubricated by adjustable bleed from primary chaincase ; guards over top and bottom runs. R.p.m. at 30 m.p.h. in top gear, 1,675.
FUEL CAPACITY : 5 gallons.
TYRES : Dunlop. Front, 3.25×19 in Ribbed. Rear, 4.00×18 in Universal.
BRAKES : $7 \times 1\frac{1}{8}$ in front ; $8 \times 1\frac{1}{8}$ in rear. Fulcrum adjusters.
SUSPENSION : Ariel telescopic front fork with hydraulic damping. Ariel link-action rear springing.
WHEELBASE : $56\frac{1}{2}$ in unladen. Ground clearance, $4\frac{3}{4}$ in unladen.
SEAT : Ariel dual-seat. Unladen height, 30in.
WEIGHT : 460 lb fully equipped, with no fuel and full oil tank.
PRICE : £225. With purchase tax (in Gt. Britain only), £271 17s. 6d. Extras : Spring frame, £16 (with P.T., £19 6s 8d).
ROAD TAX : £3 15s a year ; £1 0s 8d a quarter.
MAKERS : Ariel Motors, Ltd., Selly Oak, Birmingham, 29
DESCRIPTION : *The Motor Cycle*, 6 November, 1952.

PERFORMANCE DATA
MEAN MAXIMUM SPEED : Bottom :* 40 m.p.h.
Second :*62 m.p.h.
Third :* 79 m.p.h.
Top : 97 m.p.h.
* Valve float occuring.

MEAN ACCELERATION :

	10-30 m.p.h.	20-40 m.p.h.	30-50 m.p.h.
Bottom	2 secs	2 secs	—
Second	3.2 secs	2.6 secs	2.5 secs
Third	4.4 secs.	3.8 secs.	3.4 secs
Top	—	5.4 secs	5 secs

Speed at end of quarter-mile from rest : 85 m.p.h.
Mean time to cover standing quarter-mile : 15.4 secs.
PETROL CONSUMPTION : At 30 m.p.h., 57 m.p.g. At 40 m.p.h., 55 m.p.g. At 50 m.p.h., 54 m.p.g. At 60 m.p.h., 50 m.p.g.
BRAKING : From 30 m.p.h. to rest, 26ft 6in (surface, dry tarmac).
TURNING CIRCLE : 15ft.
MINIMUM NON-SNATCH SPEED : 13 m.p.h. in top gear.
WEIGHT Per C.C. : 0.46 lb.

Velocette

MSS

It is one of the facts of motor cycling life that 'Velocette' is a misnomer. The name of the manufacturer was Veloce Ltd (from the Latin word for 'speed') and, indeed, the first products of the company carried Veloce tank badges. However, just before the First World War a small two-stroke was added to the range, and to emphasise the different nature of the machine it was described as a Velocette, or 'little Veloce'.

The return of peacetime saw the Veloce firm – or to put it another way, the Goodman family – concentrating initially on an all-two-stroke programme and, naturally, these were continued under the Velocette name. But the coming of the 350 cc overhead-camshaft Model K engine in 1926 gave the factory a chance to get back to bigger stuff and, accordingly, the first batch of 350 cc bikes had 'Veloce', once more, on the tank sides.

'Take them away', said the dealers. 'Motor cyclists have forgotten what Veloce means by now'. And so the Goodmans had no choice but to label every bike from then on as a Velocette, regardless of engine size!

Still, that is by the way. The overhead-camshaft model was supplemented, in 1933, by a neat little pushrod overhead-valve 250 cc from the drawing board of Eugene Goodman. To reduce the weight of the valve operating gear, and so make for higher revs, the cams were located high in the timing chest and driven by a train of gears (initially straight-cut but later, in order to cut down clatter, with helical teeth).

This was the MOV, a success right from its introduction, and it was swiftly followed by a corresponding ohv 350 cc known as the MAC. Two years later, and especially for the family sidecar

man, the third of the M-series machines arrived – the 495 cc Model MSS. This was the first British bike to embody automatic ignition advance and retard, and which soon built up a healthy export trade. Indeed, as related by the late Len Moseley (*My Velocette Days*; Transport Bookman Ltd) some were sent as far afield as Japan.

Production continued up to the outbreak of the Second World War, and when the Hall Green works resumed motor cycle manufacture in 1945, the big MSS was still in the programme. Surprisingly, however, the very first peacetime machines to leave the Hall Green assembly line were about two-hundred Model GTP two-strokes featuring magneto ignition instead of the pre-war coil ignition. Ostensibly these were all earmarked for overseas markets, although a dozen travelled no further overseas than the Channel Islands.

The 495 cc MSS, together with other Velocette singles, ceased production in 1948, the reason being that the Goodman family were by then totally commited to the revolutionary flat-twin 150 cc Model LE side-valve. The LE was the 'everyman runabout' of dreams, the archetypal clean and quiet commuter machine for the masses.

Yes, well . . . Oh, certainly the potential commuter market existed. It was just that the LE was not the model for which commuters had been waiting, and the true answer was the chic little scooter as exemplified by the Vespa and Lambretta.

In the end the LE did find a niche, as silent transport for the pre-Panda beat policeman. But the numbers required for this work were insufficient to keep the factory in full production, and so the 350 cc MAC returned, initially in rigid form, but later with

Died-in-the-wool sidecar men swear that there never has been a bike to match the 499 cc MSS Velocette for sheer slogging power. A typical outfit was this 1954 marriage of an MSS and a Watsonian Monarch sidecar. Tested by Motor Cycling, *it achieved a top speed of 64 mph*

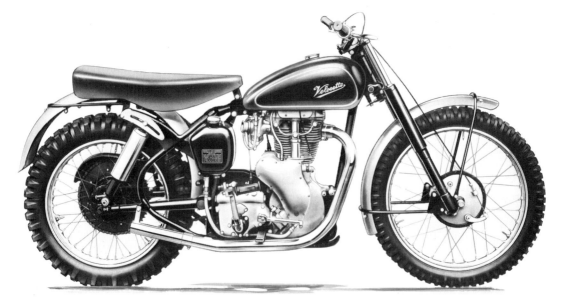

A model catalogued for some years but which never quite came up to expectations was the 499 cc MSS Scrambler, here seen in 1955 form

pivoted rear springing of unusual type. The fork itself was conventional, but the upper mountings of the rear damper units could be moved through a curved slot, to soften or harden the springing in accordance with the load on the machine.

The frame was the old traditional pattern, built by the hearth-brazing method with malleable-cast lugs, and conceding nothing to modern practice, with the rear fork grafted on.

For 1954 the MSS returned, too, but this was not the earlier MSS, even if it looked much the same. The cylinder barrel and head were now of Al-Fin light-alloy construction with bonded-in iron liner (Al-Fin was a proprietary process, operated by Wellworthy's of Lymington) but, more important still, bore and stroke dimensions had changed from the old longstroke format of 81 × 96 mm, to the fashionable 'square' 86 × 86 mm. Valve springs were of hairpin pattern.

Had Velocette's chief designer, Charles Udall at last decided to move towards modernity? In a way, maybe; but as Udall himself disclosed in an interview, the real reason was that the factory had decided to standardise on the MAC sprung frame

Far better known as a road-racer, the late John Hartle tackles a snow gulley at Panpunton, in the 1964 national Victory Trial. Most unusually, his mount is an adapted MSS Velocette

out of sheer economic necessity – and the old longstroke 495 cc MSS was just that fraction too tall. They merely shortened it to fit.

Peak power output of the MSS, on a compression ratio of 6·8 to 1, was only 23 bhp at 5,000 rpm, but the torque curve was a flat one, and a useful helping of urge was available from as low as 2,500 rpm. Which was fair enough, because the machine was designed as a slogger with the family sidecar man in mind.

For all that, the MSS found a ready sale among USA enthusiasts, who tended to skim the head, take off the lights and other non-essentials and ride flat-out across the dusty desert in the type of mass-start enduro racing of which they seemed inordinately fond.

More or less in self-defence, Hall Green had to evolve an official cross-country racer from the MSS, and this duly took its place in the catalogue as the MSS Endurance. In fact there were *two* off-road variants, the other being the MSS Scrambler; the Endurance could be considered as the Scrambler with lighting set fitted. For both, introduced in 1955, there was a high-compression engine with Amal TT9 racing carburettor and BTH racing magneto. Wheels were shod with competition-type 'knobbly' tyres and the frames, though still of time-honoured brazed lug construction, were given an extra helping of ground clearance.

On British circuits the Scrambler never did achieve very much fame or fortune (although on one occasion Billy Nicholson used one at an Easter Monday Redmarley freak hill-climb), but the Endurance version built up quite a sizeable following in America. Moreover, Tex Luce used an MSS Endurance engine, with reworked cylinder head porting and lightened and polished internals, as the basis of a very successful half-mile dirt track model; but Hall Green drew the line at adding a dirt-tracker to the now lengthy list of MSS variants.

Two more variants came into the list for 1956. Both based on the MSS engine, these were the sports-roadster 499 cc Venom and 349 cc Viper. It might be thought more feasible to have based the smaller machine, the Viper, on the existing 349 cc MAC, but in fact the same crankcase assembly was employed for both newcomers. So it made economic sense, after all.

In the years ahead, it was the Venom which took the glory – in production-machine racing and, most glorious feat of all, in capturing the 24-hour world 500 cc record at 100·05 mph. Later still there would be the Venom Thruxton, an even more rorty variation on the MSS theme. During this time, the MSS continued in production until the Velocette factory ceased bike manufacture during 1971.

ROAD·TESTS OF NEW MODELS

499 c.c. High-Camshaft MSS Velocette

INCLUSION of the 499 c.c. MSS model in the Velocette range of machines for 1954 marked the return of an old favourite rather than the introduction of an entirely new model. Nevertheless, though the latest version of the Velocette five-hundred bears an unmistakable affinity with its precursor, the new model has been modernized and re-designed in many respects.

Twenty-one years have passed since the high-camshaft, pushrod-operated overhead-valve Velocette engine made its first appearance—as a two-fifty. Two years later, following the introduction of the 349 c.c. MAC, the MSS was born to complete a trio of high-camshaft Velocettes. Those machines considerably extended the popularity of a marque already famous for the excellence of its overhead-camshaft touring and racing machines and for its high standard of engineering.

Post-war production considerations led to the discontinuance of the MSS six years ago. It re-emerges as an up-to-the-minute, single-cylinder five-hundred of exceptional quality and fine finish. It provides a high degree of riding comfort for one or two people, exemplary steering and road-holding, and an engine performance which is remarkable for the lusty power produced with complete smoothness at low and medium speeds.

Riders of various statures found that the relationship between seat, footrests and handlebar afforded a riding position which was comfortable and relaxed, even when many consecutive hours were spent in the saddle. The width across the handlebar grips, their height and their angle were such that the rider's hands rested on them naturally. All the controls on the bar could be well sited for ready operation and were smooth in use. With the footrest hangers in the 12 o'clock position, the brake and gear pedals were ideally situated and could be manipulated while the rider's insteps remained on the rests. For continued high-speed cruising the next rearward position of the footrests gave an even more suitable riding position but, with that setting, the reach to the pedals was too great for convenience. With the footrests in either position, the inside of the rider's right ankle was against the folding kick-starter crank.

Of unusual, two-level design, the dual-seat is of generous proportions, well shaped, and comfortably upholstered. With its overall length of 26½in and maximum width of 12in, it provided ample accommodation for two adults dressed in wet-weather riding kit. The pillion passenger's riding position was no less comfortable than that of the rider.

Complementary to the well-tailored riding position in furnishing a smooth and fatigue-free ride is a highly efficient system of front and rear springing. The adjustable-for-load, pivoted-fork rear suspension gave results which place it among the very best of contemporary layouts. For solo riding, the adjustment was set in its softest position. Road irregularities of all types normally encountered were absorbed without shock to the rider, whether the machine's speed was low or high. No pitching was experienced at any time, and roadholding on bumpy or undulating surfaces was of the highest order. In fact, it can truly be said of the MSS that its rider was at all times unconscious of the rear wheel. The range of adjustment provided was found to be more than adequate for pillion work.

Judged by the high standard of the rear springing, the action of the telescopic front fork was felt to be just a trifle hard, though by no means uncomfortably so. The comparative firmness became less perceptible as road speed mounted.

As is appropriate in a machine from a factory whose products have, in the past, achieved meritorious racing successes, the MSS almost steered itself. Straight-ahead steering was positive under all conditions, but it was cornering and bend-swinging which best revealed the Velocette's racing ancestry. The utmost confidence was quickly inspired by the unwavering way in which the front wheel would turn inward by just the right amount when the machine was banked into a bend or corner. This self-steering characteristic was evident at all speeds from a comparative crawl to the machine's maximum, and it operated for all normal degrees of lean. There was never any tendency for the front wheel to deviate from its allotted path, and corners of all types could be negotiated in safety faster on the MSS than on most contemporary machines. At low and medium speeds the footrest rubbers could be grounded, but that did not seriously limit cornering technique.

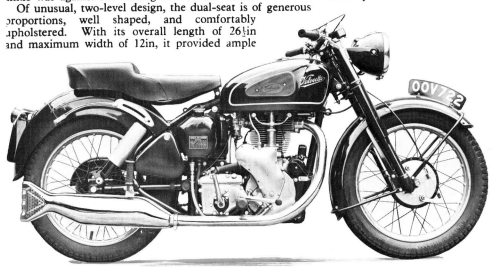

Left : well proportioned lines are enhanced by chromium-plated wheel rims and polished-aluminium engine and gear-box castings

Following pages: 1966 Venom Thruxton

A Light-alloy Single With Remarkably Smooth Power Delivery : Race-bred Steering and Road-holding Qualities

The external throttle-stop control on the carburettor provides setting for normal running and for starting

In its latest guise, the MSS engine exhibited in marked degree those pleasant attributes which characterize the well designed single and which endear the type to a large number of riders. The low- and medium-speed torque was quite exceptional. Added to good engine balance, effectively heavy flywheels and extraordinarily sweet transmission, the excellent torque resulted in an outstandingly tractable top-gear performance.

Though the engine is no sluggard in mounting the r.p.m. scale, a great deal of its charm lies in its smooth and rapid acceleration from low speeds. Whether the machine was ridden solo or two-up it was frequently throttled back to 20 m.p.h. in top gear in the normal course of traffic negotiation and was accelerated from that speed smartly and without pinking merely by opening the throttle. On steep, main-road gradients the same technique could be employed, if desired, from a speed of 20 to 25 m.p.h.

Efficient cooling is a feature of the light-alloy engine. On fast, main-road journeys no amount of hard riding tired the power unit. An extremely pleasant continuous cruising speed was 60 to 65 m.p.h., a pace which required a throttle opening of one-half or less, according to wind conditions; when main-road hills were encountered the MSS would take them in its stride without appreciable loss of speed and without need for increased throttle opening. At no engine speed was vibration perceptible through the footrests or fuel tank; a slight tremor could be felt at the handlebar but was almost unnoticable.

Mechanical noises were well subdued. A rhythmic clack from the valve gear could be identified but was not obtrusive. At small throttle openings the exhaust note was blameless. During brisk acceleration, however (though the note possessed a deep, clean-cut quality delightful to the ears of a single-cylinder enthusiast), it was considered to be too loud, particularly for built-up localities.

Achievement of prompt engine starting required a rather precise technique. When the engine was cold it was sensitive to mixture strength and, consequently, to the degree of carburettor tickling employed. A first-kick start could be effected by closing the air lever, turning the external throttle-stop control on the carburettor to the starting position, depressing the tickler lightly for a second and then, with the twistgrip in the closed position, spinning the engine rapidly by means of a long, powerful thrust on the kick-starter.

Insufficient or too much tickling were equally detrimental to easy starting. The remedy in the latter case was to open the throttle wide during operation of the kick-starter. As soon as the engine was running the air lever could be opened fully and the throttle-stop control turned to its normal running position. When the engine was warm, spinning it quickly was no less essential to a ready response though, in that case, the throttle-stop was set in its normal running position, the air lever left open and the tickler ignored. Whether hot or cold the engine would tick over reliably at a speed so low that individual power strokes could easily be counted.

Information Panel—499 c.c. High-Camshaft MSS Velocette

SPECIFICATION

ENGINE: 499 c.c. (86 x 86 mm) single-cylinder o.h.v. with fully enclosed valve gear; Duralumin pushrods, hairpin valve springs. Aluminium-alloy cylinder and cylinder head. Roller-bearing big end; crankshaft supported on taper-roller bearings. Compression ratio, 6.8 to 1. Dry-sump lubrication; oil-tank capacity, 4 pints.

CARBURETTOR: Amal with twistgrip throttle control; air slide operated by handlebar lever. Air filter.

IGNITION and LIGHTING: Lucas magneto with auto-advance. 36-watt Miller dynamo. 7½in-diameter Miller headlamp with sealed-beam light unit.

TRANSMISSION: Velocette four-speed gear box with positive-stop foot control. Bottom, 11.18 to 1. Second, 7.74 to 1. Third, 5.86 to 1. Top, 4.87 to 1. Multi-plate clutch with fabric inserts. Primary chain, ½ x 0.305in, in oil-bath case. Rear chain, ⅝ x ¼in, with guard over top run. Engine r.p.m. at 30 m.p.h. in top gear, 1,970.

FUEL CAPACITY: 3 gallons.

TYRES: Dunlop Universal, 3.25 x 19in front and rear.

BRAKES: 7in-diameter front and rear.

SUSPENSION: Velocette telescopic front fork with hydraulic damping. Pivoted-fork rear springing employing coil springs and hydraulic damping; adjustment for load.

WHEELBASE: 54½in unladen. Ground clearance, 5in unladen.

SEAT: Velocette dual-seat. Unladen height, 31in.

WEIGHT: 392 lb fully equipped, with full oil tank and one gallon of petrol.

PRICE: £175 10s. With purchase tax (in Great Britain only), £210 12s.

ROAD TAX: £3 15s a year; £1 0s 8d a quarter.

MAKERS: Veloce, Ltd., York Road, Hall Green, Birmingham, 23.

DESCRIPTION: *The Motor Cycle, 29 October 1953.*

PERFORMANCE DATA

MEAN MAXIMUM SPEED: Bottom: *37 m.p.h.
Second: *53 m.p.h.
Third: *71 m.p.h.
Top: 80 m.p.h.
*Valve float occurring.

HIGHEST ONE-WAY SPEED: 82 m.p.h. (Conditions: moderate three-quarter wind; rider wearing two-piece suit and overboots.)

MEAN ACCELERATION:

	10-30 m.p.h.	20-40 m.p.h.	30-50 m.p.h.
Bottom	3.4 secs	—	—
Second	4.6 secs	4.2 secs	4.8 secs
Third	—	5.8 secs	5.8 secs
Top	—	7.2 secs	7.2 secs

Mean speed at end of quarter-mile from rest: 72 m.p.h.
Mean time to cover standing quarter-mile: 17.8 secs.

PETROL CONSUMPTION: At 30 m.p.h., 94 m.p.g. At 40 m.p.h., 82 m.p.g. At 50 m.p.h., 72 m.p.g. At 60 m.p.h., 52 m.p.g.

BRAKING: From 30 m.p.h. to rest, 31ft (surface, dry tarmac).

TURNING CIRCLE: 18ft.

MINIMUM NON-SNATCH SPEED: 16 m.p.h. in top gear.

WEIGHT PER C.C.: 0.78 lb.

The 499 c.c. MSS Velocette

Left : detaching the tail of the rear mudguard gives access for removal of the quickly detachable rear wheel

Of average lightness in operation, the clutch was smooth and very positive in taking up the drive. A slight tendency for the clutch plates to drag was perceptible in the form of a faint clonk which could be heard and felt when bottom gear was engaged with the engine idling. All gear changes, both upward and downward, were a delight to execute. Pedal travel was short. Quick, light and simultaneous operation of the throttle, clutch and gear pedal invariably produced clean, noiseless changes.

Advantage has been taken of the engine's exceptional low-speed torque to employ closely grouped gear ratios. The 4.87 to 1 top-gear ratio enables the engine to reach its peak-power speed of 5,000 r.p.m., and the bottom-gear ratio of 11.18 to 1, though uncommonly high for a machine of this type, is in no circumstances disadvantageous; indeed, in the standing-start quarter-mile test, the Velocette put up a performance which was above average for a 500 c.c. single.

Both brakes were adequately powerful, though not so light in operation that either wheel would be locked inadvertently on wet roads. There was no trace of sponginess in the controls, and no adjustment was called for throughout the test. Incidentally, adjustment of the MSS brakes necessitates the use of spanners.

Intensity of the headlamp beam was considered insufficient for fast night riding. When the machine was ridden in rain the voltage-control unit was vulnerable to the ingress of water. As a result, when the engine was stopped, the ammeter showed a full-scale discharge and it was necessary temporarily to remove the dynamo plug to obviate running down the battery.

The speedometer fitted to the Velocette was checked for accuracy and was found to read fast progressively from 1 m.p.h. at 30 m.p.h. and 3 m.p.h. at 50 to 60 m.p.h. to 8 m.p.h. at an indicated 90 m.p.h.

For parking purposes the prop stand was considered to be among the best contemporary fittings of its type. It was accessible to operate, and it supported the machine safely on level surfaces and on all normal degrees of camber. A centre stand is provided for maintenance purposes.

Two minor criticisms arose during routine maintenance. To eliminate backlash from the throttle control it was necessary to remove the dual-seat and fuel tank to gain access to the cable adjuster. During primary chain adjustment the gear-box top front clamping nut was found to be difficult of access. The toolkit was of average quality, though a more suitable sparking-plug spanner would have been appreciated in view of the extent of the cylinder-head finning around the plug.

The highly polished surfaces on engine and gear-box castings facilitated cleaning of those units. At the conclusion of a strenuous test the engine remained completely oil-tight and only a smear of oil had found its way on to the outside of the gear box in the vicinity of the pedal pivot.

The finish of the machine is in keeping with its fine all-round performance. The new MSS unquestionably occupies a position in the forefront of single-cylinder five-hundreds.

Above: clutch adjustment is by means of a peg passed through the final-drive sprocket. Right: the dynamo is driven by a flat belt

TRIUMPH
TIGER 110

The advice chalked on the blackboard thrust out from the pits was clear enough, if somewhat superfluous. 'Slipstream Mac', it ran; and young Mike Hailwood, flat on the tank, nodded to his pit attendant father. He knew well enough that his chief opponent was the seasoned Bob McIntyre and he was, already, doing his best not to lose sight of the flying Scot.

A road-racing scene typical of the late 1950s period, perhaps? Indeed so. But in this instance the race was the gruelling Thruxton 500-mile production-machine marathon of 1958, first event of the series to carry that label (earlier meetings, run by the clock and not the milometer, had been known as the Thruxton Nine-Hour). And Mike, sharing a Triumph Tiger 110 with Dan Shorey, not only slipstreamed the 692 cc Royal Enfield

Triumph's famous Tiger 110 engine was a sportier version of the 649 cc Thunderbird seen here. In turn, the Thunderbird engine was itself a development of the original Speed Twin design, enlarged to suit American market requirements

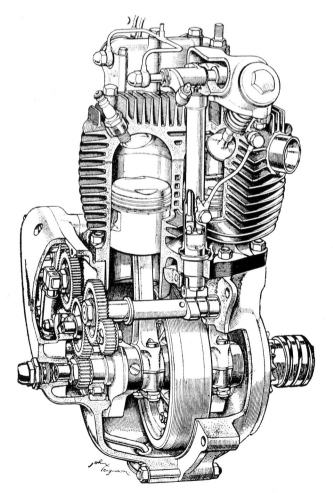

Constellation of Bob Mac and Derek Powell but, eventually, finished one lap ahead with an overall average speed of 66 mph. It is worth noting, too, that fifth place in the same event was taken by another T110 with, as one of its co-riders, a certain Percy Tait who was not exactly unknown in Triumph circles . . .

For that matter, 1958 was turning out to be a very good vintage for the 'Tee-One-Ten', because over on the far side of the Atlantic one Bill Johnson – already a record-breaker on other Triumphs – pushed a twin-carburettor-head version of a Tiger 110 through the speed trap at Bonneville Salt Flats, Utah, at 147·32 mph, to claim a new USA Class C (650 cc stock-machine) national record.

Yet that Johnson effort carried the seeds of the T110's eventual eclipse. Meanwhile, a super-sports variant of the 650 cc was on the stocks, code-named the T120. And what better catalogue name for the newcomer could there be but Bonneville!

However, to return to the beginning. Triumph got going in the immediate post-war market with the Speed Twin and Tiger 100 twins, but although these 500 cc models were perfectly acceptable to the British, the Americans were soon demanding something with more performance. Edward Turner obliged with the 649 cc Thunderbird and then, following his usual practice of allowing a design to settle down in unstressed touring form before developing it further, evolved from that basic model a high-performance edition to which he gave the name Tiger 110.

The development prototype T110 made its appearance in the 1953 International Six Days Trial, where it was ridden by Jimmy Alves, a member of the British Trophy team. That year, Britain took the main award, and no bike could have had a tougher baptism. A month later, the production version took its bow, at the Paris Salon, where it was said that the machine was primarily for export only, and very few would be released to the home market.

Right from the beginning, the T110 adopted pivoted fork rear suspension, together with an alternator to supply lighting current (although a magneto, with hand-operated advance and retard, was retained for ignition purposes). By snuggling the gearbox cosily behind the crankcase and fitting a shortened primary chaincase, the Meriden engineers had managed to keep the wheelbase only 0·5 in longer than the rigid-frame Thunderbird.

Engine changes included a beefed-up crankshaft, larger inlet valves, a compression ratio of 8·5 to 1 (instead of the Thunderbird's 7 to 1), and an increased volume of oil in circulation. Power output was 42 bhp at 6,500 rpm, notwithstanding the cast-iron cylinder block and head. From personal experience, however, I can say that the early T110 was not the sweetest of models to ride, and the power delivery was harsh, especially at low engine rpm, unless the rider juggled with the advance-retard ignition lever – and, in heavy traffic, that was not always possible.

Be that as it may, the Americans seemed to like the new Tiger 110, and were soon entering it in all kinds of events for which it

Well before his days of international racing fame, a very young Mike Hailwood here pilots an unlikely-seeming model in the production-machine Thruxton 500-mile Race of 1958. It is the 649 cc Triumph Tiger 110 which Mike and co-rider Dan Shorey took to a magnificent win, a lap ahead of the Royal Enfield twin of Bob McIntyre and Derek Powell

was never intended, strictly speaking – such as the Cambridge (Minnesota) Enduro, where, in July, 1954, it took the Light-heavyweight class award.

In Britain, the T110 found its niche in production-machine racing, finishing first, second and third in the 1955 Thruxton Nine-Hour 750 cc class, but there were better things to come with the introduction, for the 1956 season, of a new die-cast light-alloy cylinder head with cast-in austenitic iron valve seats; new, too, were steel-backed thin wall big-end bearing shells.

This time Percy Tait took 750 cc honours at Thruxton though it must be confessed that the honour was a fairly empty one, with a solid wedge of at least half a dozen BSA Gold Stars finishing ahead of him in the overall reckoning. BSA riders were the principal opposition, also, at America's unique Catalina Grand Prix meeting – a combination of road race and moto-cross – but three Tiger 110s finished fourth, fifth, and sixth. For something just a little different, Triumph provided a batch of five Tiger 110s as mounts for the TT Race travelling marshals in the Isle of Man, and the machines, collectively, covered 7,000 high-speed miles during the practice and race weeks.

One year later, Geoff Hughes and Syd Stevens brought their model home second overall in what was to be the last of the Thruxton Nine-Hour races, albeit two laps behind a three-fifty BSA Gold Star. In general the T110 had been giving good service, but at racing speeds cracks had tended to develop in the cylinder head, between the valve seat edge and holding-down-stud holes; this was put right for 1958, by providing additional metal, and by slightly reducing the valve diameter. A twin-carburettor cylinder head was offered at extra cost, but in fact this option was to remain in the catalogue for only one year, and with the coming of the Bonneville for 1959 the T110 reverted to a subsidiary role, as the halfway house between the touring Thunderbird and the super-sports Bonnie.

It was the beginning of the end for the Tiger 110, and although it did survive into the 1961 range (by which time separate engine and gearbox construction had given way to unit-construction, and the voluminous rear wheel enclosure panels known irreverently as the 'bathtub' had been adopted), by that time it was almost indistinguishable from the Thunderbird. It had a compression ratio of 8·5 to 1, as against the Thunderbird's more modest 7·5 to 1 ratio, and magneto ignition – now, at long last, with automatic advance and retard – instead of coil; but that, apart from colour schemes, was all.

In any case, another newcomer had been added to the Meriden programme. This was the 649 cc TR6 Trophy, virtually a single-carburettor version of the Bonneville, and in the years ahead it would take the role originally allotted to the T110. In time, too, the TR6 Trophy would become the Tiger 650 then, as engine size increased, the Tiger 750. Faithful shadow to the Bonneville 750, it remains in production to this day.

649 c. c. Triumph Tiger 110

Impressive O. H. V. Twin Combining Light Steering and Powerful Braking with a Performance to Delight the Sporting Rider

THE 649 c.c. Triumph Tiger 110 owes its existence largely to the demands of the American market where the primary requirement, within reasonable limits, is the highest possible power output from a given engine capacity. A tuned variant of the six-fifty Thunderbird, the T110 was introduced for 1954. Its specification included the then-new Triumph pivoted-fork rear springing and an engine incorporating a cast-iron cylinder block and cylinder head.

Most notable development for the current year is a light-alloy cylinder head of entirely new layout. The casting incorporates air passages to assist cooling; valve-seat inserts are of austenitic iron. An incidental improvement on the new head is that oil from the valve gear drains via the pushrod tubes, thus eliminating the need for external pipes. Combining a superb road potential with light handling and smooth, powerful braking, the T110 is a machine which cannot fail to impress the sporting rider. Few road burners, in truth, would ask for a higher cruising speed than the Triumph eagerly provides. Indeed, its capacity for searing acceleration and tireless, ultra-high cruising speeds is second only to the higher-performance 1,000 c.c. models of current and recent vintage.

But the Tiger 110 is not unduly obtrusive in its behaviour, for its exhaust note is reasonably well subdued no matter how hard the machine is ridden. Nor is it too intractable for use in heavy city traffic. Naturally, the high compression ratio, sporting valve timing and large port sizes necessary for such outstanding acceleration and speed from six-fifty roadsters involve some sacrifice of docility at low engine revolutions. Discreet use of the manual ignition control, however, tames the engine to a considerable degree and if, in addition, liberal use is made of the indirect gear ratios, negotiating heavy traffic need involve no irritation for the rider. Engine starting was dependable and relatively easy even in extremely cold weather, while petrol consumption was remarkably economical. In short, the T110, though primarily a high-powered sports model, is sufficiently well-mannered, manageable and economical to be employed for more modests duties without compromise.

Passing from a general survey of the model's qualities to a specific analysis of the various facets of its behaviour, it is logical to deal first with its most outstanding attribute—high open-road performance. The figures shown in the information panel speak for themselves. Yet it should be emphasized that the mean maximum speed and the quarter-mile acceleration figures would probable have been fractionally better still had less-windy conditions prevailed at the time the data were obtained. Though a very stiff wind blew only about 15 degrees off the direction of the stretch of road used, the speed loss upwind in such circumstances was not compensated by the downwind advantage.

Acceleration through the gears was scintillating and carburation clean. Even at an indicated 80 m.p.h. an exhilarating

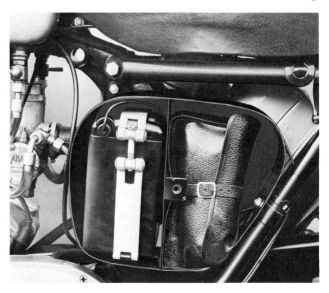

Battery and tool kit are housed in a single, partitioned container. The tool kit is adequate for routine adjustments

Finish of the Tiger 110 is shell-blue and black enamel. With many light-alloy castings polished and the usual components chromium plated, the model is very smart

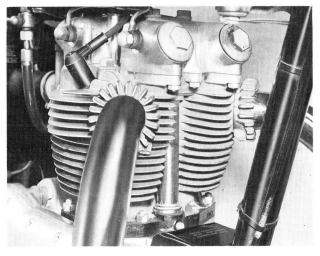

Left: Elimination of external pipes for valve-gear drainage results in a cleaner appearance of the engine. Right: Concealed between the oil tank and the battery box, the air filter did not restrict engine performance to any appreciable degree

surge forward could be produced simply by snapping the throttle wide open. To the Tiger 110, cruising at 75 m.p.h. was child's play and required only a small throttle opening. A speed of 80 m.p.h. could be held on half throttle, while a sustained 90 m.p.h. proved to be quite within the model's capabilities. The highest speedometer reading obtained with the rider sitting upright was 100 m.p.h. with a following wind.

The carrying of a pillion passenger did not substantially reduce cruising speed. With two adults (each clad in winter riding kit) occupying the dual-seat, the Triumph hummed along at a speedometer 80 m.p.h. for many consecutive miles on little more than half throttle. Opening the twistgrip fully sent the speedometer needle quickly round to the 90 m.p.h. mark. When checked for accuracy, the speedometer was found to register about 5 per cent fast at all speeds from an indicated 30 m.p.h. to the highest reading obtained—114 m.p.h. As a matter of interest the maximum-speed checks were repeated with the air filter disconnected, a bell-mouth fitted to the carburettor and the main-jet size increased from 250 to 270. No difference in speed was perceptible.

Engine vibration was detectable through the petrol tank from about 80 m.p.h. upward (or from a lower speed when the tank was full). Though pronounced, the tremor was not objectionable so long as the rider refrained from gripping the tank between his knees.

Maintenance of a steady 30 m.p.h. in built-up areas required a partially retarded ignition setting if top gear was used. Alternatively, third gear could be employed with the ignition control at full advance. Idling, once the engine had reached its normal working temperature, was slow and regular with the throttle closed and the ignition fully retarded or nearly so. With these conditions fulfilled, bottom gear could be engaged almost noiselessly; but the first bottom-gear engagement after a cold start was accompanied by an audible scrunch as a result of the relatively fast idling speed necessary to prevent stalling.

Ignition is controlled by a lever on the left side of the handlebar, though the lever is of the pattern normally used on the right side of a bar. After engagement of bottom gear on full retard, it was found desirable to advance the ignition partially or fully (by pulling the lever to the rear) before feeding in the clutch. For that reason a left-hand-pattern ignition lever would have

---

Information Panel

SPECIFICATION

ENGINE: 649 c.c. (71 × 82mm) overhead-valve vertical twin. Fully enclosed valve gear. Aluminium-alloy cylinder head. Light-alloy connecting rods; plain big-end bearings. Crankshaft supported in two ball bearings. Compression ratio: 8.5 to 1. Dry-sump lubrication; oil-tank capacity, 6 pints.

CARBURETTOR: Amal Monobloc with twistgrip throttle control; air slide operated by lever situated under seat. Air filter.

IGNITION and LIGHTING: Lucas magneto with manual control. Separate 60-watt Lucas dynamo and 6-volt, 12-ampere-hour battery. 7in-diameter headlamp with pre-focus light unit.

TRANSMISSION: Triumph four-speed gear box with positive-stop foot control. Gear ratios: bottom, 11.2 to 1; second, 7.75 to 1; third, 5.45 to 1; top, 4.57 to 1. Multi-plate clutch with Neolangite insert operating in oil. Primary chain, ⅜ × 0.305in in oil-bath case. Rear chain, ⅝ × ⅜in lubricated by bleed from primary chaincase; guard over top run. Engine r.p.m. at 30 m.p.h. in top gear, 1,760.

FUEL CAPACITY: 4 gallons.

TYRES: Dunlop; front, 3.25 × 19in with ribbed tread; rear, 3.50 × 19in Universal.

BRAKES: 7in-diameter rear; 8in-diameter front with ventilating scoops; finger adjusters.

SUSPENSION: Triumph telescopic front fork with hydraulic damping. Pivoted-fork rear springing employing coil springs and hydraulic damping; three-position adjustment for load.

WHEELBASE: 57in unladen. Ground clearance, 5in unladen.

SEAT: Triumph Twinseat; unladen height, 31in.

WEIGHT: 420 lb fully equipped, with full oil tank and approximately one gallon of petrol.

PRICE: £214; with purchase tax (in Great Britain only), £265 7s 3d. Extras: quickly detachable rear wheel, £3 (p.t., 14s 5d); prop stand, 15s 6d (p.t., 3s 9d); pillion footrests, 16s (p.t., 3s 11d).

ROAD TAX: £3 15s a year; £1 0s 8d a quarter.

MAKERS: Triumph Engineering Co., Ltd., Meriden Works, Allesley, Coventry.

DESCRIPTION: "The Motor Cycle", 27 October 1955.

PERFORMANCE DATA

MEAN MAXIMUM SPEED: Bottom: * 51 m.p.h.
Second: * 73 m.p.h.
Third: 94 m.p.h.
Top: 101 m.p.h.
*Valve float occurring.

HIGHEST ONE-WAY SPEED: 109 m.p.h. (conditions: strong near-tail wind; rider wearing two-piece riding suit and overboots).

MEAN ACCELERATION:

	10-30 m.p.h.	20-40 m.p.h.	30-50 m.p.h.
Bottom	2 sec.	2.8 sec.	2.8 sec.
Second	3.2 sec.	3 sec.	2.4 sec.
Third	—	4.6 sec	4.6 sec.
Top	—	6 sec	6.4 sec.

Mean speed at end of quarter-mile from rest: 82 m.p.h.
Mean time to cover standing quarter-mile: 16 sec.

PETROL CONSUMPTION: At 30 m.p.h., 100 m.p.g. At 40 m.p.h., 92 m.p.g. At 50 m.p.h., 80 m.p.g. At 60 m.p.h., 70 m.p.g.

BRAKING: From 30 m.p.h. to rest, 33ft (surface, dry tarmac).

TURNING CIRCLE: 14ft 6in.

MINIMUM NON-SNATCH SPEED: 18 m.p.h. in top gear with ignition fully retarded.

WEIGHT PER C.C.: 0.65 lb.

A ribbed drum and ventilation scoops are features of the 8in-diameter front brake. Stopping power was excellent

been preferred so that it could be pushed forward with the left thumb for advance while the clutch lever was still grasped.

Though temperatures below freezing point were frequently experienced during the test, engine starting was nearly always achieved at the first kick. Naturally, a vigorous thrust on the kick-start was necessary to spin the engine over compression. Prerequisites for cold starting were half retard, closure of the air lever, liberal flooding of the carburettor and a small (but not critical) throttle opening. Because of the very cold weather it was found necessary to leave the air lever closed or partially closed for the first mile or so. Situated beneath the seat, the lever was not too easy to operate with thickly gloved fingers.

Except for the common fault of a longish reach to the clutch and front-brake levers, all the other controls were quite convenient to operate and were smooth in action. (When a chain link was fitted between the lever and pivot-block of both the clutch and front-brake controls to reduce the reach required, there was still an ample range of lever movement.) The clutch was sweet yet firm in taking up the drive, and the gear pedal was pleasantly light to operate. Upward gear changes required a leisurely movement of the pedal if the dogs were to engage noiselessly. Provided engine speed was appropriately increased by slight blipping of the throttle, clean downward changes could be achieved without any pause in control movement. No difficulty was experienced in selecting neutral from bottom or second gear whether the machine was moving or at rest.

The riding position proved to be very comfortable for low and medium speeds. There was ample room on the dual-seat for a pillion passenger, though the width of the seat between the passenger's thighs was slightly too great to permit him comfortably to place his feet as far inboard on the rests as was desired. For sustained high-speed cruising, particularly against a strong wind, a position giving a more forward inclination to the rider's body would have been preferred in order to lessen the tension in his arms caused by wind pressure. Strapping luggage across the dual-seat to support the base of the rider's spine proved helpful in this connection.

As is characteristic of modern Triumph twins, steering and general handling were extremely light. This trait, coupled with the armchair riding position and the machine's smooth response to the controls, made the T110 particularly delightful to ride at speeds up to say, a mile a minute. Confidence was soon engendered and stylish riding became automatic. Stability on wet city streets was first class. Unusually little effort was needed to heel the model over and, in consequence, it could be ridden round slow- and medium-speed bends in very slick fashion. At high speeds a greater degree of heaviness in the steering would have been appreciated, especially on bumpy road surfaces and in strong, gusty winds. In such circumstances a turn or two of the steering damper had a marked steadying effect on the steering, but was by no means essential.

Both front and rear springing were distinctly firm, a feature not uncommon on high-speed machines. As a result of the firmness no components fouled the ground when the model was banked steeply on corners; that was the case whether the machine was ridden one-up with the rear springing at its softest setting or with a pillion passenger and the springing adjustment at its hardest.

Matching the machine's speed capabilities, braking efficiency was higher than the relevant figure in the performance data suggests. The reason is that the front brake was more effective at high speeds than at 30 m.p.h. Even from near-maximum speed, firm application of the brake easily evoked a squeal of protest from the tyre. Leverage in the rear-brake control was high; consequently pedal travel was longer than average and the wheel could readily be locked. After dark, main-road cruising speeds of 60 to 70 m.p.h. were possible by the light of the headlamp beam.

As a result of the extensive full-throttle riding involved when compiling the performance figures, an appreciable amount of oil leaked past the gear-box mainshaft on to the rear tyre. Also when performance data were being obtained the ammeter failed, possibly as a result of vibration. When the machine was ridden in London traffic in particularly heavy rain, some misfiring was caused by water finding its way inside the sparking-plug covers. Long main-road journeys in similar weather, however, were quite free from the bother. The firm action of the taper-cock petrol taps was appreciated (the left-hand tap controls the reserve supply), as was the fact that four gallons of fuel could be put in the tank after a few miles had been covered on reserve. Both petrol and oil tanks have large, quick-action filler caps.

With its shell-blue and black finish, the Tiger 110 is extremely smart in appearance. Possessing a performance which suggests the analogy of an iron hand in a velvet glove, it is one of the most impressive Triumphs yet produced and is justly popular among sporting riders.

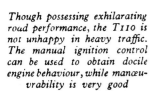

Though possessing exhilarating road performance, the T110 is not unhappy in heavy traffic. The manual ignition control can be used to obtain docile engine behaviour, while manœuvrability is very good

TRIUMPH
TIGER CUB

In the years immediately following the Second World War, the British motor cyclist had become so accustomed to linking the words 'Triumph' and 'twin', that he had almost completely forgotten the lively little 149 cc Model XO overhead-valve single of the hungry mid-1930s. So visitors to the 1952 Earls Court Show were most surprised to see, displayed among the vertical twins, a little maroon-painted lightweight described as the Terrier.

However, although the Terrier had some superficial resemblance to the pre-war model, in design it was quite new. From the drawing board of Edward Turner, it was a 149 cc (57 × 58·5 mm) unit-construction four-speeder with a most unusual bottom-half arrangement whereby the gearbox and crankcase formed a single casting; the crankshaft was inserted through the open drive-side of the unit, and the aperture was then closed by a circular door forming part of the primary chaincase inner half.

To publicise the newcomer and, at the same time, show sceptics that the factory top brass had faith in their own product, an ACU-observed round-Britain ride was put in hand, the riders being Edward Turner himself, works manager Bob Fearon, and service manager Alex Masters. Agreed, the riding schedule was none too strenuous, and each day's run somehow managed to end at a five-star hotel – but it was the thought that counted.

It was Turner's usual policy to produce a 'cooking' model, then follow it up a year later with a sportier version (Speed Twin: Tiger 100, Thunderbird: Tiger 110, 3TA: Tiger 90, and so on) but for 1954 there was a departure in that the sports lightweight, to be called the Tiger Cub, was not only 199 cc, but had a longer stroke (actual dimensions were 63 × 64 mm). That meant a different crankshaft, cylinder barrel, and head. Like the Terrier, the new Cub had plunger rear springing, but there was a dual seat instead of a saddle.

The Terrier and Cub remained in the range for the next two years, sharing such developments as a reinforced fuel tank, an improved clutch, heavier-duty oil pump, and die-cast light-alloy cylinder head. But there were signs that the Terrier was losing face (notably when 3·25 × 16 in wheels were adopted for the 1956 Cub, while the Terrier continued in unchanged form with 19 in wheels and single saddle), and it was not really a surprise to see, in the 1957 programme, that the 199 cc model reigned alone.

Well no, not exactly alone, because now there were *two* Tiger Cubs, roadster and competition, and for each there was a new frame with pivoted fork rear springing. The engine still employed plain big-end and timing side main bearings, but these were now of copper-lead on steel backings.

Back in the previous autumn, Ken Heanes had ridden a Cub to a gold medal placing in the International Six Days Trial, and the new T20C Competition Cub, equipped with lower gear ratios, higher ground clearance, and trials tyres, was a production version of the Heanes model. And at last Triumph had a competitive trials model on which to mount their works squad.

A batch of Cubs was prepared for the 1957 Scottish Six Days Trial, in which event they were ridden by Roy Peplow, Ken Heanes, John Giles, and (you had better believe it!) Mike Hailwood, but although they did reasonably well, there were still a few bugs to be shaken out.

In the following year's Scottish, the Cubs were yelping to good effect, with Artie Ratcliffe finishing third, Roy Peplow sixth, and John Giles tenth. And that was just the start, because in national trials from that point on the Tiger Cub men were to be a truly formidable force. Roy Peplow was probably the best of the early squad of Cub tamers, but in due course there would be many more – Gordon Blakeway, Ray Sayer, Scott Ellis, Gordon Farley – before the Meriden works abandoned trials support.

For a season or two, Zenith carburettors replaced Amal units, the single primary chain gave way to a duplex type, and the barrel and head were given deeper finning. For 1959 midriff enclosure panels (but, thankfully, not the full bathtub treatment of the twins) afflicted the Cub. There was a bigger (three gallon) tank, too.

And talking of enclosure, across in Utah Bill Martin constructed a long, cigar-like shell, powered it with a 199 cc Tiger Cub engine running on dope, and returned a fantastic two-way speed of 139·82 mph.

First really drastic revision of the Tiger Cub design happened in May, 1960, when the whole lower end was completely

Compact indeed was the 199 cc Tiger Cub unit. The same basic design was employed until 1966, when a completely different crankcase arrangement was adopted, mainly for manufacturing convenience. Shown here is the 1953 version, with special angled Amal carburettor

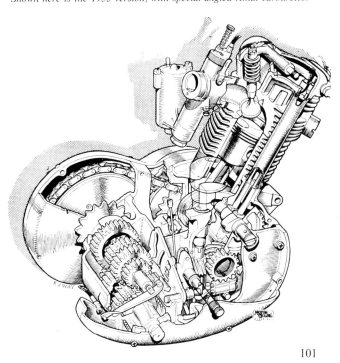

Above: *success in the International Six Days Trial encouraged the Triumph works to produce a competitions version of the Tiger Cub, listed as the Model T20C. This is the 1958 version, equipped with a Zenith carburettor used for two seasons*

The touring 199 cc Tiger Cub of 1956, with plunger-type rear springing and the small (16-in diameter) wheels new in that year's programme

redesigned. Now, there were only two main castings, joined on the longitudinal centre line. The timing-half crankcase incorporated also the gearbox shell, while the drive-half crankcase was integral with the primary drive casing. It was primarily an engineering department change, aimed at reducing production costs and speeding up assembly, and it certainly had no detrimental effect on the Cub's popularity worldwide.

Worldwide indeed, because now came a scrambles version (with 9 to 1 compression ratio, and energy-transfer ignition) and, for the USA market, an enduro model. As season followed season, so a pastoral model was added (for such agricultural duties as sheep-herding in Australia and South America); and the Mountain Cub, a trail model for the USA market – which had to be painted bright yellow so that trigger-happy hunters would not mistake it for a moose on the loose.

An addition to the roadster model was the T20SH Sports Cub, which could nip along so smartly that it earned the nickname of the 'Baby Bonnie'. The engine of the T20SH was virtually that of the scrambler with 9 to 1 compression ratio, beefed-up bottom end, increased oil supply, etc. Other desirable features included a quickly-detachable headlamp with plug-in

harness, and a two-way-damped front fork (derived from that of the BSA C15).

Understandably, youngsters were soon road-racing them, and it was the clamour for Tiger Cub races which gave rise to the British Formula Racing Club.

In the scrambles field it suffered slightly, in that it had to compete in the 250 cc class. Still, what else was a BSA C15 than an enlarged Cub with the cylinder vertical instead of sloping? But the road-going public loved the Cub, and in a 1964 *Motor Cycle* survey, 90 per cent of the contributors declared that they would readily buy another. Yet there were a number who had reservations. The Cub, it seemed, was reliable enough if given reasonable treatment. But if driven hard, it tended to knock out its main and big-end bearings.

That could have been overcome, of course, but towards the end of its life the Cub was becoming uneconomical to produce, even when it discarded its Meriden frame for that of the BSA Bantam. It had gone by 1968 . . . hadn't it? Yes, of course it had. But just imagine a Tiger Cub with an overhead camshaft instead of pushrod overhead valves, and with a capacity of 125 instead of 199 cc. That, after all, is what Honda did.

199 c.c. Triumph Tiger Cub

A Lively Overhead-valve Lightweight with Remarkable All-round Performance : Outstanding Economy and Powerful Brakes

Well revealed in the lower photograph is the neat, functional appearance of the Tiger Cub. In the view above are shown the accessible contact breaker and the rocker-box finning, a 1957 modification

WITHOUT fear of contradiction, the latest Tiger Cub can be described as an impressive lightweight. It impresses not merely by its performance against the watch but by the balance of its qualities. There is no particular difficulty in extracting plenty of power from an overhead-valve two-hundred; but that so lively a model should also have a top-gear minimum non-snatch speed of 12 m.p.h. and really brisk low-speed acceleration is cause for admiration. And when this flexible performance is coupled to good road manners and a very meagre thirst the result is an outstanding little mount which, at under £144, is remarkable value.

First impressions of the Cub are of a small, low machine although at 50¼in the wheelbase is about normal for the capacity. The low build, however, is real enough and the 16in wheels give a 29in seat unladen height which is below average. Nevertheless, the riding position is not cramped even for a tall rider, thanks to the low footrest location permitted by the narrowness of the engine unit. The relationship between seat, rests and handlebar is a happy one affording full mastery of the model, and all controls are conveniently sited save for the dip-switch which has to be located too far from the right thumb owing to the fixed pivot block of the brake lever. Hand span to brake and clutch levers is commendably short.

Although no air slide is embodied in the carburettor, the Cub

was a certain first- or second-kick starter during the admittedly mild weather of the test period. The only prerequisites were light flooding and a small but not critical throttle opening. Mechanical and exhaust noise formed one of the few points of criticism. Valve-gear clatter was audible and wide throttle openings evoked a hard, flat exhaust note of considerable volume. Unlike the other Tiger Cubs ridden, the test model had a slightly erratic tickover which could not be rectified by normal carburettor adjustments.

Once on the move carburation was satisfactory save that when the throttle was opened suddenly there was a momentary hesitation before the engine responded. The high degree of economy obtained in the steady-speed tests, and quoted in the data panel, was paralleled in normal running: in spite of extensive town work and full use of the Cub's agility, consumption averaged around 100 m.p.g.

Provided the clutch plates were freed before starting, by actuating the kick-starter with the handlebar lever raised, bottom-gear engagement was quiet. The clutch has bonded-on Neolangite facings and was as sweet and light in action as one expects of a Triumph. Synchronized operation of the controls gave delightfully quick gear changes except upward between second and third when a slight pause was necessary if the meshing of the dogs was not to be felt; pedal travel was a good compromise between lightness of action and convenience. There was no detectable gear noise in the indirect ratios. Neutral was easy to find from either bottom or second gear but the gear-position indicator on the nacelle left no room for doubt.

It would be difficult to envisage a more enjoyable machine to ride in traffic than the Tiger Cub. The combination of light weight, a trials-type steering lock and admirable low-speed punch made it more nippy under such conditions than the majority of two-wheelers. Such is the flexibility that second-gear starts necessitated no undue clutch slipping and it was, in fact, felt that a closer-ratio gear box would be an improvement. In selecting the ratios, however, the manufacturers have borne in mind the desirability of easy steep-gradient restarts with two up.

One of the most remarkable features of the Cub is its ability to climb quite steep gradients in top gear. Muswell Hill, probably North London's most severe main-road acclivity, was tackled at the legal 30 m.p.h. and even on the steepest section there was no difficulty in maintaining speed—a feat which many machines of more imposing capacity can scarcely equal.

So brisk was the top-gear acceleration that only when absolute maximum pick-up was required was third gear engaged at derestriction signs, yet if desired that ratio could be retained up to an indicated 50 m.p.h. or more (the speedometer recorded 1 m.p.h. fast at 30 m.p.h. and the optimism increased to 4 m.p.h. at 60 m.p.h.). The eagerness apparent in traffic was well maintained outside built-up areas and was coupled with complete tirelessness. As a result the model was habitually cruised at a genuine 55 m.p.h., a speed which enabled averages of 40 m.p.h. or more to be readily attained. No matter how hard the model was driven it never pinked on premium-grade fuel and remained almost completely oil tight. Only when pulling hard at low engine speeds was there any roughness in the power delivery and the engine was particularly sweet at the cruising speed just mentioned. The additional weight of a pillion passenger caused little falling-off in performance.

The low weight and light steering makes for some sensitivity to gusty cross winds, but the handling qualities are, in general, fully up to the performance. Such are the cornering abilities that on really sinuous going there can be few quicker and less tiring mounts. The stands and exhaust system are well tucked away and the footrests could be grounded on corners only if extreme methods were employed. An innovation for 1957, the pivoted-fork rear suspension proved an excellent compromise for solo or two-up riding and the Girling units had ample rebound damping to control any pitching tendency. In comparison the front fork was on the firm side and its action was audible on rough surfaces. Slight oil leaks from the fork legs developed during the test.

Both brakes were thoroughly reassuring in their progressive response but their great power was not truly revealed until the crash-stop tests were carried out. That such a creditable mean stopping distance should have been recorded with drums of only 5½in diameter may seem surprising but such drums are, in fact,

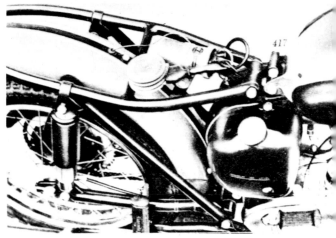

The new rear sub-frame and pivoted-fork springing are of sturdy design and the rectifier and coil are located under the seat

some 13 per cent more effective with 16in-diameter than with 19in rims. Wet roads did not cause any deterioration of the brakes and revealed that the mudguarding was of rather higher-than-average efficiency.

Though its shape is a big improvement over the earlier pointed-nose pattern, the twin-seat gave the impression of being on the hard side after riding spells of much over two hours, and for a long-legged rider the upper edges of the knee grips became noticeable. It was considered that the grips could with advantage project less from the narrow but commendably capacious tank.

The nacelle-mounted horn had a pleasant, arresting note. The ample power of the headlamp would have been more effective if it were possible to set the beam higher. Accessibility of valve-clearance adjusters and contact breaker is noteworthy, and the coil and rectifier are reached after removal of the seat, a task involving merely the slackening of three nuts. Equally accessible is the battery; for topping-up it has only to be withdrawn from its compartment in the tool box. The prop stand could hardly be bettered for its accessibility, neat stowage and stability on cambered surfaces; very little effort is needed to bring into use the low-lift centre stand.

INFORMATION PANEL

The Triumph Tiger Cub

SPECIFICATION

ENGINE: Triumph 199 c.c. (63 x 64mm) overhead-valve single. Steel connecting rod with plain big-end bearing. Crankshaft supported in ball bearing on drive side and plain bearing on timing side. Compression ratio, 7 to 1. Dry-sump lubrication; oil-tank capacity, 2¼ pints.

CARBURETTOR: Amal Type 332, without air slide. Oil-wetted gauze-element air filter.

IGNITION and LIGHTING: Lucas RM13 alternator with coil ignition; auto-advance and emergency-start switch position. Lucas 6-volt, 8-ampere-hour battery charged through a rectifier. Lucas 5½in-diameter headlamp with 30/24-watt bulb in pre-focus light unit.

TRANSMISSION: Four-speed gear box in unit with engine; positive-stop foot control. Gear ratios: bottom, 19.0 to 1; second, 13.1 to 1; third, 8.35 to 1; top, 6.35 to 1. Multi-plate clutch with bonded-on moulded inserts running in oil. Primary chain, non-adjustable, ⅜ x 0.205in in oil-bath case. Rear chain, ½ x 0.205in with guard over top run. Engine r.p.m. at 30 m.p.h. in top gear, 2,830.

FUEL CAPACITY: 3 gallons.

TYRES: Dunlop 3.25 x 16in studded front and rear.

BRAKES: 5½in diameter x 1in wide front and rear.

SUSPENSION: Telescopic front fork with hydraulic damping. Pivoted-fork rear springing with Girling hydraulically damped suspension units.

WHEELBASE: 50½in unladen. Ground clearance, 4¼in.

SEAT: Triumph dual-seat; unladen height, 29in.

WEIGHT: 231 lb fully equipped, with full oil tank and approximately ¼ gallon of petrol.

PRICE: £116. With purchase tax (in Great Britain only), £143 16s 10d.

ROAD TAX: £1 17s 6d a year; 10s 4d a quarter.

MAKERS: Triumph Engineering Co., Ltd., Meriden Works, Allesley, Coventry.

DESCRIPTION: The Motor Cycle, 25 October 1956.

PERFORMANCE DATA

MEAN MAXIMUM SPEED: Bottom: *29 m.p.h.
Second: *42 m.p.h.
Third: 55 m.p.h.
Top: 63 m.p.h.
* Valve float occurring.

HIGHEST ONE-WAY SPEED: 67 m.p.h. (conditions: moderate tail wind; rider wearing two-piece suit and overboots).

MEAN ACCELERATION:

	10-20 m.p.h.	20-30 m.p.h.	30-40 m.p.h.
Bottom	1.5 sec	—	—
Second	1.8 sec	2.0 sec	3.0 sec
Third	3.0 sec	3.4 sec	4.1 sec
Top	—	4.8 sec	5.4 sec

Mean speed at end of quarter-mile from rest: 56 m.p.h.
Mean time to cover standing quarter-mile: 21.8 sec.

PETROL CONSUMPTION: At 30 m.p.h., 130 m.p.g.; at 40 m.p.h., 111 m.p.g.; at 50 m.p.h., 90 m.p.g.

BRAKING: From 30 m.p.h. to rest, 32ft (surface, dry tarmac).

TURNING CIRCLE: 11ft 6in.

MINIMUM NON-SNATCH SPEED: 12 m.p.h. in top gear.

WEIGHT PER C.C.: 1.16 lb.

Norton
MODEL 99

One of the experiments carried out by Edward Turner during his spell at the Ariel works in the 1930s, was to remove the front crankshaft of an Ariel Square Four, and run the engine as a vertical twin. The experiment, which gave considerable food for thought, was watched by two other members of the Ariel design staff of the time, Val Page and Bert Hopwood; and it could well be claimed that it was the inspiration for many of the British vertical twins which were to follow in subsequent years – Page's 650 cc Model 6/1 Triumph, and post-war 498 cc Ariel KH, Bert Hopwood's 497 and 597 cc Norton Dominators and 648 cc BSA Golden Flash, and Edward Turner's own 498 cc Triumph Speed Twin and derivatives.

Hopwood had served a lifetime in the Midlands motor cycle industry, starting as tea-boy in the Ariel foundry, but in due course he graduated to the drawing office, and when Edward Turner was put in charge of Triumph in 1936, Bert went with him as assistant designer and, therefore, had a considerable hand in the detailing of the Speed Twin, the machine that was to set a fashion to the world.

Bert's opportunity of stepping out from Turner's shadow

The main characteristic of the Norton twin was the front-mounted single camshaft; with all four pushrods rising at an angle between the two cylinders. This is the 1958 version of the 597 cc Dominator 99 engine, in which year a crankshaft-mounted alternator was first employed

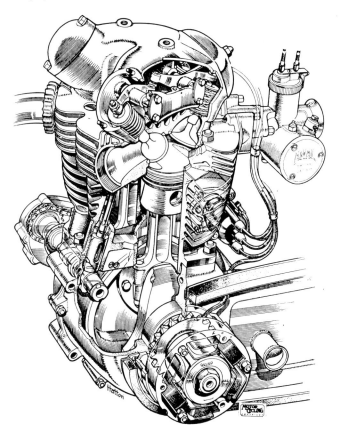

came in 1947, when he took up the position of Norton chief designer. There, his first task was to bring out a new Norton gearbox, followed by a redesign of the ES2 and 16H engines. Immediately after came the first engine for which Hopwood was wholly and personally responsible, the 497 cc Norton Dominator introduced in 1948. And then it was off to Small Heath, to produce the famous A10 Golden Flash. A busy man . . .

He was, however, back at the Norton works by 1955, and within a few months the 597 cc version of the Dominator twin was under way. Between times, the road-racing Manx Nortons had been grabbing the limelight, with their McCandless-designed duplex-loop Featherbed frames, and the Norton firm cashed in on track success by evolving a roadster edition of the Featherbed layout, using commercial-quality tubing instead of the more expensive Reynolds 531 material.

First Dominator to emerge in Featherbed guise was the 497 cc Model 88, joined for 1956 by the 597 cc Model 99. These were the original 'wideline' twins, the nickname derived from the broad spacing of the frame top tubes. In later years there would be 'slimline' versions, the top tubes being cranked inward in the region of the dual seat nose, to afford a more comfortable riding position.

Early Dominators employed all-iron engines, but the 497 cc Dominator 88, on joining the range for 1955, introduced such features as a light-alloy cylinder head and full-width wheel hubs. These were inherited by the 597 cc Dominator 99 of the following year.

To this point a chromium plated fuel tank with frosted silver top and side panels had been fitted, but an economy was effected for 1957 by using all-painted tanks adorned with separate, chromium-plated side panels framed in plastic beading. Traditionalists might well have mourned, too, the change from the D-shape footrest rubbers used since vintage days, to ordinary round rubbers.

Magneto ignition and separate direct-current dynamo had sufficed for the Dominator's electric equipment thus far, but modernity in the form of the crankshaft-mounted alternator was waiting around the corner, and was adopted for the 1958 season. In order to avoid expensive redesign work, Nortons kept the changes to a minimum, eliminating the front-mounted dynamo, but retaining the magneto drive chain which now served to drive a distributor with advance-and-retard unit incorporated. To save making a new drive-side crankcase half, the stator of the Lucas RM15 alternator was carried on a spider spigoted to a boss on the crankcase exterior.

Among the extras listed by Nortons was a 'full rear chaincase' but in practice this was a snare and delusion because a gap existed between the fore part of this chaincase, and the gearbox sprocket, and into this gap an accumulation of assorted road muck found its way. In any case, an inadequate rear chain had always been the Achilles heel of the Norton (they persisted in using a ½-in wide chain, despite constant pleas from customers) and one customer who specified the 'full chaincase' came to the

The world-renowned 'featherbed' duplex tubular frame is shown to good effect in this view of the 1961 597 cc Dominator 99 Standard. A further model (the 99 de Luxe) featured large, pressed-steel enclosure panels, shrouding the carburettor and extending rearward to the registration plate

cynical conclusion that its effect was to shorten rear chain life from its usual 8,000 miles to something nearer 4,000 miles.

From the USA came the inevitable demand for more and yet more performance, and so the early part of 1958 saw the announcement of a twin-carburettor set-up, for which an increase of some 8 to 10 per cent in performance was claimed. The Bracebridge Street works were prepared, also, to polish Dominator cylinder heads internally, and fit larger-diameter inlet valves to order.

Lineal descendant of the Dominator was the Norton Commando, which remained in production into the 1970s. The engine was eventually enlarged to 850 cc, canted forward from the vertical and carried on a rubber mounting system

But the Americans wanted more, and to satisfy them the Nomad Enduro was evolved. This machine employed the old brazed-lug Norton cradle frame, into which was slotted a 597 cc Dominator 99 engine souped-up by the fitting of twin $1\frac{1}{16}$-in Amal Monobloc carburettors, a more sporting camshaft, and high-compression pistons which gave a compression ratio of 9 to 1.

The 'Slimline' Featherbed frame, mentioned earlier, was one highlight of the 1960 range, and with it came a new-style fuel tank, painted all over and with a long, die-cast styling flash (incorporating miniature knee-grip rubbers) on each side. Nor was that all, because the Norton folk had become caught up in the craze for tinware draped around the rear wheel. This embellishment was first seen on the 250 cc Jubilee twin, and the disease then spread to the vertical twins, and the 1960 catalogue illustrated the Norton 88 de Luxe, and 99 de Luxe. Fortunately, more discerning customers could still order the standard 88 and 99, undraped at the rear – and, what's more, with a saving of around £6 on the cost.

Previously offered at extra cost, the bigger inlet valves were now fitted as standard, but the major engine change was a new cylinder block and head for the 597 cc model, featuring an increased area of finning.

In Britain, the Dominator had not been considered to date as a machine with a racing potential, even though American users had begun to chalk up victories. Especially for the USA market, Nortons brought out the 597 cc Manxman (and without even a passing nod to the Excelsior firm, either) with a special racing camshaft and flat-based cam followers, plus two-rate valve springs, and barrel-shaped tubular light-alloy pushrods. This was soon followed by a European version known as the 597 cc Dominator Sports Special, in essence the Dominator 99 with Manxman modifications, geared to a top speed of 115 mph.

Joe Craig, the legendary Norton race chief, had been killed in a car accident, and racing development was now in the hands of Doug Hele; but Doug's hands were tied because the AMC Group, in overall command of Norton destiny, were running into a trading loss and wanted to cut back on what they saw as a drain on their capital.

Could the Dominator design be used as the basis of a new, and cheaper, racer? To find out, Doug tweaked a 497 cc Dominator unit and mounted it in a Manx frame, then entered Tom Phillis on the resulting Domiracer for the 1961 Senior TT. It is a part of TT history that Tom finished an astonishing third, having turned in a lap at 100·36 mph.

But the sands were now running out fast, and 1962 saw the end of the Bracebridge Street works. Soon, AMC themselves had gone, but at least the Dominator concept survived, eventually to become NVT's Norton Commando of the 1970s.

MOTOR CYCLE

ROAD TESTS OF NEW MODELS

597c.c. Norton Model 99

Flashing Acceleration, Hairline Steering, Tremendous Braking Power : A Notable Sports Twin

THERE has never been any doubt as to the rôle of the 597 c.c. Norton Model 99 twin: it is a high-performance roadster intended primarily for solo use. The wide popularity of vertical-twin five-hundreds shortly after the war soon led to the introduction of models of similar layout but larger capacity. Most of the newcomers were dual-purpose machines, equally suitable for fast solo touring or hauling a sidecar. But the Model 99, first marketed in 1956, is not intended to woo the sidecarrist. Its duplex-loop frame has no sidecar lugs and is of the type made famous first on the factory racing models (in 1950) and subsequently on the Manx production racers and the Model 88, forerunner and smaller brother of the 99.

Superb steering, extraordinarily powerful braking and a delightful gear change combine with surging acceleration to justify the Norton's claim to be a sporting roadster. From its inception the Model 99 took advantage of the development of the smaller twin in having the so-called Daytona camshaft and a light-alloy cylinder head. The cumulative effect of improvements made in the past two years furnishes a good example of the way a sports model's manners can be enhanced by detail changes. The raucous exhaust of the early models has been subdued to a note which, though throaty, is not offensive. Use of light alloy for the pushrods and elimination of the dynamo and its drive (a crankshaft-driven A.C. generator is standardized for 1958) have contributed to a reduction in mechanical noise. Detail appearance has been tidied up. Finally, a scarcely noticeable but much appreciated refinement is the use of plastic covering for the control cables. The covering ensured that the initial sweetness of the controls was maintained in spite of many hours of riding in vile weather.

The adoption of an alternator was naturally accompanied by a change to coil ignition and the easy starting claimed for that system was very evident. Provided the air lever was closed and the

carburettor well flooded under cold conditions, no more than one swing of the kick-starter was required to set the engine running. After a cold start in chilly weather the air lever was opened in two of three stages covering the first mile or so to ensure unhesitant response to throttle opening during the warming-up period. An emergency position for the ignition switch is provided to enable the engine to be kick-started if the battery is flat. With the switch in that position the only additional requirement for a sure start was a really hearty thrust on the pedal.

Behind the crankcase mouth may be seen the distributor cover which conceals the contact breaker and auto-advance unit

Idling was slow and even once the engine was warm and, though petrol consumption was a little heavier than average in the lower speed ranges, carburation was clean at all throttle openings. There was no tendency to blurred running at 30 m.p.h. in top gear and pick-up from that speed was brisk as, indeed, it was right up the scale.

As would be expected, the most vivid acceleration was obtained by using the gear box to the full, and although the 99 had no vices for town riding it was on the open road that it showed up to best advantage. On full throttle, with the rider sitting upright, the model quickly reached its level-road top speed of an indicated 90 m.p.h.—quickly enough, that is, to outstrip a number of sleek sports cars of comparable or slightly higher top speed. Half throttle was sufficient to cruise at 75 m.p.h. or a little more while a throttle setting of two-thirds kept the speedometer needle in the 80 to 85 m.p.h. range as long as road conditions permitted. (Speedometer flattery was roughly constant throughout the range at five per cent.)

The engine was utterly tireless and, within its compass, the only considerations which dictated the speed to be sustained on long journeys were a vibration period and the riding position (unless a backrest was improvised). Felt through the handlebar and tank, the tremor became noticeable just before 65 m.p.h. was reached (in top gear), peaked at about 70 m.p.h. and faded out at 75 m.p.h. Beyond reasonable criticism for low and medium speeds, the riding posture was rather upright owing to the upward sweep of the handlebar and to the forward positioning of the footrests relative to the seat. Hence the rider had to exert an appreciable pull on the bar to counter the effect of wind pressure on the body. In the same context, the lower frictional characteristics of the plastic handlebar grips (as compared with rubber) served to increase the effort required, especially in wet weather. A considerable improvement resulted from a change to rubber grips but it was felt that a similar effect could be achieved with plastic grips if the material were more resilient or the knurling deepened.

Width of tank and seat between the rider's thighs is above average (11½in) and made it slightly awkward for riders of average height to put their feet to the ground. The rear part of the seat is of ample proportions for a pillion passenger and is well shaped for comfort. With the exception of the horn button (which is set rather low on the left side of the handlebar), all controls are excellently sited and proved smooth in operation.

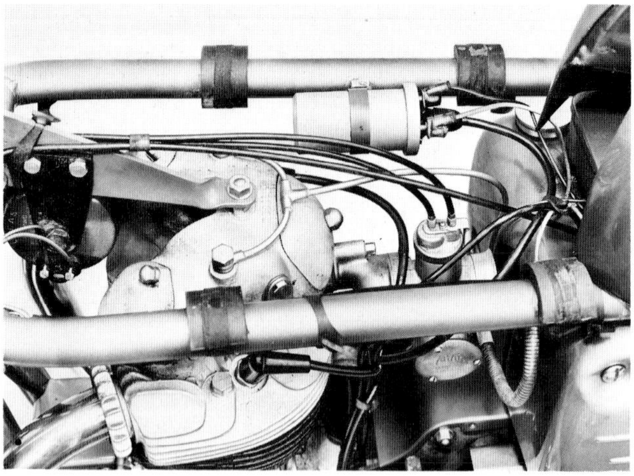

Above: Normally concealed by the petrol tank, the ignition coil is bolted to a lug welded to the upper run of the right-hand frame tube. Below: The 597 c.c. engine has a light-alloy cylinder head

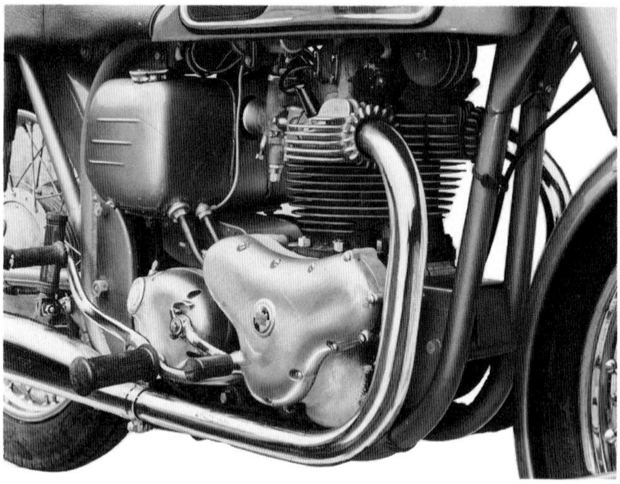

INFORMATION PANEL

SPECIFICATION

ENGINE: Norton 597 c.c. (68×82mm) overhead-valve vertical twin with light-alloy cylinder head. Valve gear operated from a single camshaft. Light-alloy connecting rods with steel-back, micro-babbitt shell big-end bearings. Crankshaft supported in roller bearing on drive side and ball bearing on timing side. Compression ratio, 7.4 to 1. Dry-sump lubrication; oil-tank capacity, 4½ pints.

CARBURETTOR: Amal Monobloc; air slide operated by handlebar lever.

IGNITION and LIGHTING: Coil ignition with automatic advance. Lucas RM15 60-watt A.C. generator driven by left end of crankshaft. Lucas 6-volt, 12-ampere-hour battery charged through rectifier. Lucas 7in-diameter headlamp with pre-focus light unit.

TRANSMISSION: A.M.C. four-speed gear box with positive-stop foot control. Gear ratios: bottom, 12.1 to 1; second, 8.03 to 1; third, 6.04 to 1; top, 4.53 to 1. Multi-plate clutch with moulded inserts running in oil. Primary chain, ½×0.305in in oil-bath case. Rear chain, ⅝×¼in with guard over top run. Engine r.p.m. at 30 m.p.h. in top gear, 1,750.

FUEL CAPACITY: 3½ gallons.

TYRES: Avon: front, 3.00×19in Speedmaster; rear, 3.50×19in Safety Mileage.

BRAKES: Front, 8in diameter×1¼in wide; rear, 7in diameter×1¼in wide; finger adjusters.

SUSPENSION: Norton telescopic front fork with hydraulic damping. Pivoted-fork rear springing employing Girling hydraulically damped shock absorbers with three-position adjustment for load.

WHEELBASE: 55½in unladen. Ground clearance, 5½in unladen.

SEAT: Norton dual-seat; unladen height, 31½in.

WEIGHT: 413 lb fully equipped, with full oil tank and approximately half a gallon of petrol.

PRICE: £235. With purchase tax (in Great Britain only), £293 3s 3d.

ROAD TAX: £3 15s a year; £1 0s 8d a quarter.

MAKERS: Norton Motors, Ltd., Bracebridge Street, Birmingham, 6.

DESCRIPTION: *The Motor Cycle*, 5 September 1957.

PERFORMANCE DATA

MEAN MAXIMUM SPEED: Bottom: *45 m.p.h.
Second: *68 m.p.h.
Third: *91 m.p.h.
Top: 93 m.p.h.
*Valve float occurring.

HIGHEST ONE-WAY SPEED: 96 m.p.h. (conditions: moderate side wind; rider wearing two-piece plastic suit and overboots).

MEAN ACCELERATION:

	10-30 m.p.h.	20-40 m.p.h.	30-50 m.p.h.
Bottom	2.4 sec	2.2 sec	—
Second	4.2 sec	3.4 sec	3.2 sec
Third	—	4.4 sec	4.4 sec
Top	—	7.2 sec	6.8 sec

Mean speed at end of quarter-mile from rest: 80 m.p.h.
Mean time to cover standing quarter-mile: 16 sec.

PETROL CONSUMPTION: At 30 m.p.h., 78 m.p.g.; at 40 m.p.h., 73 m.p.g.; at 50 m.p.h., 68 m.p.g.; at 60 m.p.h., 60 m.p.g.

BRAKING: From 30 m.p.h. to rest, 27ft (surface, dry tarmac).

TURNING CIRCLE: 17ft.

MINIMUM NON-SNATCH SPEED: 20 m.p.h. in top gear.

WEIGHT PER C.C.: 0.69 lb

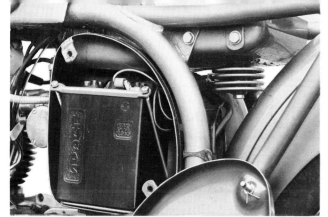

The alternator charges the enclosed battery through a rectifier which is bolted to the underside of the tool tray beneath the seat

In the matter of wheel suspension the makers have compromised in favour of short firm movements, especially at the front, to obviate all possibility of pitching. At the expense of a hard ride on bumpy surfaces the rider has the advantage of precision handling at very high speeds. Once initial overtightening of the head races had been rectified, steering was absolutely first rate. In all circumstances it inspired the highest confidence; indeed, it was one of the most prominent factors in the joy of riding the 99. On a straight path the Norton steered itself irrespective of speed or surface irregularities. And all that was necessary to cut a stylish line on any variety of bend or corner was to heel the model over by leg pressure. There was never a waver from the front wheel nor a chop from the rear, so that a line could be chosen almost to the breadth of a hair. But a more generous steering lock would have been appreciated when turning about in a narrow road or manhandling the model in a confined space.

Braking power was more than a match for the speed of the 99. Either wheel could be locked by panic action but the controls were sensitive enough to preclude such a mistake otherwise. The slight heaviness in front brake operation which resulted from the use of an unusually thick cable on earlier models has been eliminated by a change to a cable of normal weight. Travel of the rear-brake pedal is a shade long. On the debit side, comparatively frequent adjustment for wear was required on both brakes and the finger adjuster on the rear control was awkward to use owing to the proximity of the left-hand silencer.

Gear changing was a joy. No deliberation was called for in the movement of the controls. Pedal operation was light and textbook methods gave text-book results: rapid, smooth and noiseless changes. The slight stiffness in engaging bottom gear which was a feature of some of the earlier A.M.C. boxes has been cured by an alteration in the rating of the selector spring. Neutral selection from bottom or second gear was simplicity itself whether the model was rolling or stationary.

The only criticism of the box concerned rather wide spacing of the third and top ratios and a slight whine when the engine was pulling in either of the intermediate gears. However, the lowish third gear gave a very useful burst of acceleration from 40 to 65 m.p.h. As is shown by the mean maximum speed figures in the information panel, the 99 is overgeared in top. Indeed, in one direction the model was just as fast in third gear as in top. But although the mean maximum speed would doubtless be raised and top-gear flexibility enhanced by use of an engine sprocket having one tooth fewer, the overgearing was not really obtrusive, for the engine pulled lustily in the middle speed ranges.

Extremely light to withdraw, the clutch took up the drive abnormally quickly in the last fraction of lever movement. But the delicacy required for a smooth getaway was soon mastered and was subsequently quite automatic. In a rapid succession of four full-throttle quarter-mile sprints from a standing start, the free movement in the control cable increased perceptibly as a result of expansion of the friction material; but there was never the slightest trace of slip or drag and cable clearance returned to normal as soon as the clutch had cooled down. Since the clutch adjuster is situated in the centre of the pressure plate (there is also an external cable adjuster on the gear-box cover), a detachable panel in the rear dome of the primary chaincase would be a boon, so that adjustment could be effected without removing the left footrest, brake pedal and chaincase outer half. Incidentally, removal of the outer half of the case does not disturb the alternator.

During a test comprising just under 1,000 miles of hard riding the engine and gear box retained their oil well, there being only faint smears at some of the joints at the end of the test. Slight seepage occurred from the oil-tank filler cap and chaincase inspection cover. A small pool of oil formed under the crankcase breather when the model was parked at the end of a run. At 1,200 to 1,500 m.p.g. oil consumption was rather high. The rear chain ran dry and required adjusting and oiling at frequent intervals. Intensity of the headlamp beam was well up to average and the offset of the dipped beam precluded offence to oncoming traffic.

Most routine maintenance tasks were easily carried out with the standard tool kit (which is carried in a shallow tray under the dual-seat). The exception was adjustment of the contact-breaker points. The auto-advance and contact-breaker unit is situated behind the crankcase mouth in the place previously occupied by the magneto; the adjustment is inaccessible and thereby liable to invite neglect by owners who are not fastidious. When raising the 99 on to its centre stand for maintenance work it was found helpful to use the left footrest as one lifting point. The foot of the prop stand operates close to the machine's centre line and hence a firm, level surface is necessary if the risk of toppling is to be avoided.

In appearance the Model 99 is a winner. Its lines are handsome and the polychromatic grey finish blends tastefully with the polished aluminium and chromium plating. Framed in plastic beading, the separate chromium side panels give a distinctive aspect to the petrol tank, while the cleaning-up process mentioned earlier results in a pleasing absence of bittiness.

The 597 c.c. Norton Model 99 twin

VIPER

Although, in general, the motor cycling public looked upon the Velocette as a sturdy machine built by conscientious engineers for a connoisseurs' market, one gets the sneaking feeling that the company (in other words, the Goodman family) would have sold many more bikes, if only they could have added a touch of modernity to the design.

By the 1950s, for example, other makers were using lighter, all-welded tubular frames; and yet Velocette, right to the bitter end, stuck with the malleable-lug, hearth-brazed heavy frame that echoed 1920s practice. To take another point, the peculiar Velocette clutch, located inboard of the final-drive sprocket, no doubt worked very well when set correctly; but to riders not steeped in Velo lore the design was distinctly off-putting, and it is interesting to speculate on how many possible purchasers decided, instead, to buy a BSA, or an Ariel, or something else with a clutch that looked familiar.

To be brutally frank, the electrics were pathetic (an alternator-equipped model was on the stocks, but the factory closed down before it could be put into production). And what other British single needed a special paragraph on starting technique in the rider's handbook?

A remote ancestor of the Viper was the 248 cc MOV which appeared in the summer of 1933, a Eugene Goodman design and the first of the M-range of pushrod, overhead-valve Velocette singles. This was followed for 1935 by the 349 cc MAC. By June of the same year (Velocette never were particularly fussy about reserving new models or production changes for autumn announcement) the 495 cc MSS had arrived, and so the family of high-camshaft singles was complete.

In the course of time the MOV would disappear, and the remaining MAC and MSS would acquire pivoted-fork rear springing and a telescopic front fork, but there were few other changes and, externally at least, the 1955 Velocette singles looked much as they had done for the past 20 years.

By this time, however, demand was rising for something with a more spirited performance than the MAC or MSS could produce. In earlier days, the answer would have been the overhead-camshaft KSS, but post-war economics had caused this model to be dropped.

Designer Charles Udall set to work and the result, unveiled in October, 1955, was a pair of sporty overhead-valve models, the 349 cc Viper and 495 cc Venom, each benefitting from the factory's road-racing experience by the adoption of a bi-metal Al-fin cylinder with cast-iron liner, and by a cylinder head in light alloy.

The two models were really one, because the Viper was not based on the touring MAC but, instead, employed the same bottom-end assembly as its bigger Venom sister. Viper bore and stroke dimensions were 72 × 86 mm (compared with the 68 × 96 mm dimensions of the MAC). Other specification details included a high-compression, split-skirt piston, and enclosed hairpin valve springs. A chromium-plated fuel tank and mudguards, set off by black or willow green paintwork, made the Viper a handsome machine indeed.

With its over-90 mph potential, the new Viper would have been a possible answer to the overwhelming BSA Gold Star dominance of the Isle of Man Clubmans TT – if only it had been introduced a year or two earlier. But the Clubmans TT had folded. Still, production-machine racing was beginning to catch public imagination, and in the 1957 Thruxton Nine-Hour Race a Viper co-ridden by Eddie Dow and John Righton held a creditable third place until a dropped-in valve brought retirement.

The classic high-camshaft layout of the pushrod overhead valve Velocette engine is seen to good effect in this cutaway drawing of the 349 cc Viper, which featured a light-alloy cylinder barrel and head, and totally-enclosed hairpin valve springs

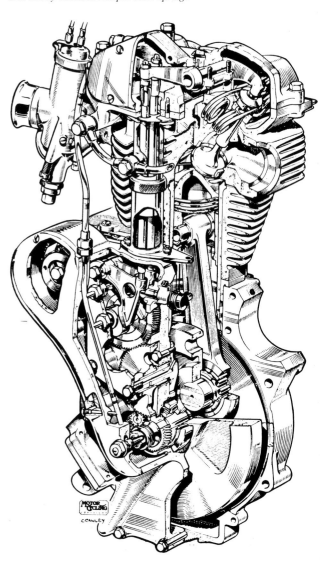

Preceding pages: 1965 Viper Veeline

In later years the Viper was indeed to achieve a modest degree of racing success, but it was fated to be overshadowed by the 495 cc Venom, and in the end it was the Venom which was given further development to produce the ultimate in super-sports Velocettes, the Venom Thruxton.

One move which met with little enthusiasm from the motor cycling fraternity, and with even less from die-hard Velocette fans, was the adoption of glass-fibre panels which encased everything below cylinder-base height. This was an economy measure, the covers obviated the need for polishing the light-alloy castings of the timing cover and gearbox end cover. In fact New Hudson had tried something similar (but in pressed steel) as far back as 1932, with a notable lack of success and only Francis-Barnett, with their pre-war Cruiser, had scored any sort of hit with engine enclosure.

Still, the message must have got through, because although the covered-up Viper and Venom were continued, from 1960 they were now partnered by the Viper Clubman and Venom Clubman, in which the lower works were once again left naked and unashamed. And there was rather more to it than that, because, in the interests of clubman and production-machine racing, these were equipped with TT Amal carburettors, BTH racing magnetos, and close-ratio gearboxes. Compression ratio was raised (9·3 to 1, on the Viper), a solid-skirt piston replaced the split-skirt type, and rear-set footrests were provided.

The following year brought yet another variant, the Viper Veeline which featured a roadster-type dolphin fairing. When applied to the tuned model, the fairing gave rise to the Viper Clubman Veeline, which was quite enough of a mouthful for anyone. Up to this time, both the Viper and Viper Clubman had been fitted with a chromium-plated fuel tank, and Velocettes were certainly the last British firm to do so. Now, however, the Viper Clubman had a new and rather ugly 4½-gallon tank with square lines, painted all over, bearing the Velocette name in a rectangular clear-plastic panel, and trimmed by a horizontal band of corrugated, anodised alumium.

For two more years, the chromium-plated tank was listed for the standard Viper, but by 1962 that model, too, was using the big square tank.

Meanwhile, a Venom had gained the world 500 cc 24-hour record at Montlhéry, and in July, 1963 an attempt was made on the 350 cc long-distance records at the same venue, with Velocette sales director Bertie Goodman again as a member of the riding team. Unhappily, ignition bothers set in after the first six hours (at which time the average speed was just over 105 mph), and with no hope of achieving the target 12-hour or 24-hour records, the attempt was abandoned for the day. A restart was made next morning, but speed was down, and after an hour and a half the engine failed.

Another attempt was made to produce an economy model in the early 1960s, using the old-style three-gallon fuel tank and an all-painted finish but, somehow, a Velocette in grey-blue with a horizontal cream band on the tank did not look right.

Motor Cycle road-tested the Viper again in 1966, and found it to be much as it had been in 1958, so far as all-out performance was concerned, a shade less lively in acceleration, but rather better on fuel economy. But for the Viper, and for Velocettes as a whole, time was fast running out. Coil ignition at last replaced the time-honoured magneto in July, 1968. A Velocette range was announced for 1970, but it no longer included a 350 cc model, and before long the factory had ground to a complete halt.

Previously available on the Clubman version only, the squared-off 4¼-gallon fuel tank with anodised-alloy styling band became a standard fitment on the Velocette Viper from 1963 onward

349 c.c. Velocette

A REMARKABLY FINE MOTOR CYCLE : ALL-ROUND PERFORMANCE WELL ABOVE THE

EXCEPT that the engine is geared to turn over comparatively fast and revels in doing so, there is little to suggest to the uninitiated rider that the Velocette Viper is a three-fifty. Judging from the evidence of the speedometer, he might well conclude that he was riding a lively five-hundred, for the Viper will send the needle round the dial to the 75 or 80 m.p.h. mark in third gear (according to conditions of wind and gradient) and then hold that speed in top on about two-thirds throttle. And, with the rider crouching but clad in full plastic weather kit, over 90 m.p.h. is possible.

The impression of high performance gained on road test owed nothing to speedometer flattery: at two per cent fast, the speedometer had a higher than average standard of accuracy. What is praiseworthy is that such a sporting performance is achieved in a three-fifty for such a meagre sacrifice in the more prosaic but none-the-less important qualities of docility, unobtrusiveness and ease of riding When it is stated that the engine revels in spinning fast, that should not be taken to imply that the Viper is intractable or in any way unhappy at lower engine speeds. In suburban districts with a 40 m.p.h. speed limit the model proved to be quite lively with upward gear changes made at about 20, 30 and 40 m.p.h. And on town roads, with their 30 m.p.h. limit, the Viper ran perfectly sweetly in top gear at the legal maximum speed. Indeed, even greater proof of the engine's flexibility (and of the efficiency of the face-cam transmission shock absorber on the engine shaft) is the minimum non-snatch speed of 14 m.p.h. in top gear and the fact that it was possible to carry out a 10-to-30 m.p.h. acceleration test in third gear in spite of the close grouping of the Viper's gear ratios.

But the prime joy of riding the Viper was to make full use of its engine power on the open road and, for that purpose, upward gear changes were best made at about 35, 55 and 75 m.p.h. Riding the Viper in that fashion, it was found possible to average 55 m.p.h. on long non-stop runs over fast arterial

roads. Third gear was used extensively on runs of that nature; but that was no disadvantage since all gears were quite free from whine, and the only noticeable difference between top and third was in the relationship of engine and road speeds. For all practical purposes the engine was smooth throughout its speed range: such tremor as could be felt (between 60 and 65 m.p.h. in top gear) was so slight as to be scarcely worthy of mention.

Time was when obtrusiveness went hand in hand with sporting performance, especially in the smaller capacity classes. Judging by the Viper, improvements have been made in that respect. It is true the model has a clean-cut and healthy exhaust note but it is of a pleasant character and not a bit out of place on the open highway. In built-up areas, however, to avoid giving offence to bystanders it was necessary to avoid hard acceleration. The low level of mechanical noise was commendable, especially so in a sports model with light-alloy cylinder and head: only a slight rhythmic clack from the piston was audible. Unquestionably the fine-pitch helical timing gears with an outrigger plate, light-alloy pushrods and long quietening ramps on the cams contribute much to the mechanical quietness.

The use of auto-advance on a super-sports single is another indication of progress in engine design. The mechanism is properly matched to the engine characteristics and the rider is relieved of the need to juggle an ignition lever to prevent back-firing when starting or to obtain a slow tick-over or smooth low-speed pulling.

The kick-starter on Velocette singles is rather low geared and the Viper repaid use of the starting technique stipulated in the owner's handbook. That involves turning the engine on to compression, then farther forward by one slow stroke of the kick-starter before administering the starting thrust. A first-kick response was the rule rather than the exception, provided the carburettor float tickler was used only sparingly when the engine was cold and not at all when it was hot. In fact, sufficient

Viper

...ERAGE : FIRST-CLASS FINISH

Right: The 7½-in diameter front brake is within a full-width, light-alloy hub and has a lining area of 23 sq in. Both brakes were extremely powerful and impervious to rain

Extreme right: Most routine maintenance jobs can be carried out easily. The contact-breaker points are readily accessible.

mixture enrichment for cold starting could usually be obtained merely by closing the air lever, which could be reopened fully as soon as the engine fired. Idling was slow and reliable whatever the engine temperature and carburation was devoid of flat spots under all conditions.

Engagement of bottom gear when stationary sometimes required the clutch to be partially fed in while upward pressure was maintained on the gear pedal. In every other respect the gear box was a joy to use. All changes, up or down, were clean, light, fast and positive. As implied earlier, the Viper's gear ratios are closer than those of its touring counterpart, the 349 c.c. MAC (though not so close as the racing ratios obtainable at option). This enhanced both the pleasure of the gear change and the range of usefulness of bottom gear which, at 12.62 to 1, permitted a speed of just over 40 m.p.h.

Though it is of little more than academic interest, the high bottom-gear ratio actually detracted slightly from the Viper's getaway during the full-throttle, quarter-mile acceleration tests, otherwise the relevant figures in the information panel might have been even better. In ordinary riding, the only occasions when bottom gear proved a shade too high were when starting from rest two-up in a built-up area. Then the use of a small throttle opening for quietness (rather than a large opening and some clutch slipping) resulted in a comparatively moderate get-

Drive to the Miller dynamo is by a vee-belt from a pulley on the engine shaft. The belt is adjusted by turning the dynamo in its clamp

INFORMATION PANEL

SPECIFICATION

ENGINE: Velocette 349 c.c. (72 x 86mm) overhead-valve single with Wellworthy Al-Fin cylinder barrel and light-alloy head. Duralumin pushrods; hairpin valve springs. Roller big-end bearing. Crankshaft supported in two taper-roller bearings. Compression ratio, 8.5 to 1. Dry-sump lubrication; oil-tank capacity, 4 pints.

CARBURETTOR: Amal Monobloc; air slide operated by handlebar lever.

IGNITION and LIGHTING: Lucas magneto with auto-advance. Miller 36-watt dynamo and Varley 6-volt, 12-ampere-hour battery. Miller 7in-diameter headlamp with pre-focus light unit.

TRANSMISSION: Velocette four-speed gear box with positive-stop foot control. Gear ratios: bottom, 12.62 to 1; second, 8.73 to 1; third, 6.64 to 1; top, 5.5 to 1. Multi-plate clutch with fabric inserts operating in oil. Primary chain, ⅜ x 0.305in in pressed-steel, oil-bath case. Rear chain, ⅜ x 0.305in with guard over top run. Engine r.p.m. at 30 m.p.h. in top gear, 2,170.

FUEL CAPACITY: 3¼ gallons.

TYRES: Dunlop 3.25 x 19in; rear, Universal; front, ribbed.

BRAKES: Front, 7½in. diameter x 1⅛in wide; rear, 7in diameter x 1in wide.

SUSPENSION: Velocette telescopic front fork with hydraulic damping. Pivoted-fork rear springing employing Woodhead-Monroe hydraulically damped shock absorbers with adjustment for load.

WHEELBASE: 53¼in unladen. Ground clearance, 6¼in unladen.

SEAT: Velocette dual-seat; unladen height, 31in.

WEIGHT: 364 lb fully equipped, with full oil tank but no petrol.
PRICE: £207; with purchase tax (in Great Britain only), £258 4s 8d.
ROAD TAX: £3 15s a year; £1 0s 8d a quarter.
MAKERS: Veloce, Ltd., York Road, Hall Green, Birmingham, 28.
DESCRIPTION: *The Motor Cycle,* 12 September 1957.

PERFORMANCE DATA

MEAN MAXIMUM SPEED: Bottom*: 43 m.p.h.
Second*: 62 m.p.h.
Third*: 82 m.p.h.
Top: 88 m.p.h.
*Valve float occurring.

HIGHEST ONE-WAY SPEED: 91 m.p.h. (conditions: moderate three-quarter wind; rider wearing two-piece plastic suit and overboots).

MEAN ACCELERATION:

	10-30 m.p.h.	20-40 m.p.h.	30-50 m.p.h.
Bottom	3.4 sec	3.3 sec	—
Second	5.4 sec	5.2 sec	4.6 sec
Third	8 sec	8 sec	7.4 sec
Top	—	9 sec	11 sec

Mean speed at end of quarter-mile from rest: 74 m.p.h.
Mean time to cover standing quarter-mile: 18.2 sec.

PETROL CONSUMPTION: At 30 m.p.h., 85 m.p.g.; at 40 m.p.h., 80 m.p.g.; at 50 m.p.h., 70 m.p.g.; at 60 m.p.h., 60 m.p.g.

BRAKING: From 30 m.p.h. to rest, 28ft (surface, dry tarmac).

TURNING CIRCLE: 16ft.

MINIMUM NON-SNATCH SPEED: 14 m.p.h. in top gear.

WEIGHT PER C.C.: 1.04 lb.

away and a trace of pinking. Neutral was easy to find from bottom or second gear, whether the machine was moving or at rest. Smooth and positive in action, the clutch was unaffected by abuse.

For all-round road work it would be difficult to improve on the Viper's riding position. It provides a very relaxed posture yet no perceptible pulling on the bar is required when high speeds are sustained for long periods. At the end of a full day in the saddle not a trace of discomfort was felt. Although seat

The rear suspension is adjustable for load by altering the position of the top attachments of the Woodhead-Monroe suspension units

height (31in) is not below average, the shape of the seat nose makes it easy for short riders to place their feet firmly on the ground at traffic halts. Proportions and padding of the seat are ample for passenger carrying, and the pillionist's position is as comfortable as the rider's.

Disposition of the controls is well-nigh faultless and all were smooth to operate The only criticisms are of a minor nature and to some extent based on personal preference. First, the combined horn button and dip-switch was mounted 2½in too far inboard on the left side of the handlebar and could not be moved nearer the grip because there was insufficient free length of horn wire. Secondly, the lighting switch in the right-hand

side of the headlamp cowl would be more convenient to operate if it were transposed with the ammeter on the left.

As is evident from the crash-stop figure shown in the information panel, braking power was immense. No matter whether speed was high or low, the Viper could be brought to rest extraordinarily quickly and smoothly with both tyres shrieking in protest. Yet so sensitive and progressive were the controls, and so free from sponginess, that no qualms at all were felt in braking as heavily as was safe on wet roads. Moreover, no brake efficiency was lost during hours of riding in teeming rain and on flooded roads.

It is difficult to appreciate why a steering damper is fitted for the need to use it was never felt at any time during the test. The Viper virtually steered itself. All that was required of the rider on bends or corners was to bank the model to the appropriate degree, whereupon it would follow the curve without a waver. While it was just possible on slow corners to ground the footrest on the left and the silencer clip on the right, the degree of banking required to do so was much more than is normally used.

A shade on the firm side at low speeds, front and rear springing combined to give leech-like roadholding and a comfortable ride. Recoil damping of the rear suspension seemed a little short of the ultra-high standard usual on Velocettes and slight oil seepage from the shock absorbers at the end of the test suggested they were below par. Even so, there was never any pitching worthy of the name—only the realization of how high is the normal level of control taken for granted in the Woodhead-Monroe units.

With the exception of the minor oil seepage just mentioned and the customary film of lubricant thrown off the rear chain, the Viper was commendably oil-tight. And cleaning after a long ride in filthy weather was a relatively quick affair, thanks in part to the high polish on the aluminium castings and mudguard blades. Apart from the light-alloy parts, the finish is in serviceable black enamel and chromium plating.

Both the centre and prop stands are fine examples of their type. Routine adjustments are readily accessible except that the petrol tank must be removed to get at the valve-clearance adjustment and the carburettor top. A good-quality tool kit is standardized. For night riding the headlamp beam permitted speeds of 60 to 70 m.p.h. to be used on unlit main roads.

The Velocette Viper offers a blend of pep and docility which is quite remarkable in a three-fifty. And the price of the blend is nothing more than a slightly over-average petrol-consumption rate at speeds below 50 m.p.h. One of the few criticisms ever made of Velocette singles is that they lack uniformity of line. That charge carries little weight with the connoisseur who puts his model's behaviour before its eye-appeal. To such an enthusiast, what is right looks right. And justly so in the case of the Viper—which is a joy to ride and a pride to own.

ARIEL
LEADER

There can be no doubt at all that the Ariel Leader was a very surprising motor cycle, but the biggest surprise of all was that it should have originated in a factory that seemed firmly wedded to a four-stroke programme – not only side-valve and overhead-valve singles, but also vertical twins and, of course, the Square Four. True, Ariels had introduced a two-stroke once before; but that had been back in 1916, and First World War conditions had prevented it from reaching the production stage.

Ariel's veteran designer, Val Page, was responsible for the Leader, and it was said that he and his drawing-office team had been given a completely free hand to produce an ultra-modern two-fifty with built-in weather protection, using whatever method of construction they deemed necessary.

The project got under way in 1955, and it was to be three years before the result reached the production stage. A copybook exercise in the use of steel pressings, the machine was based on a tremendously rigid boxed beam, from which the engine unit was suspended at two points, with the rearmost engine mounting serving also as the pivot for the rear fork.

Further pressings formed the dummy tank (within which was parcel carrying space), legshields, headlamp cowl, and tail unit. Front suspension was by trailing-link fork, the stanchions of which were also pressings. The rear fuel tank was housed within the frame beam, and access to the filler cap was obtained by hingeing up the dual seat. Detachable side panels married with the lines of the machine as a whole, and kept the engine and gearbox unit completely hidden from view.

The engine was a 249 cc two-stroke twin, with the cylinders inclined forward at 45 degrees, and featured light-alloy pressure die-cast cylinder heads with part-spherical combustion chambers. The crankcase was not split, and that necessitated a built-up crankshaft assembly, with the two halves inserted into the crankcase then held together by a socket-headed drawbolt.

Although the gearbox shell was cast integrally with the crankcase, the gears and shafts were actually manufactured on Ariel's behalf by the Burman company (and just as an aside, there was a plan to use the same gearbox internals for a 250 cc overhead-camshaft Velocette, of which development was never completed).

Fork design was especially ingenious, because hydraulically-damped spring units were concealed within the fork leg pressings, and the die-cast trailing links, of heat-treated light alloy, were so arranged that the wheelbase remained constant, with the claimed advantage of minimal tyre wear.

Standard equipment included a generously proportioned windscreen with, just below it, a pressed-steel instrument panel. Numerous optional extras were listed, embracing a cast light-alloy rear carrier, direction-indicator lamps, styled-in pannier cases, and a chromium-plated rear bumper.

Understandably, the tooling-up costs for a machine so radically different from anything that had gone before were truly immense, and it took a large dose of courage on the part of the Ariel company (and, in particular, their managing director, Ken Whistance) to take the decision to go ahead.

Some of the necessary pressings were produced by Carbodies of Coventry (a BSA subsidiary), while others were obtained from Concentric Pressed Products. To justify the initial outlay, volume production was put in hand, and that meant a tailing-off of four-stroke models.

Yes, the Leader sold, but not in the quantities for which Ariel had hoped, and so for 1960 a second two-stroke twin was evolved. This was the Arrow, a model which retained the main pressings of the Leader, but discarded the inbuilt legshields, dashboard and windscreen. The tail, too, was rather less elegant, and there was a simpler pressed-steel superstructure.

With the coming of the Arrow, four-stroke production at the Selly Oak works was brought to an end, and it certainly appeared that Ariel's 'bold bid for economic suicide' (to quote *Motor Cycle*) had turned out to be nothing of the kind. Improvements were made from time to time, and these embraced higher-compression cylinder heads, better front brake plate anchorage, and larger-capacity fuel tanks.

A third variant appeared in January, 1961, in the form of the Sports Arrow (popularly called the Golden Arrow, from the colour of its dummy tank pressing), with enlarged inlet tract and $1\frac{1}{16}$-in instead of $\frac{7}{8}$-in choke Amal Monobloc carburettor. A pretty little machine, with much chromium plating on the engine side cover, front fork link cover plates, toolbox lid, and so on, and whitewall tyres to complete the picture, the Golden Arrow found plenty of customers in Britain.

Crankcase and gearbox of the Ariel Leader were combined in a single casting. This meant that the crankshaft had to be made in two pieces, inserted from each side and held together in the middle by a longitudinal socket screw

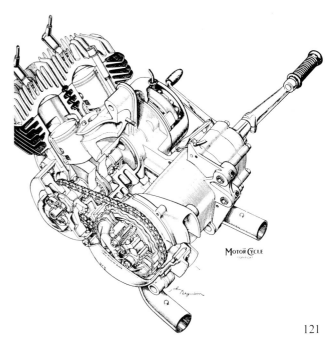

MOTOR CYCLE

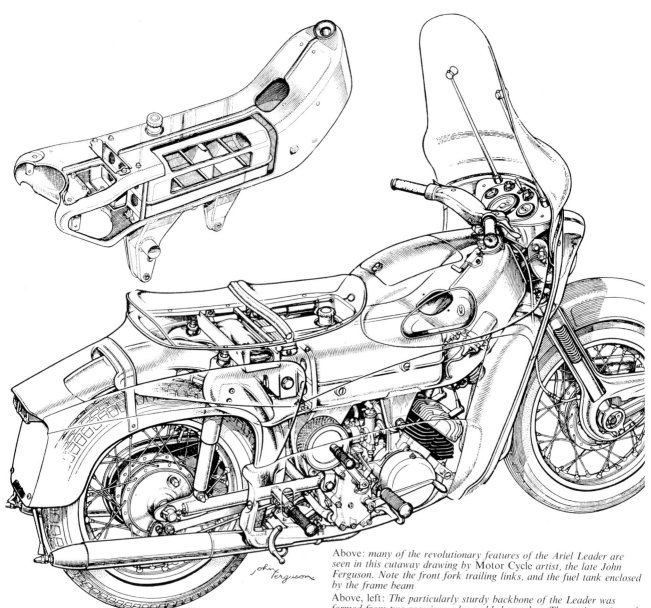

Above: *many of the revolutionary features of the Ariel Leader are seen in this cutaway drawing by* Motor Cycle *artist, the late John Ferguson. Note the front fork trailing links, and the fuel tank enclosed by the frame beam*

Above, left: *The particularly sturdy backbone of the Leader was formed from two pressings edge-welded together. The engine unit, and pivoted rear fork, were carried by brackets from the underside of the beam*

Exports were low, however, and American enthusiasts would not have a pressed-steel frame bike at any price. That was a pity, because the Arrow could fly, and tuned examples were soon being seen on home racing circuits, and even in the Isle of Man, where first Mike O'Rourke, and later Peter Inchley, produced the best results by British machines in the 250 cc class for many years. Experiments began with a tubular-framed Arrow (and there were rumours that, had it ever been put into production, the name would have been the Ariel Red Hunter; now wince, ye traditionalists!) but although this reached the road-mileage test stage, it was not proceeded with.

Responsibility for design and development of the Arrow and Golden Arrow belonged to Bernard Knight (who, earlier, had been one of the design team involved with the BSA Bantam), because Val Page was by then well past retiring age. However, Val had remained at his drawing board for a specific reason. Ariel, in the late 1950s, were engaged in a project which employed a straight-four 400 cc overhead-camshaft engine, and he wanted to see this through to finality, as his swan song.

Essentially, the straight-four was intended for an Army contract, but it was planned that surplus production could be diverted to motor cycle use and, accordingly, Val Page had designed a kind of Super Leader.

This model, the prototype of which still exists, suspended the straight-four engine from a Leader frame beam. There was shaft drive to the rear wheel, but the Leader pressings camouflaged the whole thing so successfully that, when stationary, only the twin headlamps gave a hint that the machine was rather special.

Sad to relate, development of the four was reaching finality when the government of the day ordered a massive cutback in military spending, and the hoped-for contract failed to materialise. The outcome was closure of the Selly Oak works, and transfer of Ariel production to the parent BSA plant at Small Heath. Last member of the Ariel two-stroke family was the Arrow 200, a 199 cc twin added in May 1964. Ostensibly, it was designed to creep under the 200 cc level and so gain favourable quotes from some insurance companies. In fact, it was a way of using up some of the stocks of Arrow parts cluttering up the Small Heath works, and before another year was out the Arrow, and the Leader, were no more.

IN laying out the Leader, Ariels aimed at a roadster providing a new level of refinement in motor cycling. The sprightly performance and superlative handling of the thoroughbred solo were considered essential features, but were to be married to cultured manners and the sort of conveniences demanded ever more insistently, such as built-in weather shielding, accommodation for luggage, enclosure of mechanism, sleek lines and cleanliness in use.

The makers have achieved their aim and more. A pressed-steel, beam-type frame of great torsional rigidity, in conjunction with a very ingenious trailing-link front fork and a conventional pivoted rear fork, contributes to a magnificent blend of steering and comfort. The potentialities of the parallel-twin two-stroke engine have been thoroughly exploited to combine pep with sweetness. Not only are the conveniences mentioned inherent in the basic layout; they are supplemented by a host of other highly practical features—such as extensive thief proofing and a lever for

ROAD TESTS OF NEW MODELS

249 c.c. Ariel Leader

Sprightly Two-stroke Twin with Excellent Roadholding and Steering : Built-in Weather Protection : Many Practical Features

trimming the headlamp beam—and an extraordinarily useful range of items available at extra charge.

Most of the Leader's attractive features have, at some time or other, been incorporated in earlier designs or offered as accessories, but never before has a motor cycle provided a more complete and coherent answer to the plea for progression along "civilized" lines.

For some 1,500 miles the model under test was used, with and without a passenger, for business and pleasure trips varying in length from a few miles to a few hundred. For much of the mileage the weather was wet and the roads were often awash. With the exception of a peaked safety helmet, no special clothing was normally worn—just a lounge suit, light raincoat and kid gloves. In other words the rider dressed as he would to travel in an open sports car; and he arrived at his destination just as clean and dry. Only when riding through a succession of freak storms was it found desirable to wear a really waterproof coat and, perhaps, light leggings. (Riders who do not wear spectacles found it an advantage to use goggles in rain.)

On the longer journeys the Leader's comprehensive luggage capacity was greatly appreciated. The test model was equipped with the full range of extras, including panniers and carrier. Normal weekend kit, with spare shoes and change of clothing, was comfortably stowed in the detachable, shaped plastic bags in the lockable panniers. On the cast-aluminium carrier behind the dual-seat two suitcases could be secured by the adjustable, 1in-wide rubber straps provided. No less useful was the box, with lockable hinged lid, incorporated in the upper mid-section of the body. Its capacity for holding items which might be required during an outing—maps, flask, sandwiches, waterproof overalls and so forth—was remarkable. When the Leader was parked the box was handy for holding the rider's helmet, and there was room left for oddments such as scarf and gloves.

The steering lock and the securing clip for the hinged dual-

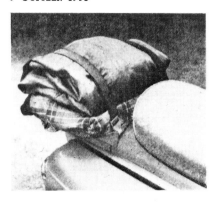

Left: A cast-alumin-ium carrier, complete with rubber straps, is available at extra charge. An idea of the amount of gear that could be accommodated is evident from this picture

Fuel-tank filler cap, battery and tool compartment are reached simply by hinging up the dual-seat which has a moulded plywood base

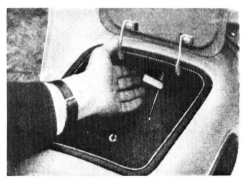

The steering lock (seen here) and the lock for the dual-seat are operated from the box in the body top

seat are both operated from inside the box; hence, by locking the box lid, not only can the model be rendered proof against theft but the fuel tank, battery, tools and tyre pump (all housed under the seat) can be safeguarded, too.

When the Leader was delivered for test the engine was only partially run in. Nevertheless an effortless cruising speed of about 50 m.p.h. on a quarter throttle was soon being used. The performance figures shown in the information panel were compiled when the total mileage was only 1,500; and though by then the model was quite capable of withstanding full throttle indefinitely, it was felt that slightly better figures could probably be obtained after two or three times that mileage. (Incidentally,

contrary to the usual practice with a naked machine, all performance data were obtained with the rider normally seated.)

Except when revved to the limit the engine was delightfully smooth and revelled in hard work. Under average conditions a cruising speed of a genuine 60 m.p.h. could be maintained as long as desired—which is praiseworthy for a two-fifty two-stroke—and required a throttle setting of around two-thirds to three-quarters. (On full throttle, the Leader lapped the Motor Industry Research Association's high-speed circuit at an average speed of over 64 m.p.h.) Yet the engine two-stroked exceptionally well under light load and was perfectly happy and unobtrusive when one was burbling along at well below 30 m.p.h. in top gear.

The torque peak of the engine occurs fairly high up the r.p.m. scale and this tends to give the Ariel Leader a dual personality. If upward gear changes are made early to keep engine speed low, it is a model of docility; but if the engine is allowed to spin fast by suitable use of the gear box, then acceleration and climb are quite sprightly. Indeed, it was commonplace to cover 140 to 145 miles in three hours, inclusive of normal traffic delays and fuel stops. The usual drill when refuelling was to take on 1½ gallons of petrol and a half a pint of oil—those being the largest convenient quantities approximately consistent with the recommended petroil ratio of 25 to 1.

INFORMATION PANEL

SPECIFICATION

ENGINE: Ariel 249 c.c. (54 x 54mm) two-stroke twin with separate iron cylinder barrels and light-alloy heads. Roller big-end bearings. Crankshaft supported in three ball bearings. Compression ratio, 8.25 to 1. Petroil lubrication; mixture ratio, 25 to 1.

CARBURETTOR: Amal Monobloc with strangler for cold starting. Felt air filter.

IGNITION and LIGHTING: Coil ignition with fixed timing. Lucas RM13/15 50-watt alternator driven by right-hand end of crankshaft. Lucas 6-volt, 13-ampere-hour battery charged through rectifier. Lucas 6in-diameter headlamp with pre-focus light unit.

TRANSMISSION: Four-speed gear box in unit with the engine; positive-stop foot control. Gear ratios: bottom, 19 to 1; second, 11 to 1; third, 7.8 to 1; top, 5.9 to 1. Multi-plate clutch with Neolangite facings operating in oil. Primary chain, ⅜ x 0.225in in cast-aluminium oil-bath case. Rear chain, ½ x 0.305in in pressed-steel case. Engine r.p.m. at 30 m.p.h. in top gear, 2,650.

FUEL CAPACITY: 2½ gallons.

TYRES: Dunlop white-wall 3.25 x 16in; rear, Universal; front, Lightweight Reinforced ribbed.

BRAKES: 6in diameter x 1⅛in wide front and rear; fulcrum adjusters.

SUSPENSION: Ariel trailing-link front and pivoted rear forks, both employing Armstrong hydraulically damped shock absorbers.

WHEELBASE: 51in unladen. Ground clearance, 5in unladen.

SEAT: Ariel dual-seat; unladen height, 31in.

WEIGHT: 330 lb equipped with all available extras (pannier cases and bags, luggage carrier, prop and front stands, trafficators, parking light, smiths' eight-day clock, neutral indicator and inspection lamp) but without fuel.

PRICE: £168. With purchase tax (in Great Britain only), £209 11s 7d. Price does not include extra equipment mentioned.

ROAD TAX: £1 17s 6d a year.

MAKERS: Ariel Motors, Ltd., Selly Oak, Birmingham, 29.

DESCRIPTION: *The Motor Cycle*, 17 July 1958.

PERFORMANCE DATA

(Obtained at the Motor Industry Research Association's proving ground, Lindley)

MEAN MAXIMUM SPEED: Bottom: 24 m.p.h.
Second: 40 m.p.h.
Third: 57 m.p.h.
Top: 67 m.p.h.

HIGHEST ONE-WAY SPEED: 69 m.p.h. (conditions: negligible wind; rider normally seated)

MEAN ACCELERATION:

	10-30 m.p.h	20-40 m.p.h	30-50 m.p.h
Second		6 sec	5.5 sec	—
Third	10 sec	9 sec	9.5 sec
Top	—	16.6 sec	16 sec

Mean speed at end of quarter-mile from rest: 57 m.p.h.
Mean time to cover standing quarter-mile: 22 sec.

PETROIL CONSUMPTION: At 30 m.p.h., 90 m.p.g.; at 40 m.p.h., 82 m.p.g.; at 50 m.p.h., 73 m.p.g.

BRAKING: From 30 m.p.h. to rest, 33ft (surface, dry tarmac).

TURNING CIRCLE: 14ft 6in.

MINIMUM NON-SNATCH SPEED: 13 m.p.h. in top gear.

WEIGHT PER C.C.: 1.32 lb.

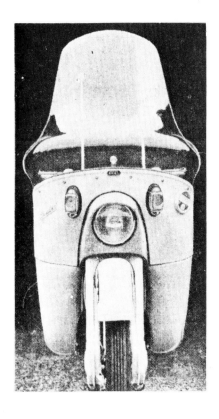

A front view of the Leader gives an excellent impression of the weather protection provided. The windscreen is attached to the top of the weathershield and supported by substantial vertical rods. Flashing - light indicators flank the headlamp

The exhaust note had a crisp edge, which mellowed slightly as the miles totted up and carbon formed in the silencers, but was by no means objectionable. Mechanical noise was negligible and an air silencer (formed by the rear engine-attachment bracket) subdued induction roar.

Little effort was required to spin the engine by means of the kick-starter and cold starting was child's play. Provided the strangler was closed and a few moments were allowed for the carburettor to fill after the tap was turned on, a first-kick response was the rule, but in any case no more than three or four prods were ever required. (The strangler control and petrol tap protrude through the left-hand side panel.) Only about a quarter-mile had to be covered before the strangler could be opened fully; restarting, with the engine warm, required only a light thrust on the pedal.

Idling was better than average for a two-stroke and, with the engine ticking over slowly, bottom gear could be engaged noiselessly—with the sole proviso that, before the first gear engagement of the day, the clutch plates were freed by operating the kick-starter with the clutch withdrawn. Clutch engagement was smooth. A leisurely technique was required for a clean change from bottom gear to second; the other two upward changes could be made more quickly and well repaid careful matching of the control movements. Clean downward changes demanded a synchronized blip of the throttle; the best results were achieved by setting the throttle stop for idling and removing every trace of backlash from the throttle cable, so that the response to blipping was a mite quicker than if the throttle was set to close completely. Neutral was easily selected from bottom or second gear. The indicator light (an extra) in the instrument panel serves also as an ignition warning light when the gears are in neutral—a minor but appreciated feature. Slight transmission noise was audible in the indirect gears.

Not adjustable for load, the springing proved to be a remarkably good compromise for riding with or without a passenger. In the former instance it was only a shade on the firm side and in the latter well-nigh perfect. In both cases roadholding was exemplary. Complementary to the fine roadholding was steering of a lightness and precision which were a joy to the connoisseur and a source of great confidence to the beginner. Another aspect of performance to reach the same high standard was braking, which was smooth, powerful and controllable. A sensible innovation is a second stop-light switch so that use of either brake operates the light.

Well shaped and deeply padded, the dual-seat was praised by both riders and passengers. The riding position was relaxed and comfortable though short riders might prefer a slightly lower seat and a footrest setting two or three inches farther forward. There is an ample range of adjustment for the rear-brake and gear pedals and, though the positions of the clutch and front-brake levers on the handlebar cannot be altered, they are reasonably well sited just above the plane of the rider's forearms. To clear the windscreen, the levers are comparatively short; consequently it was found advisable to maintain a close setting in the control cables.

Worthy of special praise is the fingertip positioning of the dipswitch and trafficator switch beneath the left handlebar grip. (Trafficators are extra.) The trimmer for the headlamp beam operates in a slot in the middle of the instrument panel and has a range suitable for all machine loadings between the extremes of a light rider and two persons with luggage. Intensity of the beam was adequate for normal speeds after dark and full lamp and ignition load on the battery was balanced by the alternator at 30 m.p.h. in top gear.

Clever design has ensured ease of maintenance in spite of extensive shielding. The brake adjusters are readily accessible, as are the sparking plugs (from the front of the engine). Removal of the side panels—which involves undoing five coin-slot screws on each side and first detaching the gear pedal and kick-starter on the right—gives access to the carburettor, contact breaker and gear box, and to clutch and primary-chain adjustments. The tail of the body may be hinged upward for rear-wheel removal and, if panniers are fitted, that is a necessary preliminary to rear-chain adjustment, too, unless a box spanner is available to fit the spindle nut.

A retractable lifting handle can be brought into use when pulling the machine on to its centre stand; the prop stand is extra, as is the two-piece, detachable front stand normally stowed in the tool tray. Other extras not already mentioned were a speedometer trip recorder, eight-day clock, low-consumption parking lamp and inspection lamp with 4ft of flex.

The Leader's elegant lines are enhanced by white-wall tyres and a two-tone finish combining light Admiralty grey with oriental blue or cherokee red. Such is the appeal of the model's outstanding convenience, cleanliness, roadworthiness and appearance that the Leader cannot fail to be the forerunner of a new trend and a yardstick by which future designs will be judged.

Left : The flashing-light indicators are actuated by a long, easily operated lever. Right : Plan view of the facia which houses the ammeter, speedometer, clock (or medallion), light and ignition switches and, between them, the manual beam-setting lever for the headlamp

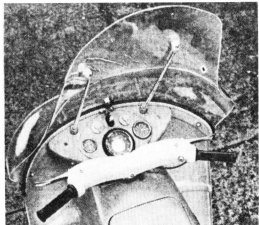

A·J·S
MODEL 16

Because some dastardly road-tester once wrote a mildly critical remark about an AJS (or maybe it was a Matchless) the top brass of the big AMC factory at Plumstead, south-east London, steadfastly refused to supply the motor cycling press with road test machines throughout the 1950s. Only towards the end of the era was this policy relaxed slightly, to the extent that a press tester would be permitted to ride a model around and record his impressions of it. But to click a stopwatch and publish performance figures was strictly taboo, so would-be purchasers had to guess at the 'What will it do?' bit.

Rather than miss out AJS-Matchless altogether, it was felt we ought to include this double-helping impression of the long-serving 347 cc AJS Model 16 in solo and sidecar trim, written by one-time *Motor Cycle* staffman David Dixon.

Not that there was any genuine AJS ancestry in the Model 16, anyway, because its true forebear had been the 347 cc Matchless G3L of Second World War fame. Even that model had been merely a weight-saving exercise carried out by Plumstead works director Bert Collier, using the pre-war-type G3 Clubman as the basis. For service reasons, as many parts as possible remained common to the G3 and G3L and, externally, the main difference was that the G3L (the 'L' stood for 'Light') had skimpier finning on the cylinder barrel and head.

Where the G3L did make history, of course, was that it was the first British production motor cycle to feature a hydraulically-damped front fork. The new patented AMC Teledraulic fork afforded a total movement of 6·280 in, and that was quite something when compared with the 3·375 in movement of the girder fork fitted to the G3.

Many thousands of Matchless G3L models were built for the allied forces from 1941 on, and it was understandable that the model would continue into post-war production in virtually unaltered form – save that khaki had given way to black enamel, and the exhaust pipe and silencer were chromium plated. The AJS Model 16, announced in mid-1945, was a companion to the Matchless GL, and the only essential difference between the two was that the Matchless carried its magneto at the rear of the cylinder barrel, whereas the AJS magneto was at the front.

In retrospect the distinction seems singularly pointless, but there were traditionalists who wanted an AJS and would not have a Matchless at any price and, of course, vice versa. So maybe such 'badge engineering' (which was to continue right through the 1950s) did have some justification.

Neither AJS nor Matchless adopted plunger-type rear springing, and the Model 16 retained its rigid rear frame until 1949, when pivoted fork suspension controlled by hydraulically-damped spring units of Matchless's own design and make became available at an extra cost of £20 6s 4d (including purchase tax), equivalent to £20.32.

These units were, at first, quite slim, and not the famous 'Jampots' (so named from the large diameter of their upper works), first adopted for 1951.

Other 1951 modifications included a die-cast light-alloy cylinder head with austenitic iron valve-seat inserts, and, in the interest of compatible expansion rates, pushrods of Hiduminium 44 light alloy. By this time, the combined Matchless and AJS ranges had expanded considerably, and in the AJS range the rigid-frame roadster Model 16M now had companions in the Model 16MS springer, Model 16MC rigid-frame Competitions, and Model 16MCS spring-frame Competitions.

There were not, as yet, separate trials and scrambles specifications. The off-road machine was a plain 'Competitions' model, and it was up to the purchaser to use it as he wished.

Changes came but slowly. For 1953, the old-style separate saddle and rear mudguard pillion pad were abandoned in favour of a dual seat. For 1954 the main visible change was that wheel hubs were now full-width, although there were also a few internal modifications – lighter flywheels, higher-lift cams, larger inlet port – aimed at producing a livelier performance. Automatic ignition advance, adopted on the 500 cc models the previous year, spread to the 347 cc models also for 1955 (although manual advance-retard levers were still fitted to the competitions version), as also did use of a Lucas rotating-magnet magneto.

These, however, were petty differences, and not until the

Kent farmer Gordon Jackson was one of the kingpins of the motor cycle trials scene of the 1950s (before becoming equally well-known in the world of car trials). Always well placed in the Scottish Six Days Trial, he was outright winner in 1956, and in this photograph he is shown tackling Kinloch Rannoch hill on the second day of the event

Derived from Jackson's trials-winning model, this is the production version of the 347 cc AJS Model 16MC Trials for 1957. That year, a new all-welded frame with additional ground clearance was featured

September, 1957, announcement of the next season's models was there any major change in the Model 16. Magneto ignition had been dropped in favour of a crankshaft-mounted Lucas RM15 alternator, and this meant a redesign of the bottom-half assembly to accommodate the lengthened drive-side engine shaft.

At the same time, the old pressed-steel primary drive cover, a perpetual source of oil leaks, was replaced by a cast light-alloy casing. A new four-speed gearbox made by AMC themselves, had superseded the familiar Burman box a year previously.

This, more or less, was the position at the time the road impression reprinted here was conducted.

Of the subsequent history of the model, a duplex frame graced the 1960 Model 16, but at the same time a new lightweight 350 cc came into the range, and it was thought that the Model 16 would soon be pensioned off. Not so, however, for it was to undergo a face-lift for the subsequent season. Bore and stroke dimensions changed from the earlier 69 × 93 mm, to a new longstroke

configuration of 74 × 81 mm, valve diameters were increased, and maximum power output went up from 19 to 23 bhp at 6,200 rpm.

So far, so good, but creeping into the Matchless-AJS programme was a rash of transatlantic jazziness, expressed in big, gaudy, metal tank badges, and in unfamiliar model names where, in the past, numbers had served. So the Model 16 became the 16 Sceptre and, for 1964, it changed its dimensions yet again, this time to 72 × 85·5 mm. The new bottom-end assembly, claimed the makers, was derived from scrambles practice and it featured steel instead of cast-iron flywheels, a steel connecting rod, and a big-end bearing having large-diameter rollers in a dural cage. Even the oiling system was modified, with a Norton gear pump replacing the plunger pump. There was a still bigger inlet valve, and compression ratio had by now gone up to 9 to 1.

In the AJS catalogue, the model was still shown as the 16 Sceptre, but it had left its Second World War parentage far, far behind and had become a different animal altogether.

Although the Model 16C designation was retained for 1964 that year's trials machine embodied a redesigned, short-stroke 348 cc engine in which the pushrods were housed in cast-in cylinder barrel tunnels. There were other essential changes, such as a Norton-type geared oil pump

ROAD IMPRESSIONS OF NEW MODELS

347 c.c. Model 16 A.J.S.

By DAVID DIXON

FAMOUS SINGLE PUT THROUGH ITS PACES IN SOLO FORM

THE plot sounded good to me. The 347 c.c. Model 16 A.J.S. would be available for a couple of weeks in solo form. After that it would be harnessed with a Wessex Sports sidecar for a further period. Most, of course, are familiar with the Model 16: orthodox, proved to the hilt, a roadster with all the flywheel effect and low-speed punch one normally associates with those magnificent trials models on which Gordon Jackson and others do such incredible things on mud and rocks, weekend in and weekend out, the country over.

I felt at home the moment I cocked my leg over the saddle. Everything about the riding position was just right. Some might have found the handlebar a shade long and the tank a trifle wide between the knees. But there was no impression of being on the biggish model the A.J.S. *looks* to be. Once under way in traffic, the machine was as docile and tractable as a horse going to hay. In spite of its top hamper, the A.J.S. could be filtered through traffic gaps in effortless style. Low-speed steering was excellent if a trifle heavy. And a really good steering lock proved most helpful in maneouvring the machine in confined spaces.

Mechanical quietness has for long been a feature of the A.J.S. singles and the model under review was exemplary in that respect. A whine from the primary chaincase was audible, but only just. Apart from that there was merely a gentle rustling from the valve gear. Not a trace of piston slap could be detected whether the engine was hot or cold. Provided that the throttle was used with discretion, exhaust quietness was average for a single. When the throttle was tweaked hard, however, the exhaust took on a stentorian note which though pleasant, perhaps, to those who appreciate that sort of thing was not so much fun for pedestrians.

When delivered, the A.J.S. had covered only 280 miles. Even allowing for that, the performance was sprightly if not super-sporting. Good engine tractability and sweet transmission encouraged normal upward gear changes at 15, 20 and 30 m.p.h.

in traffic. In the initial stages a comfortable cruising speed was around the 50 m.p.h. mark. Fully run-in, the engine would push the job along at 65 m.p.h. plus all day long without, as it were, turning a hair. Throughout there was virtually no vibration.

The clutch was light to operate, smooth in its take-up of the drive and impervious to abuse. A caress of its lever was all that was necessary when changing gear. The gear box, too, came in for high praise. Pedal movement is moderately light and moderately brief and the length of the pedal is such that upward and downward changes could be made merely by pivoting the right foot on its rest. For the sheer delight of it, the gear box was used rather more than was necessary; it can therefore be assumed that my overall fuel-consumption figure of 77 m.p.g. could reasonably be improved upon.

I am something of a fuss-pot where handling is concerned and in that respect the A.J.S. was good but not perfect. I mean nothing derogatory: what I am trying to get across is that the Model 16 is a touring rather than a super-sporting mount and it has, for one thing, a $3\frac{3}{4}$ gallon tank. The top hamper is such that the machine has to be put round corners, and a conscious effort has to be made when it is being cranked swiftly from lock to lock. The A.J.S. was rock steady over most types of road surface and straight-head steering was above reproach.

Oddly enough—for the A.J.S. front fork is normally soft in action—the front suspension proved to be on the hard side, the result, it was felt, of tightish oil seals and bushes. The rear springing was adequately soft. From high or low speeds, the braking was first class and both tyres could be made to squeal without the wheels being locked. I would have felt happier had a rear stop light been fitted.

Those deep, stylishly valanced mudguards were truly effective. I know—I rode through a couple of downpours! But as the rear guard extends well down behind the wheel and does not have a detachable tail piece, wheel removal was a difficult, exasperating

business. Accessibility for other routine maintenance jobs, on the other hand, was excellent and the tool kit was commendably comprehensive. Small points I liked were the knurled finger adjusters for both brakes, the slotted cover in the cast-aluminium chaincase giving access to the clutch thrust-rod adjustment, a sensibly large fuel reserve and the stout rubber retaining strap that effectively eliminates chafing of the battery. I failed to see the point of fitting a 120 m.p.h. speedometer: too many figures clutter the dial.

How would the machine perform with the sidecar? The outfit was taken to the Isle of Man for a two-week period. With the Wessex fitted, what a beautifully balanced outfit it looked! Favourable comment was forthcoming from all who saw it. And the handling was even better, if that were possible, than was the outfit's appearance. Unladen, the lean-out of the machine was 1in and the toe-in of the sidecar wheel was ¾in. With the sidecar empty there was a barely noticeable pull to the right; with a load in the chair and the steering damper screwed down by one turn, straight-ahead steering was hands-off. Heavy-duty sidecar springs had been fitted to the front fork.

For the run to Liverpool I left London a little before 7 p.m. and just managed to catch the 1 a.m. boat—and Liverpool was 217 miles away by the route I took. When London was left behind the speedometer registered only 550 miles, so I had to beware of flogging the engine too hard. Yes, I'll admit I was a trifle worried. However, after starting cautiously, I soon found that the outfit would whistle along quite happily at 50 m.p.h. on the 6.48 to 1 sidecar top gear (the solo top ratio is 5.8 to 1). Even with a luggage load which included Vic Willoughby's leathers and my own—and enough stationery to start a business—the chair wheel was inclined to lift on sharpish left-handers. But there seemed to be no limit to the speed at which the outfit could be driven round right-hand bends; overall there was a feeling of absolute tautness.

As the miles totted up and time grew short, I forgot my scruples about new engines. The throttle was tweaked harder, the exhaust assumed an urgent note and the exhaust pipe turned from straw colour to blue. The speed rose from 50 to 60 m.p.h. The landing stage was reached at exactly 1 a.m.! Gang-planks

AND LATER WITH A WESSEX SPORTS SIDECAR ATTACHED

Above left: The Model 16 is finished in black and chromium and the tank is lined in gold. Above: The author pauses during an out-of-town run on the solo. On the right the A.J.S. and Wessex outfit is in the Isle of Man—by the new Bungalow near the summit of Snaefell

were already being pulled away from the ship's side as I purchased my tickets and hustled the outfit up the ramp and on to the deck. It says much for the handling and alignment of the outfit that after a cup of tea I felt fresh enough to have started all over again. Though there was no brake on the sidecar wheel, the A.J.S. stoppers had proved more than adequate and, even when applied hard, halted the outfit in a perfectly straight line. The overall average speed was 38 m.p.h. and that included stops for re-fuelling and direction finding; petrol consumption worked out at 57 m.p.g. The lighting had proved good enough to allow the use of all the available performance. On the return trip from Liverpool to London a week later, the average was stepped up to 40 m.p.h. and the fuel consumption improved to 58 m.p.g.

Everyone who drove the outfit in the Island was impressed with its handling and surprised, too, at the way in which that 347 c.c. power unit coped with every situation. The secret of obtaining the best results was, of course, to keep the engine on the boil. A standing start on a 1 in 6 hill in Douglas was made three-up. Even though the all-up weight was in the region of 40 stones, the outfit pulled away smoothly.

A lap of the Mountain course with me in the sidecar proved stimulating. The construction of the sidecar is interesting. A stressed-steel middle section forms a backbone to which glass-reinforced plastic nose and tail sections are bolted. Four steel plates bolted to the middle section provide pick-up points for the connections to the machine. No fewer than seven straight tubes from the sidecar pick up to five points on the machine, making an extremely rigid, cross-braced structure. Wheel suspension is of the plunger variety: the stub axle is carried by a light-alloy bracket which slides on two vertical guides; movement is controlled by an Armstrong spring-and-hydraulic unit.

Rather a lot of engine and transmission noise was transmitted via the connections and bulkhead; doubtless it could be overcome by better insulation. The seating position was quite comfortable, though care had to be taken to keep one's calves away from the steel body former. There was ample leg and elbow room. A footrest is provided but it was too far forward for all

The power unit remained remarkably clean externally. The contact breaker is reached by removing the cover plate on the end of the timing chest

but tall passengers. Draught from the left side was traced to air deflected upward from the integral wheel fairing. Ease of entry and exit was aided by the hinged screen and a cast light-alloy step. Luggage-carrying capacity in the boot behind the seat was admirable: there seemed to be no end to the amount of gear that could be stowed.

All in all, in both solo and sidecar forms, the Model 16 proved itself a thoroughly sound proposition for the enthusiast who requires robust and reliable transport for everyday use.

Below: The battery is housed in a compartment on the left-hand side and retained by a rubber band—a feature that ensures against chafing of the case. The bottom picture shows the rocker clearance being adjusted The job is easily carried out with the tank in position

SPECIFICATION

ENGINE: A.J.S. 347 c.c. (69 x 93mm) overhead-valve single; crankshaft supported in two ball bearings on drive side and a bronze bush on timing side; caged roller big-end bearing; light-alloy cylinder head; compression ratio, 7.5 to 1.

CARBURETTOR: Amal Monobloc; air slide operated by handlebar lever.

TRANSMISSION: A.M.C. four-speed gear box; positive-stop foot control. Solo gear ratios: bottom, 15.48 to 1; second, 10.26 to 1; third, 7.83 to 1; top 5.8 to 1; sidecar ratios: 17.3, 11.47, 8.74 and 6.48 to 1. Multi-plate clutch with oil-resistant friction material and incorporating vane-and-rubber shock absorber. Primary chain, ½ x 0.305in in cast-aluminium oil-bath case. Final drive by ⅝ x ⅜in chain; guard over top run.

BRAKES: 7in diameter front and rear.

SUSPENSION: Telescopic front fork with two-way hydraulic damping. Pivoted rear fork controlled by three-position adjustable Girling units incorporating hydraulic damping.

WHEELS and TYRES: 19in-diameter wheels with straight-pull spokes and light-alloy full-width hubs. Dunlop 3.25 x 19in tyres, ribbed front. Universal rear.

ELECTRICAL EQUIPMENT: Lucas RM15 a.c. generator with emergency-start switching. Coil ignition. Lucas 7in-diameter headlamp with pre-focus light unit containing pilot bulb and 30/24-watt main bulb. Lucas 6-volt, 12-amp-hour battery.

FUEL CAPACITY: 3⅞gallons.

OIL CAPACITY: 4 pints.

DIMENSIONS: Wheelbase, 56in; ground clearance, 6½in; seat height, 32in.

PRICE: £185 10s; with purchase tax (payable only in Great Britain), £223 15s 3d.

MANUFACTURERS: A.J.S. Motor Cycles, Plumstead Road, Plumstead, London, S.E.18.

WESSEX SIDECAR

CONSTRUCTION: monocoque; stressed sheet-steel middle section, glass-reinforced plastic nose and tail. Hinge-up screen, canvas hood, canvas-and-celluloid all-round screens. Wheel axle carried by light-alloy bracket sliding on two vertical guides; movement controlled by Armstrong spring unit with hydraulic damping. Avon Triple Duty 3.25 x 19in tyre.

DIMENSIONS: Overall length, 7ft 9in; seat back to footrest, 45in; seat to hood, 30in; width at elbows, 35in; seat back, 16½ x 16½in; seat 16½ x 17in.

PRICE: £93; with purchase tax, £112 3s 7d. Chromium-plated bumper, £2 10s extra.

MANUFACTURERS: Wessex Sidecars Ltd., High Street, Othery, near Bridgwater, Somerset.

Greeves
SPORTS TWIN

When the name Greeves is mentioned the mental image conjured up will almost certainly be a sporting one; Bryan Wade, perhaps, leaping a moto-cross model high over a crest with the front fork on full lock – or Derek Adsett cleaning a rocky stream bed in a national trial, or maybe a string of would-be road racers following their teacher on those dull blue, and very forgiving Silverstone track bikes.

Indeed, so great was the Greeves factory's emphasis on sporting lightweights, that it tends to be forgotten that they made road bikes, too. Not very many, true, but right from the start in late 1953 to the end of roadster production in 1966, there was always at least one two-stroke twin in the range.

Motor cycles, however, were a sideline, because the mainstay of the firm was the three-wheeled Invacar invalid carriage, built in considerable numbers to Ministry of Pensions contract. Even though this was government work, it was none too easy to get around the materials shortages and delivery delays that plagued British industry in the 1950s, and to get the Invacars through on time involved a great deal of wheedling and personal visits by the two principals of the firm, Bert Greeves, and his cousin Derry Preston-Cobb (himself a victim of paralysis and for whom Bert had built the very first, prototype Invacar).

By 1953, the supply position was beginning to ease, and Bert Greeves could at last get down to fulfilling a personal ambition. A keen motor cyclist for many years, he had always seen himself as a motor cycle manufacturer, and now the chance came. In fact there had been experimental Greeves machines around the South Essex area from 1951 on, and most unusual they were, too. Suspension on the Invacar three-wheeler was by a patented rubber-in-torsion device, and the same scheme was adopted for the bikes also.

At the front, the torsion-rubber units were carried at the base of tubular fork stanchions, and pivoted in them were short leading links which carried the front wheel spindle. Rear wheel suspension was by a pivoted fork, rods from which were connected to similar torsion-rubber units mounted just below the seat. Manually adjustable friction dampers were fitted to each rubber unit.

Unconventional enough so far, but by far the biggest break with tradition came in the frame construction, where the front-down member was a massive girder in cast light alloy, with the steel top tube cast in place. Engine cradle plates, too, were flanged light-alloy castings and these, like the front-down beam, were products of the small aluminium foundry which Bert Greeves had recently added to his Thundersley works.

The original late-1953 range announcement dealt with 197 cc Villiers-powered singles in roadster, scrambles, and trials trim, but at the Earls Court Show that November (where Greeves were exhibiting for the first time) there was a surprise. This was the attractively-named Fleetwing, powered by the recently-introduced 242 cc British Anzani two-stroke twin, an engine derived from a motor boat unit and featuring a crankshaft with a hollow, ported middle section that served as a rotary inlet valve.

By 1955 the roadster twins had grown to three, the original Fleetwing having been joined by the 'Standard' and by a 322 cc version, named the Fleetmaster. The general public had yet to be convinced of the practicality of the revolutionary Greeves cast light-alloy frame, and it was probably the low level of roadster sales that had prompted the addition of the cheaper 'Standard' frame of all-welded tubular construction, with proprietary rear damper units instead of rubber-in-torsion springing (although the system was retained at the front of the model).

The smaller Anzani twin was a pleasant machine to ride, but a mean maximum speed of only 61 mph (obtained in a *Motor Cycle* road test in May, 1955) could hardly be described as a sparkling performance; neither could a standing-start quarter-mile time of 22·8 sec. The tubular frame Standard 242 cc twin was continued unchanged for 1956 – possibly to use up engines already held in stock – but the more expensive alloy-beam Fleetwing had been dropped. By now, too, Armstrong rear damper units had replaced rubber-in-torsion rear springing throughout the range.

The Fleetwing name returned for the 1957 season, still with a two-fifty twin, but the engine unit was now the Villiers 249 cc Mark 2T, the first twin to be produced by the Wolverhampton concern since the 344 cc in-line Pullman of 1927. The Standard twin was still listed with the 242 cc British Anzani unit, as also was the 322 cc Anzani-engined Fleetmaster.

Producing 15 bhp at 5,500 rpm, the new Villiers unit was a

First twin-cylinder two-stroke to emerge from the Villiers factory since the late 1920s, the 249 cc Mark 2T was announced for the 1957 season. The manufacturers had made a valiant effort at producing a streamlined 'power egg' unit

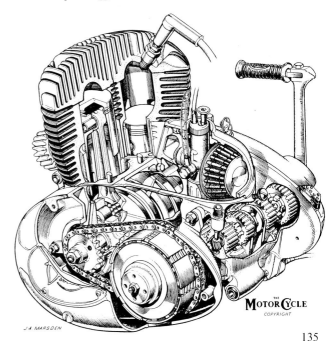

A novelty for the 1962 Greeves 25DCX Sportsman Twin was the use of glass-fibre front fork shrouds and handlebar cowling. The colour scheme of banana yellow and light blue was somewhat off-putting, too

slow-revver by two-stroke-twin standards. To some extent it was a double-up of the 122 cc Mark 10D single, retaining the same 50 mm bore, but with a slightly longer stroke, and featuring an ingenious roller-bearing centre main journal located in a plate which was sandwiched between the two crankcase halves, so avoiding the necessity of having to use a split bearing. The crankshaft was entirely pressed-up, and had seven separate components.

This was a much more lively model than the earlier Fleetwing, with a 70 mph top speed, brisker acceleration, and at the same time better fuel economy. It still looked rather gawky, despite the bigger dual seat, twin-drum front brake (Oh, come now; it wasn't as quick as all that!), and a somewhat clumsy headlamp mounting.

Throughout the Greeves factory's existence, its output of roadster machines was always overshadowed by the competitions side. Typical action is shown here by Dave Bickers, on a Greeves-barrelled 246 cc Villiers single, leading BSA works rider Arthur Lampkin in the 1961 Gloucester Grand National

At this point, perhaps we should turn aside from the story of the roadster twin, to examine the momentous happenings at Greeves on the competitions side. Brian Stonebridge had joined the company as development engineer and competitions manager, and his presence was soon felt.

Hurtling his 197 cc Greeves around the demanding Hawkstone Park moto-cross circuit in April, 1957, Stonebridge not only won the 250 cc event by a street, but calmly annexed the 350 cc Hawkstone Championship – and that was just the start. At Thirsk, and at the televised Wakefield scramble the day after, he lined up his little 197 cc with the five-hundreds and finished each time in second place, splitting the formidable pairing of Jeff Smith (BSA Gold Star) and Ron Langston (Ariel Red Hunter).

Success after success followed – the Lancashire Grand National, the Sunbeam Point-to-Point, and even standard time in that most punishing of all events, the Scott Trial – and nobody could doubt the unbreakability of the Greeves light-alloy beam frame any more.

Lessons learned on the circuits were passed on to the roadster models also, and the new 249 cc Greeves Sports Twin for 1959, featured in the road test which follows, was not only a much more handsome beast but, also, the frame geometry was based on scrambles experience. The machine was lighter than its predecessor by some 20 lb – and, surprise, surprise!; it was £20 cheaper!

The 1963 Greeves range still included the 25DC Sports Twin, but there were two more models employing the Villiers 2T unit. Glass-fibre was all the rage, and the newcomers (25DD Essex Twin, and 25DCX Sportsman) were rather gaudy efforts with humpy glass-fibre tanks, plastic mudguards and faired front rubber-in-torsion units. The Sportsman had, also, a handlebar fairing.

At the end of 1963, unhappily, Villiers replaced the faithful Mark 2T with the 17 bhp Mark 4T two-fifty, and this was a harsher, more revvy engine lacking much of the likeable smoothness of the earlier unit. The last Greeves twin was the Mark 4T-powered East Coaster of 1966, and when this was discontinued later in the year the famous rubber-in-torsion front fork went, too (competitions models had long since switched to the 'banana' front fork with external spring units). From that point, right through to 1977, the factory eschewed roadsters and concentrated on competitions only.

249 c.c. Greeves Sports Twin

Scrambles-bred Lightweight Capable of Mile-a-minute Cruising with Superb Handling and Roadholding

NORMALLY one might be excused for thinking that there is no resemblance between scrambling and main-road touring. However, equip a successful scrambles machine as a roadster and the relationship becomes clear: it is at once realized to what a high degree development the fierce fire of competition can elevate a machine so that its behaviour is wholly delightful and often exciting in terms of ordinary road use. All this is so in the case of the Greeves Sports Twin. True, its power unit—the Villiers four-speed 2T engine—is no longer used in the factory scramblers. That apart, the basic design features of the Sports Twin are the same as employed for the competition mounts. They include the light-alloy beam forming the front-down member of the frame and the pivoted front fork controlled by rubber in torsion and Girling hydraulic dampers. The machine has a most businesslike appearance. Its performance—not only as regards the engine but also in terms of steering, roadholding and braking—place it straight in the sports-machine category.

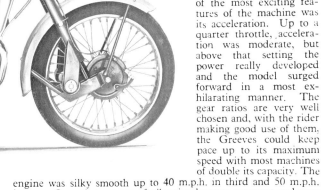

The Greeves possesses a businesslike air

The 25DB was impressive from the first moment of sitting astride. The riding position is just about spot on for tall riders and for those of average height. Although the footrests are not adjustable, their position affords a comfortable knee angle. The two-gallon fuel tank is only eight inches wide at the rear. At 28½in the handlebar width is greater than is usual for a lightweight but the almost straight section and slight upward tilt of the grips give a natural hand position. In delivery trim the controls were ideally positioned and light in operation. Towards the conclusion of the test the clutch became stiff to operate, a condition that was remedied by lubricating the cable. The 80 m.p.h. speedometer, which was easily read at all speeds, is set in a neat pressing which houses the headlamp. At 50 m.p.h. the speedometer registered 52 m.p.h. An anti-theft ignition lock is provided on the crankcase. Turning the key to the off position short-circuits the contact breaker, when the key can be removed and pocketed.

With the plunger-operated air control fully closed and the throttle between one-eighth and one-quarter open, two dabs on the kick-starter invariably brought the engine to life from cold; flooding was unnecessary provided the float chamber was allowed time to fill to its normal level. The engine was sensitive to mixture control and the plunger required to be opened gradually during the first mile of running. When warm, the engine started readily on one depression of the kick-starter.

Before the first start of the day it was necessary to depress the kick-starter with the clutch withdrawn in order to free the plates; otherwise a loud clash resulted as bottom gear was engaged. Light and smooth in operation, the clutch could be faulted only in two circumstances: following a very rapid change into top gear there was a slight amount of slip for a second or so; and after prolonged use in heavy traffic the plates expanded to the extent of causing drag which resulted in noisy changes. Clutch operation soon returned to normal on getting clear of a traffic crawl. The gear pedal was pleasantly light to operate and its travel was reasonably short. Under normal conditions gear changing, both up and down, was noiseless but it was possible to produce an audible clash from the gear box if ultra-fast changes were attempted in the indirect ratios; top-gear engagement was quiet at all times even when snap changes were made.

On the open road one of the most exciting features of the machine was its acceleration. Up to a quarter throttle, acceleration was moderate, but above that setting the power really developed and the model surged forward in a most exhilarating manner. The gear ratios are very well chosen and, with the rider making good use of them, the Greeves could keep pace up to its maximum speed with most machines of double its capacity. The engine was silky smooth up to 40 m.p.h. in third and 50 m.p.h. in top. Over that a trace of vibration became apparent and over 60 m.p.h. slight high-frequency vibration was noticeable at the handlebar; however, the tremors would almost have passed unnoticed had they not been highlighted by the engine's exceptional smoothness lower down the scale.

Although the exhaust system is of the Siamesed pattern, utilizing one Villiers silencer, the degree of quietness was such that full-throttle acceleration could be used whenever practicable without offence to bystanders. On the other hand, if the mood called for pottering, the engine would two-stroke evenly and pull smoothly in top gear at just over a dozen miles an hour, though a certain amount of chain flutter was evident under conditions of very light loading

The steering, roadholding and general handling are of such a high order that the full performance of the Sports Twin could be used with safety whenever possible. Surprisingly high averages could be maintained over long distances whether the route consisted of winding secondary roads or trunk roads. The

Left : The enclosed frame mid-section has two compartments and houses the tool kit and battery ; the lighting switch and horn are in the forward face. Above : Front and rear brake drums are radially ribbed. Right : The Siamesed exhaust system tucks away below the primary chaincase

comfortable cruising speed was 55 to 60 m.p.h. and this could be maintained seemingly indefinitely even over bad surfaces. Indeed, so delightful was the handling that whenever a choice of route offered, secondary roads were invariably chosen. Bend swinging at all speeds was sheer joy: without any conscious effort the model could be cranked over to either side until a footrest grounded.

With a passenger aboard, the handling was virtually unimpaired but the centre-stand legs grounded rather easily on sharpish corners. Front and rear suspensions were perfectly matched and, though very soft around the static-load position, there was absolutely no tendency for the machine to pitch or roll; nor did either suspension bottom or top at any time. Road shocks seemed hardly to exist; yet proof that the front suspension was doing a fine job on rough surfaces was provided by the unsprung light-alloy mudguard which could be seen bobbing up and down like a cork in choppy water.

Good brakes are essential on a sports machine. The Greeves was equipped with ribbed drums which are an optional extra on the model. Deceptively powerful at high or low speeds, both brakes were capable of making the tyres squeal without inadvertent locking of the wheels. Hard application of the front brake caused the front end of the machine to rise sharply.

Only in minor features of the Sports Twin could reasonable ground for criticism be found. For instance, a certain amount of groping was necessary to reach the lighting switch which is mounted underneath the seat on the front of a neat pressing which encloses the horn and battery. The horn gave such a ridiculous squawk that it caused amusement to pedestrians. A careful watch on the fuel level was required as there is no reserve. The tool kit was barely adequate for routine maintenance: there was no spanner to fit the cylinder-head bolts and the plug spanner, which also fits the wheel-spindle nuts, broke rather easily when the rear-wheel nuts were being tightened following chain adjustment.

Points which impressed included a good driving light which allowed safe night cruising at 55 m.p.h., the easily operated centre stand, additional front-brake adjustment by means of extra holes in the cam-lever yoke, and the excellent all-round finish. The power unit remained oiltight except for seepage from the rear of the primary chaincase which spread a film of oil over the exhaust pipe and silencer. The rear chain was well lubricated by oil which found its way on to the gear box sprocket. Adjustment of the rear chain was required only once every 500 miles.

Smartly finished in two-tone blue and chromium plate, and with gold lining of the tank, the Greeves Sports Twin proved itself one of the liveliest and most diverting lightweights on the road. It is a machine to give endless fun without ostentation and is assured of a niche in the hearts of many sporting riders.

INFORMATION PANEL

SPECIFICATION

ENGINE: Villiers 249 c.c. (50 x 63.5mm) two-stroke twin with separate iron cylinder barrels and light-alloy heads. Roller big-end bearings. Crankshaft supported in one ball and two roller bearings. Compression ratio, 8.2 to 1. Petroil lubrication; mixture ratio, 24 to 1.

CARBURETTOR: Villiers, with plunger for cold starting. Fabric air filter.

TRANSMISSION: Villiers four-speed, foot-controlled gear box in unit with engine. Gear ratios: bottom, 17.52 to 1; second, 10.89 to 1; third, 7.59 to 1; top 5.73 to 1. Multi-plate Neolangite-bonded clutch operating in oil. Primary chain ⅜ x 0.225in in oil-bath case. Rear chain, ½ x 0.305in with guard over top run. Engine r.p.m. at 30 m.p.h. in top gear 2,375.

IGNITION and LIGHTING: Villiers flywheel generator with contact breaker and low-tension ignition and lighting coils; remote h.t. coils; rectifier. Varley 6-volt, 9-amp.-hour battery; Miller 5½in-diameter sealed-beam light-unit with 30/24-watt main bulb and pilot bulb.

FUEL CAPACITY: 2 gallons.

TYRES: Avon; front, 2.75 x 19in Speedmaster; rear, 3.25 x 18in Safety Mileage.

BRAKES: 6in diameter x 1in wide front and rear.

SUSPENSION: Greeves pivoted front fork employing rubber in torsion and Girling hydraulic dampers. Pivoted rear fork controlled by Armstrong spring-and-hydraulic telescopic units.

WHEELBASE: 53in unladen. Ground clearance 6½in unladen.

SEAT: Greeves dual-seat; unladen height 31½in.

WEIGHT: 294 lb fully equipped and with 1 gallon of petroil.

PRICE: £160 2s 5d; with purchase tax (in Great Britain only), £193 2s 11d. Extra: ribbed brakes, £4 7s 1d.

ROAD TAX: £1 17s 6d a year.

MAKERS: Greeves Motor Cycles, Church Road, Thundersley, Essex.

DESCRIPTION: The Motor Cycle, 30 October 1958.

PERFORMANCE DATA

MEAN MAXIMUM SPEED: Bottom: 33 m.p.h.
Second: 42 m.p.h.
Third: 57 m.p.h.
Top: 69 m.p.h.

HIGHEST ONE-WAY SPEED: 70 m.p.h. (conditions, moderate tail wind, rider wearing two-piece suit and overboots)

MEAN ACCELERATION:

	10–30 m.p.h.	20–40 m.p.h.	30–50 m.p.h.
Bottom:	4.1 sec	—	—
Second:	5.6 sec	5 sec	—
Third:	9.2 sec	9.6 sec	8 sec
Top:	—	14.2 sec	15.4 sec

Mean speed at end of quarter mile from rest: 64 m.p.h. Mean time to cover standing quarter mile: 20.5 sec.

PETROIL CONSUMPTION: At 30 m.p.h., 112 m.p.g.; at 40 m.p.h. 92 m.p.g.; at 50 m.p.h. 64 m.p.g.; at 60 m.p.h., 52 m.p.g.

BRAKING: From 30 m.p.h. to rest, 33ft (surface, dry tarmac).

TURNING CIRCLE: 14ft.

MINIMUM NON-SNATCH SPEED: 13 m.p.h. in top gear.

WEIGHT PER C.C.: 1.18 lb.

Excelsior

Douglas

Triumph

VINCENT

Velocette

Royal Enfield

ARIEL

A·J·S

SUNBEAM

BSA

Greeves

Norton

Excelsior

Douglas

Triumph

VINCENT

Velocette

Royal Enfield

ARIEL

A·J·S

SUNBEAM

BSA

Greeves

Norton